MOTHERS OF FEMINISM

MOTHERS OF FEMINISM

The Story of Quaker Women in America

MARGARET HOPE BACON

1817

Harper & Row, Publishers, San Francisco

Cambridge, Hagerstown, New York, Philadelphia, Washington
London, Mexico City, São Paulo, Singapore, Sydney

FIRST EDITION

Library of Congress Cataloging-in-Publication Data

Bacon, Margaret Hope.
  Mothers of feminism.

  Bibliography: p.
  Includes index.
  1. Women, Quaker—United States—History.   I. Title.
BX7748.W64B33   1986   289.6'088042   85-45712
ISBN 0-06-250043-0

  86 87 88 89 90 RRD 10 9 8 7 6 5 4 3 2 1

In memory of my mother
Myrtle Hope Borchardt

Contents

Acknowledgments

I was fortunate to be granted a T. Wistar Brown Fellowship at Haverford College in order to do the research on this book, and I spent many happy weeks in the Quaker Collection of the Haverford College Library. To its curator, Dr. Edwin Bronner, and his colleagues, Elizabeth Potts Brown, Diana Alten, Eva Myers, and Sheila Hallowell, I owe a special debt of gratitude for their unflagging helpfulness in finding books for me in the library and responding to emergency calls from my home, even from Maine. The staff of Magill Library uniformly supported my work. Barbara Curtis, a former staff member, read the manuscript for accuracy, sharing the task with her husband, John. ·

I was also aided by Rosalind G. Wiggins, Curator of the Archives of New England Yearly Meeting of Friends; Damon Hickey and Carole Treadway of the Friends Historical Collection, Guilford College, North Carolina; Peter Parker and Cynthia Little of the Historical Society of Pennsylvania; G. William Frost, Albert Fowler, and Jean Soderlund of the Friends Historical Library, Swarthmore College; and Alice Bacon Long of the Treasure Room at Westtown.

For permission to quote from manuscript sources I am indebted to the Quaker Collection, Haverford College Library; the Friends Historical Library, Swarthmore; the Historical Society of Pennsylvania; Friends Historical Collection, Guilford College; the Treasure Room, Westtown School; and Archives of the New England Yearly Meeting of Friends. I would also like to thank especially Cora and Robert Emlen for making available to me portions of the journal of Sarah Foulke Farquhar Emlen held privately by the Emlen family.

Among scholars who encouraged my work, allowed me to read their papers, and to quote from those papers I should mention first my friend Amelia Fry of the Oral History Project of the Bancroft Library of the University of California. Phyllis Mack of Rutgers University, Judy Wellman of the State University of New York at Oswego, Kathy Barry of Brandeis University, Judith Middleton of Vanderbilt University, Susan Lynn of Stanford University, Dana Greene of St. Mary's College, Carol Stoneburner of Guilford College, Hugh Barbour of Earlham College, and Thomas Hamm of Indiana University were also extremely helpful and generous. Others who shared thoughts and manuscripts include Katherine Smedley, Elizabeth Walker, William Taber, and Claire Ullman.

In response to my appeal, Quaker women from all over the country wrote to me regarding their thoughts and feelings about present-day feminism within the Society of Friends. They are unfortunately too numerous to be listed here. For help in collecting opinions I would especially like to thank the Women's Committee of Philadelphia Yearly Meeting; Carolyn Smith, who aided me in distributing questionnaires; and Nancy Whitt, the editor of *The Friendly Nuisance*.

For his patience, his support, and his proofreading I am grateful to my husband, S. Allen Bacon.

Despite all this outpouring of help, there may be errors in this manuscript. If so, the fault is entirely my own.

Introduction: The First Feminists

On July 13, 1848, five women sat around a mahogany tea table and planned a revolution. Six days later the revolution began; in the small town of Seneca Falls in upstate New York the world's first woman's rights convention was held, and a Declaration of Women's Rights was proclaimed and signed by one hundred participants. Any question about the historical significance of this event was soon dispelled by the vehemence of the reaction, as both the press and the clergy denounced these desexed females for stepping out of their sphere.

Of the five women who planned the convention, four were members of the Religious Society of Friends, or Quakers, as they are more familiarly known. The fifth, Elizabeth Cady Stanton, had come to the tea party to see her old friend and longtime role model, Lucretia Mott from Philadelphia, a Quaker minister who had been advocating women's rights for the past forty years.

Although Quakers had been numerous in the colonial period and had predominated for a time in New Jersey and Pennsylvania, they represented only a tiny percentage of the American population by 1848. Yet their influence in such fields as the abolition of slavery, the reform of prisons, the fair treatment of Native Americans, and especially the rights of women was far in excess of their numerical strength. It has been estimated that Quaker women comprised thirty percent of the pioneers in prison reform, forty percent of the women abolitionists, and fifteen percent of suffragists born before 1830.[1] Susan B. Anthony, who joined the women's rights movement in 1852 and carried it forward until 1906, was a Quaker, as was Alice Paul, the author of the Equal Rights Amendment, who often credited her Quaker background for her long and determined struggle for women's rights.

The pioneer role that Quaker women played in the development of feminism in this country had its origins over two hundred years before the convention at Seneca Falls. The Society of Friends itself, born during a period of religious ferment in England, became the first sect to embody a concept of the spiritual equality of men and women within its church government and discipline, liberating Quaker women to preach and prophesy as well as to share responsibilities. The experience Quaker women had accumulated in public speaking, holding meetings, taking minutes, and writing epistles prepared them for leadership roles when the time was ripe for a women's rights movement to emerge.

Because of the prominent role that Quaker women played in the development of the women's movement, many Quaker values became embedded in its ideology and practice. The use of nonviolence in protecting the early conventions against angry mobs, the insistence on including women of all races and walks of life in meetings, the tradition of working for consensus rather than making decisions hierarchically, the ties between the women's movement and the peace movement, the tendency toward a broad rather than a narrow focus on issues—all represent values of the Society of Friends.

Of course other religious groups, especially the Unitarians and the Methodists, also contributed to these traditions. Nevertheless, it is easier to understand some of the threads in the women's movement today if one knows something of their Quaker antecedents.

There is, however, another and more compelling reason to look at the 340-year history of the Quaker experiment in finding practical applications for the doctrine—first stated by William Penn—that "in souls there is no sex."[2] Although Quakerism at times had been a closed society, it lived always within the larger society and could not resist being affected by the surrounding culture. For much of Quaker history, the concept of the equality of women and men contradicted values of the people with whom Friends did business and shared civic roles. Inevitably, tension existed between the values held by the Religious Society and those held by the world. From the earliest days, therefore, a struggle took place between those women and their male allies who wanted to broaden the concept of spiritual equality into social, economic, and political roles, and those who were alarmed at such a development. The history of the Society of Friends in America can be seen, therefore, as a microcosm of the long struggle for gender equality in society at large. One can learn about the slow process of social change and the difficulties of reconciling creative new insights with the ways of the world by studying the Friends' successes and failures in realizing the original vision.

Although Quakerism developed first in England, I have limited myself, after the first chapter, to telling the story of the struggle for gender equality in America. A strong women's rights movement with a large Quaker leadership first developed in the United States. The political and social climate of the American colonies apparently helped the Quaker testimony of gender equality to blossom. Feminist aspirations then spread to England from the United States. Anne Knight, an early British Quaker feminist, was much influenced by Lucretia Mott, and Ray Strachey, a prominent British suffragette, was a descendant of one of the strongest of American feminist families, the Whitalls. Today, of course, there are strong Quaker feminists among Quaker women not only in Great Britain, Ireland, Australia, and Canada, but around the world. Since the American experience is the one I know best, however, it is the one I can present as a case study in the development of gender equality.

My own experience over a forty-year period has been almost entirely within one branch of the Religious Society of Friends in America, the branch that retains the silent meeting for worship and holds a strong philosophy of social action. Today there are several other branches of modern Quakerism. While I have tried to read about and to interview Quakers of all persuasions for this book, undoubtedly I reveal a bias toward the branch I know best, whose values coincide with mine.

Although I have written about many Quaker women, this is not a book about them exclusively, but also about feminism within the Society of Friends. Beginning with George Fox, many male Quakers have shared the struggle for equality. Quaker feminists today insist that this struggle is the duty of both men and women. I have tried to tell the story of this struggle rather than merely to catalog all the important Quaker women.

Finally, there is a danger of sounding smug when one picks out the women of a particular persuasion from the vast procession of foremothers. I can only say that Quaker women today are anything but smug. They worry that praise of past heroes blinds us to the needs and demands of the moment, and they fear that currently the Society is making little effort to rid itself of the subtle sexism that has crept into its being over the years. "What we have to fear most is basking in our past glories and not facing the facts of today," one Quaker woman cautions me.[3]

But if the performance leaves much to be desired, the dream is still intact. Out of the same spiritual roots as the testimony on the equality of women and men in the Society of Friends came a set of values traditionally regarded as "feminine." The practice of love, humility, empathy, peacemaking, and philanthropy has not been set aside for women only but has been shared by men and women equally. Friends have believed that these are in fact Christian values to which all owe allegiance. Although many Quaker men have been involved in the world of business and politics where values usually assigned to men, such as aggression and power, have been emphasized, the history of the Society has moved consistently toward refraining from assigning values on the basis of gender. To wed the two sets of values, to combine assertiveness and love as Jesus did, is the dream today of many Quaker men and women. This is also the vision of an androgynous society entertained by the modern feminist movement.

1. Quaker Women in Puritan England

Great ideas are often born before their time. In turbulent eras of human history, they burst forth and command public attention, only to disappear again in a more conservative era and remain lost from view until they are reborn in another period. Some ideas of human liberty have been born time and again in this fashion. In the quiet interludes, they are kept alive by small communities of men and women somewhat withdrawn from society, just as the monks kept alive the love of learning during the Dark Ages.

In the period from 1640 to 1660, England experienced a burst of new ideas, some great and some perhaps less so, as the Protestant Reformation played itself out and created a series of radical Puritan sects. At the same time, the changeover from a society controlled by the nobles of church and state to one dominated by the merchant class produced social upheaval, while the accompanying enclosures of the land left large numbers of workers and laborers adrift.

Concepts of political democracy, of common ownership of the land, of the leveling of class differences, and even of a primitive form of communism all thrived during this yeasty period, much to the dismay of propertied and influential people. The authority of both church and state was questioned as men and women took seriously the consequences of their newly acquired freedom to read the Bible for themselves and to reason with their peers about its message.

All of Puritanism can be viewed as an expression of the newly found belief that the human soul could directly encounter its Creator. But whereas the conservative wing of the Puritan movement hedged this new freedom with restrictions about who had the authority to interpret the Bible correctly and to administer the sacraments, the Separatists, and particularly the radical sects—the Brownists, Independents, Baptists, Millenarians, Familists, Diggers, Ranters, and Seekers—began to question the need for the ordained ministry, to refuse to pay tithes, and to declare that the Bible could only be understood in the light of the Holy Spirit within. Some gave up church attendance and met in homes; some worshiped in silence, dressed plainly, and refused to use the pagan names—Monday, Tuesday, Wednesday, Thursday, etc.—for the days of the week. Some of the more radical sects saw no need for training at Oxford or Cambridge, since the inner Light alone was sufficient for interpreting the Scriptures. This Light was defined as the capacity of each human soul to receive Divine illumination. Worst of all, from the point of view of many, the radicals allowed women to interpret the Scriptures and occasionally to preach. Even the women who pushed carts through the streets selling oysters, it was complained,

> Locked their fish up
> And trudged away to cry, "No bishop."

The reaction against women's preaching was particularly virulent at this time in the established church and the right and center of the Puritan movement, because of the increased orthodox emphasis on the role of the male as head of his household and ultimate source of authority. As the nobility's control of church and state receded, many feared anarchy would prevail unless each householder were made responsible for his wife, his children, and his workers. A family was described in current Protestant literature as a "little church and a little commonwealth," as well as a school for training servants and women in subjugation.[1]

Women had played a role in heretical spiritual movements in England since the Lollards of the fifteenth century, and prior to the English Reformation, women had exercised some authority in the church as abbesses of convents. In many senses, they had lost power in the hundred years after the Reformation, and the radical Puritan sects gave them a chance to regain it. Through radical sectarian movements, women could challenge the increasingly male orientation of Puritan theology and infuse it with some of the so-called feminine values.

But while women preached among the Ranters, the Baptists, and a few other sects, only the Quakers—a group that grew up around several charismatic figures in the early years of the Commonwealth, and which was composed of many former Ranters, Seekers, and Independents—permitted women to preach and prophesy on the basis of equality and to play an acknowledged role in church government. All students of the Puritan movement agree with Geoffrey Nuttall, a distinguished present day British scholar of the religious enthusiasts of the period, who said, "There had been certainly nothing previously like equality *on this scale.*"[2]

The Society of Friends is generally regarded by historians as being at the far left of the radical Puritan movement, although some scholars continue to link it also with continental mysticism. In either case, Friends did not so much develop new ideas as carry the ideas of the period to their logical conclusion. While most of the other sects either disintegrated as a result of their anarchism or disappeared under the persecution of the Restoration in 1660, the Quakers survived. They brought their new ideas to the American colonies and have embodied many of the concepts of the 1640s and 1650s, developing them in light of new times and what Friends call "a continuing revelation." No concept better illustrates this principle than their continuing testimony on the equality of women.

George Fox

The fact that the Quakers were able to establish a structure preserving the concepts of liberty and equality developed during the Commonwealth era and yet restraining members from

George Fox. Permission from the Quaker Collection, Haverford College Library, Haverford, PA. Photo by Norman Wilson.

the excesses of unbridled religious anarchy is due in no small measure to the talents of two remarkable people. Although Quakerism had several leaders in its early days, George Fox is known today as its founder. He kept a detailed journal of his search for truth and his experiences in the birth of the Society, and it was undoubtedly he who helped give it organized form. If he was the father of Quakerism, Margaret Fell, his *helpmeet* as he called her, and later his wife, was its nursing mother. Coming from very different backgrounds and possessing different though complementary skills, these two nurtured the infant Society of Friends until it was able to resist persecution and preserve order without losing its enthusiasm.

George Fox was born in 1624 at Fenny Drayton in Leicestershire. His parents were the weaver Christopher Fox, who had won the reputation in his village of "righteous Christer," and Mary, a woman reportedly descended from the martyrs persecuted by Queen Mary in the previous century. Mary Fox was recognized as being more learned than her neighbors. Seeing that her son was of a solitary and religious temperament, she did not urge him to play with the other children of the village but supported him in his seriousness and inwardness, according to William Penn, his friend who wrote the preface for the first edition of George Fox's *Journal*. "His mother, taking notice of his singular temper, and the gravity, wisdom, and piety that very early shined through him, refusing childish and vain sports and company when he was very young, she was tender and indulgent over him, so that from her he met with little difficulty."[3]

George Fox did not write a great deal about either of his parents in this journal, but when his mother died in 1673, he wrote that his spirit was in travail, "For I did in verity love her as ever one could a mother."[4] Her acceptance of his withdrawn behavior as a child must have contributed to the self-confidence and the loving nature that contemporaries perceived in him.

Thus encouraged by his mother, George Fox spent many solitary hours reading his Bible and meditating. As an adolescent, he was apprenticed to a cobbler who also kept sheep. Out on the lonely moors watching the sheep, George Fox continued his religious struggles. Finally at age nineteen, he left home and began a pilgrimage up and down England, looking for someone who could answer his spiritual yearnings. Although he wrote in his journal that he had "great openings," he found none who spoke to his condition, as he put it, until 1647. In that year he had a religious experience and heard a voice that said:

"There is one, even Christ Jesus, that can speak to thy condition;" and when I heard it, my heart did leap for joy . . . and this I knew experimentally.[5]

Christ himself was the Inward Teacher, "the true Light that lightest every man who cometh into the world," as stated in the Gospel according to John (1:9). For this reason George Fox, and Friends after him, always spoke of the Light with a capital L. But the potential to respond to the Light was present in every person, whether he or she had known about Christianity. Fox therefore believed that "there was that of God," as he put it, in the American Indian, in the African black, in all men and women everywhere. This was the religious basis for a holy community in which no one had dominance over another, and there would be no further reason for war. The Quaker insistence on using only the plain language of the people, *thee* and *thy*, rather than you and your, using full Christian names, instead of titles, declining to take off their hats to anyone, and refusing to take oaths or serve in the army, all stemmed from this central concept.

Even prior to this watershed experience and long before he began to articulate a peace testimony, George Fox had been developing his concept of the equality of men and women. He wrote in his journal that he had met a people who believed that women had no souls, "no more than a goose." He reproved them, pointing out that Mary had said, "My soul doth magnify the Lord." Shortly thereafter he met a woman in Nottinghamshire, Elizabeth Hooten, who was to become the first Quaker woman minister. Forty-seven at the time she first met George Fox, she was deeply stirred by his religious fervor, and later, when he began to gather a band of followers, originally called the Children of the Light, she attached herself to him. She spent the rest of her life supporting the new movement, either in jail or traveling in the ministry. Her husband was at first so opposed to her conversion that they came close to parting, but later he became convinced of the truth of the Quaker message and supported her.

In 1648 George Fox attended a meeting in a "steeplehouse" of Presbyterians, Independents, Baptists, and Anglicans, at which a woman asked a question and the priest replied that he did not permit women to speak in the church. George Fox disputed him, saying that a church was "a spiritual household," not "an old house made of lime, stones, and wood," and that in the true church, of which Christ was the head, a woman might prophesy and speak. "It broke them into pieces and confused them, and they all turned against me into jangling," he recorded.[6] This was the first of many disputes that George Fox entered over the right of women to speak in church.

As the Quaker movement grew, and more and more women began to travel in the ministry, George Fox was constantly called upon to defend this right against the charge of the priests that women were to remain silent in the churches, according to the apostle Paul's injunction. In 1656 he wrote a tract arguing for women's right to prophesy. Its full title was: *The Woman learning in Silence: or, the Mysterie of the womans Subjection to her Husband, as also, the Daughter prophesying, wherein the Lord hath, and is fulfilling that he spake by the Prophet Joel, I will pour out my Spirit unto all Flesh.*

George Fox argued that men and women were "helpsmeet" before Adam's transgression and fall, and that after the fall the husband ruled over his wife. But through Christ they were restored to their original state and were again helpsmeet, or equal. The biblical injunctions against women speaking did not apply to those who had received salvation through Christ. He used the Bible to argue that women had often served as prophets. The apostle Paul, who in 1 Timothy 2 wrote that women should keep silent in the churches, elsewhere commended women like Priscilla and Phoebe, who were coworkers in the early church. Mary Magdalen had first declared that Christ had risen. George Fox noted that Paul interpreted Scripture according to the measure, or Light, given him; likewise, Paul's readers could only understand Scripture in light of the teaching of Christ in their hearts.

As the controversy over women's preaching continued, even within the ranks of the newly formed Society of Friends, George Fox wrote a second tract, *Concerning Sons and Daughters, and Prophetesses speaking and Prophesying in the Law and the Gospel*, in which he again used the Bible to illustrate that women had served as prophets, and to refute Paul's negative injunctions more specifically. Paul, he claimed, was speaking of a particular group of women in a particular church, women who had not yet been reborn in Christ, nor therefore raised to the level of helpsmeet. Paul had not meant to condemn the preaching of all women.

In addition to these two tracts, George Fox wrote extensively about women's ministry in his journal, in his many epistles to the nascent meetings of the Society of Friends, and in other publications defending the Quaker movement. If the Holy Spirit is accessible to all human beings, he argued, then no one has the right to quench it. In one of his epistles, he wrote in defense of women's meetings, "And what spirit is this, that would exercise lordship over the faith of any? And what a spirit is this, that will neither suffer the women to speak amongst men, nor to meet themselves to speak?"[7]

Although George Fox could be extremely irritating and abrasive to the magistrates and priests who opposed him, he could also be tender and nurturing, and many regard this as the reason for his leadership in the Society of Friends. William Penn wrote of him:

So meek, contented, modest, easy, tender, it was a pleasure to be in his company. He exercised no authority but over evil, and that everywhere and in all, but with love, compassion, and long-suffering, a most merciful man, as ready to forgive as unapt to take or give offense. Thousands can truly say he was of an excellent spirit and savour among them, and because thereof, the most excellent spirits loved him with an unfeigned and unfading love.[8]

George Fox's journal is full of images of the Holy Spirit nurturing eternal life in men and women. He speaks of the bread of life, and the living food of the living God, and of being gently led by the love of God. Many other early Friends used the language of nurturance, likening the love of God to that of a mother who holds her nurslings to her breast. These maternal images of God were not unique to the Quakers at this time, but the early Friends' use of such language is striking. They spoke of the presence of the Spirit in worship as a "tendering" experience, which resulted in feelings of love and compassion for one another and for all humankind. They compared the love of God to the love of a nursing mother, and the care of Christ to that of a mother hen for her chicks.

George Fox felt called not only to confound false teachings but also to bring men and women to the liberating experience that he had himself known. Although his journal frequently describes his arguments with priests and magistrates in harsh terms, his epistles and letters written to the members of the Society of Friends and to Quaker meetings are gentle and sensitive. In turn, his followers and colleagues turned to him for advice and counsel and for the "bread of life."

Margaret Fell

In 1652 George Fox came to Lancashire and there met and converted a large group of Seekers. The birth of the Society of Friends, originally called Children of the Light, is usually dated from this time, though in fact there were meetings as early as 1648. In the same year he made a noteworthy convert. She was Margaret Fell, the wife of Judge Thomas Fell of Swarthmoor Hall near Ulverston. At the time of George Fox's arrival, she was thirty-eight, the mother of eight children, and the busy

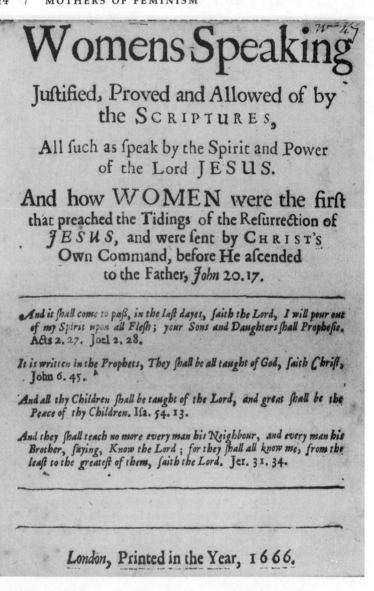

Womens Speaking

Juſtified, Proved and Allowed of by the SCRIPTURES,

All ſuch as ſpeak by the Spirit and Power of the Lord JESUS.

And how WOMEN were the firſt that preached the Tidings of the Reſurrection of JESUS, and were ſent by CHRIST'S Own Command, before He aſcended to the Father, *John* 20.17.

And it ſhall come to paß, in the laſt dayes, ſaith the Lord, I will pour out of my Spirit upon all Fleſh; your Sons and Daughters ſhall Propheſie. Acts 2.27. Joel 2.28.

It is written in the Prophets, They ſhall be all taught of God, ſaith Chriſt, John 6.45.

And all thy Children ſhall be taught of the Lord, and great ſhall be the Peace of thy Children. Iſa. 54. 13.

And they ſhall teach no more every man his Neighbour, and every man his Brother, ſaying, Know the Lord ; for they ſhall all know me, from the leaſt to the greateſt of them, ſaith the Lord. Jer. 31. 34.

London, Printed in the Year, 1666.

Title Page of *Womens Speaking.* Permission from the Quaker Collection, Haverford College Library, Haverford, PA. Photo by Ted Hetzel.

manager of a large country home with its bake and brew sheds, its gardens and stables and looms and apprentices. She possessed a searching, religious nature, and when George came to her household and began to preach his message of the Seed of Christ within and the need to return to a primitive Christianity in which Christ himself taught his people, she was deeply moved. A few days later, when George Fox spoke in the parish church and rebuked those who tried to understand the Scriptures without the illumination of the Spirit of Christ, she suddenly burst into tears and cried to the Lord, "We are all thieves, we are all thieves, we have taken the Scripture in words, and know nothing of them in ourselves."[9]

From that day on, Margaret Fell was a tower of strength to the new Quaker movement, putting her home as well as her energies into it wholeheartedly. Her husband, though never himself convinced, felt a deep sympathy for the Friends and used his influence to protect them from the hostile magistrates and priests in the region.

Swarthmoor Hall, as a result, became a hub for Quaker activities. Margaret Fell corresponded with many of the men and women who traveled up and down England proclaiming the Quaker message, the First Publishers of Truth, as they were called. She coordinated their efforts and assisted their families financially when they were in jail as a result of the religious persecution they suffered for many years. She also traveled extensively, visiting Quaker families and meetings and going to London on several occasions to plead with the king and parliament to free George Fox and other Friends from jail. So important was her role in sustaining the Quakers in the time of adversity and in helping the infant movement to grow and thrive, that she was called the Nursing Mother of Quakerism. But like George Fox, she was able to move comfortably from nurturing to political action in behalf of her beloved Society.

While Judge Fell lived, he was able to protect Margaret Fell from persecution, but after his death she served several long jail sentences and was threatened with praemunire, the loss of her entire estate. While she was serving a four-year sentence in Lancaster Prison, she wrote a pioneering book, *Women's Speaking Justified, Proved and Allowed by the Scriptures, all such as speak by the Spirit and Power of the Lord Jesus.* This was the first such book written by a woman since the Reformation, and it has long been considered a milestone in the history of women. In it Margaret Fell argued from both the Old and the New Testament that women had often played prophetic roles; she reinterpreted the difficult passages in Paul's epistles; and she spoke of the role of women in first proclaiming the message of the resurrection:

Mark this, you that despise and oppose the message of the Lord God that he sends by women; what had become of the redemption of the whole body of mankind, if they had not cause to believe that the message that the Lord Jesus sent by these women, of and concerning His resurrection?[10]

In 1669, eleven years after the death of Thomas Fell, Margaret and George Fox were married. Margaret was fifty-five, George ten years younger. Both had written extensively about marriage and had helped to develop a simple ceremony in which the man and woman took one another "in the presence of God and these our friends." George Fox said that his marriage was a symbol of "the Church's coming up out of the wilderness," and of "the redemption of all marriages out of the Fall." When he was asked by an elderly Puritan why he was marrying, since marriage was only for the procreation of children, he answered that he felt such things beneath him, and that his marriage was a "testimony that all might come up out of the wilderness to the marriage of the Lamb."[11]

George Fox was determined to demonstrate that their marriage was between equals. Prior to the marriage he met with Margaret Fell's children to get their approval and to assure them he sought no advantage through his connection with their estate. Thereafter, he was scrupulous to pay his own way, even carefully matching Margaret's gifts to him with those to her of equal worth. Throughout the twenty-two years of their marriage George Fox spent only four years in residence at Swarthmoor Hall. The two were more often apart than together, both serving additional jail sentences as well as traveling in the service of Friends, George Fox to the American colonies and the continent. In the last years of his life, when he might have sought the comforts of home, George was in London, lobbying for freedom from persecution. Both George and Margaret looked upon the marriage as primarily a spiritual partnership, and neither hindered the other's following their leading. Margaret outlived George by eleven years and continued to travel and to counsel the Quakers until her death.

Persecution and Liberation

The persecution of the Quakers began soon after the group came into being and continued until 1689. Friends were punished for their refusal to pay tithes to support the local ministers, to show respect for the magistrates by taking off their hats in the presence of their betters, to take oaths, to refrain from interrupting church services, and to be married by priests. Many of these ideas were shared by other Separatists, as we have seen, and Oliver Cromwell did what he could to protect Friends, but local magistrates and priests were not as tolerant. A local judge gave Friends the sobriquet of Quakers when George Fox suggested that the magistrate ought to tremble in the sight of the Lord. "You are the Quaker, not I," the judge said. By 1660 the Quakers had decided that they could not serve in the army, and for this refusal too they were jailed. With the return of Charles II to the throne of England in 1660 and the Conventicle Act aimed at destroying the nonconforming churches, persecution mounted. Perhaps as many as 15,000 were imprisoned, and 450 died. Their patient and persistent acceptance of suffering has often been cited as an antecedent to the modern practice of nonviolence. Their actions spoke to

Quaker Woman Preaching, by Egbert Van Heemkerk. Permission from the Quaker Collection, Haverford College Library, Haverford, PA. Photo by Ted Hetzel.

the conscience of many and led to the passage of the Toleration Act of 1689.

Some of the Quakers' suffering perhaps seems self-inflicted. In the grip of religious enthusiasm, many first-generation Quakers went to extremes to witness to their newfound faith. In 1653 two Quakers—Mary Fisher, about twenty, and Elizabeth Williams, an older unmarried woman—traveled to Cambridge to argue with the young theologians about their beliefs. When the scholars taunted them by asking foolish questions, the women announced that their college was a "Cage of Unclean Birds." Summoned, the mayor of Cambridge issued an order that they be whipped until the blood ran down their backs. The following year two other young women, Elizabeth Fletcher and Elizabeth Leavens, made the same trip and were beaten so severely that Elizabeth Fletcher never recovered, though the following year she returned and went naked through the streets of the city "as a sign against the hypocritical profession they made there."

Witnessing to the truth by going naked or wearing sackcloth or carrying a pan of coals on their heads won the early Friends, particularly the women, the suspicion of insanity. Elizabeth Adams stood before Parliament for two days with a great earthen pot upside down on her head. When people asked her what it meant she replied, "Many things are turned and turning."[12]

Yet, what material exists today about the lives of these enthusiasts[13] reveals that the vast majority lived sane and well-regulated lives aside from their religious duties. Their extravagant acts were undertaken, they felt, under the direct leading of the Holy Spirit. They dared not disobey, not so much for fear of punishment but for fear of being separated from the love of God. The ecstatic descriptions many of the early Quaker women have left of their conversion experiences suggest a state not unlike that of having fallen deeply in love. To protect these feelings of joy and of sweet peace, they were willing to follow wherever the Spirit led. When not under the direct leading of that Spirit they cared for their families and conducted their part in the Quaker business meetings in tranquillity.

Among early Quakers were the many former Ranters. Most radical of all the groups, the Ranters believed all strong urges were divine in origin, and accepted no external limits on their behavior. In its early days Quakerism was tinged with Ranterism. George Fox himself sometimes gave way to strange impulses, but he came in time to see the danger of confusing such states with divine promptings, and he often warned against "vain imaginings," mistaking one's own desires for revelations of the Spirit. Perhaps as a result of his own experience George Fox became interested in the phenomenon of mental illness, and he felt he had sometimes been able to cure those who were distracted.

In 1656 James Nayler, who had been one of the leaders of the early Quaker movement, allowed the enthusiasm of two women followers to overturn his judgment. They led him into the city of Bristol on horseback, holding the bridle and chanting "Holy, Holy, Hosannah" while a crowd cheered. Arrested for blasphemy, James Nayler was convicted by Parliament and punished by being whipped through the streets of London, having a hot rod bored through his tongue, and being imprisoned. After his release in 1659 he was reconciled with George Fox, but he was attacked by highwaymen and died shortly thereafter.

The Nayler incident sent shock waves through the Quaker movement, which was just beginning to gain a foothold in the New World on the island of Barbados, and in Holland. Critics used the episode to discredit Quakerism. The concept of freedom from sin through Christ, which had played such a major role in George Fox's own conversion experience and led to a doctrine of perfectionism, was modified, and men and women were taught to be on their guard against the voice of evil, which Friends called "the Reasoner."

As a result of the Nayler affair, opponents produced an increased outpouring of anti-Quaker literature, and Quakers answered with a stream of defending tracts. More important, however, was George Fox's perception that Friends in a locality must meet together regularly and in orderly fashion, so that they might check one another to see if one person's sense of a holy leading met a corresponding answer in the souls of his or her peers. This was the beginning of the Quaker meeting for business and the birth of that delicate balance between individual freedom and group authority, which has lain ever since at the heart of Quakerism.

Men and women Friends had met together for worship from the beginning, but the establishment of the business meeting at first caused some confusion. The first business meetings in the city of London appear to have been for men, although women may have attended with their husbands. There was also a regular Two Weeks Meeting for men, and this group apparently decided to establish a comparable meeting for women to take care of the poor. In 1659, when a storm of persecution broke over the Friends, this women's meeting could not adequately address the widespread suffering and destitution, and one of its members, Sarah Blackbury, appealed to George Fox for additional aid. George was inspired, he wrote in his journal, to establish a new women's meeting, the Box Meeting, which met weekly and kept its funds for the relief of suffering in a box. In addition to the relief of those in prison and their families, the two women's meetings took care of orphans and widows and oversaw the placement of maids.

The Box Meeting and the Women's Two Weeks Meeting were so successful, and the women so clearly demonstrated their capacity to handle business and keep accounts and records, that George Fox later used them as organizational models. In the late 1660s he developed a definite organization for Quakerism by setting up a system of preparative, monthly, quarterly, and yearly meetings for business which gave Friends in neighborhood, township, county, and regional areas pastoral responsibility for their members. He urged Friends to establish women's business meetings parallel to the men's meetings on each level.

These separate women's meetings became a subject of intense controversy and even schism within the young Society. Some critics felt that too much organization was being developed, destroying the freedom that had been enjoyed by the Society in the early days, and that women's meetings were an unnecessary complication. Why not allow women to continue to meet with the men? Some of these critics may have had women's interests in mind, but the majority knew that in the presence of men women would be too timid to raise their voices in matters of business. Particularly objectionable to some critics was the fact that the women's meetings were to oversee the first steps in preparing a young couple for marriage. Two Quaker ministers in Westmoreland, John Story and John Wilkinson, began to agitate against the separate meetings.

George Fox rose to the defense, arguing against his critics with his usual vigor. "There is [sic] some dark spirits that would have no women's meetings, but as men should meet with them, which women cannot for civility and modesty's sake speak amongst men of women's matters, neither can modest men desire it, and none but Ranters will desire to look into women's matters."[14]

Margaret Fell was the target of much hostility from the group that argued against the separate women's meetings. She and George Fox continued to defend such meetings, George with mounting passion. In 1676 he wrote an epistle, "An Encouragement to All the Faithful Women's Meetings," in which he cited biblical justifications for women's assemblies and argued with sarcastic humor against his adversaries: "Now Moses and Aaron, and the seventy elders, did not say to those assemblies of the women, we can do our work ourselves, and you are more fit to be at home to wash the dishes; or such-like expressions, but they did encourage them in the work and service of the Lord."[15]

But having mustered every biblical argument he could think of, George Fox rested his case on the immediacy of the leading he felt: "And if there was no Scripture for our Men and Womens meetings, Christ is sufficient."[16] While George Fox cannot be called a feminist, since that would mean reading history backwards, his respect for women, his appreciation of their buried talents, and his willingness to battle for their rights led the Society toward gender equality in the centuries that followed. He might not have been so persistent if he had not had the support and comradeship of Margaret Fell. Theirs was the first of a long series of Quaker marriages to practice equality, and the result was a burst of creativity for both partners.

Not surprisingly, one of the strongest women's meetings was the one in Lancashire in which Margaret Fell and her daughters took part. Sarah Fell in particular was known for her excellent clerkship and her careful keeping of record books. An early epistle of this meeting addressed to all women's meetings everywhere repeated the familiar biblical arguments and gave specific instructions for the conduct of women's meetings in overseeing marriages, regulating the conduct of their members, relieving the needs of the poor, and keeping good accounts and records.

Ultimately the women's business meetings prevailed. Prejudice against women in public life did not vanish overnight, however, even within the Society of Friends. Efforts were made to subdue Quaker women who spoke too long or too passionately in the mixed assemblies for worship, and to limit the authority the women's meetings exercised. As British Friends grew wealthy and conservative toward the end of the seventeenth century, they borrowed from their Puritan counterparts the concept of male authority in the household and ultimately in the church. Some Quaker women shared this view, and some of the early women's meetings were poor, shallow, and circumscribed. Others gained strength as they ultimately challenged the men to share power equally. This happened first in the American colonies.

2. The Traveling Women Ministers, 1650–1800

Quaker women were not only active in the spread of the Quaker message in the British Isles, they played an important role in planting the Seed, as they called it, in the New World. The first traveling Quaker ministers to reach the American colonies were women and throughout the colonial period women nurtured the growth of Quakerism up and down the Eastern seaboard. They preached in public places, met with the small groups of Quakers beginning to form in different colonies, prayed with families, and endured hardships for the sake of the message of a direct relationship between God and humans. Their bravery and their effectiveness as channels of the Holy Spirit were further evidence of God's intention that men and women be equal, the Quakers thought. In time, their exploits came to have an effect on the developing American culture.

In 1655 Mary Fisher, the young woman who had preached to the students at Cambridge, set off for the New World with Ann Austin, an older woman and the mother of five children. They landed first in Barbados, where Quakers had made a small settlement, then set out after several months for New England. On July 11, 1656, they sailed into Boston Harbor on the *Swallow*, the first Quakers to arrive in the Massachusetts Bay Colony.

The Puritans of Boston, however, were already on guard against the Quaker heresy. Their theocracy rested on the combined authority of church and state, an authority they perceived as threatened by the Quaker doctrine of a direct relationship between God and the individual. In addition, they were alarmed by the women preachers. Authority in Puritan Boston was vested in the male as the head of his family unit. While women were enthusiastic members of the new community and dominated the church congregations numerically after 1660,[1] their participation in developing church policy was not encouraged. In 1638 Anne Hutchinson had been tried and excommunicated for preaching a covenant of grace rather than works to groups of women and men who met in her home. The authorities regarded the covenant of grace as antinomian, elevating individual conscience and subjectivism over external authority, but they were also threatened by Hutchinson's refusal to accept a woman's proper place. Hugh Peters, a Massachusetts minister, scolded Hutchinson: "You have rather been a husband than a wife, and a preacher than a hearer; and a magistrate than a subject, and so you have thought to carry all things in Church and Commonwealth as you would have not been humbled for this."[2]

The arrival of the two Quaker women, both dangerous heretics and unsubmissive women, was therefore exceedingly alarming. The deputy governor, Richard Bellingham, ordered that they not be allowed to land until they were stripped naked, searched for signs of witchcraft, and all their tracts confiscated. They were then imprisoned for five weeks, where no one could speak to them, until the master of the *Swallow* was able to transport them back to Barbados.

This was only the beginning of the Quaker invasion of New England. Two days after the *Swallow* left, another ship arrived carrying eight Quakers, four of them women. These too were searched and imprisoned, and the shipmaster was fined. In 1657 Mary Dyer, a former member of the colony who had sided with Anne Hutchinson and had moved to Rhode Island, arrived in Boston from England with another Quaker woman, Ann Burden. Mary Dyer had been converted to Quakerism during a visit to England in 1652, and she had remained there five years as a traveling minister. The authorities were particularly frightened of her possible influence. They imprisoned her, held her incommunicado, and banished her and her companion to Rhode Island.

The following year the Massachusetts General Court passed a law banishing Quakers on pain of death. Hearing that two British Quakers were being held in prison in Boston in the summer of 1659, Mary Dyer traveled to Boston to visit them and was herself imprisoned. All three were banished under threat of execution. Within a month Mary Dyer had returned with a group of Quakers determined to "look their bloody laws in the face." Sentenced to death and led through the streets to the gallows with drumbeat, Mary was reprieved after her legs and arms were bound and the rope placed around her neck. She did not feel she could accept this stay of sentence, however, and she returned to Boston the next spring, 1660. This time she was sentenced and hung. Today her statue stands on the grounds of the Boston State House as a symbol of freedom of conscience.

The year following Mary Dyer's death, 1661, Elizabeth Hooten, George Fox's first convert and now a woman of sixty-one, arrived in the New World with Joan Brocksopp, intending to visit jailed Quakers in Boston. Since no ship's captain would carry them to the Bay Colony, they sailed to Virginia, planning to make the journey overland. A Friend in Virginia volunteered to take them to Rhode Island by ketch. In Rhode Island they attended a general meeting of Friends before proceeding to Boston. When Elizabeth Hooten and Joan Brocksopp attempted to visit the Boston prisoners, they were taken to Governor Endecott, who placed them in jail until the General Court could decide upon their fate. Their sentence was to be escorted two days' journey into the wilderness, and there to be abandoned. Elizabeth Hooten wrote of the occurrence in her journal:

. . . & there they left us towards the night amongst the great rivers & many wild beasts y' useth to devoure & y' night we lay in the woods without any victualls, but a fewe biskets y' we brought with us which we soaked in the water, so did the Lord help & deliver us & one caried another through the waters & we escaped their hands.[3]

The two made their way to Rhode Island, and from there to Barbados. They returned to England after making another unsuccessful attempt to visit Boston. The following year Elizabeth Hooten sailed back to New England with her daughter, intending to purchase a house in Boston where visiting Friends might be cared for. Although she had King Charles's permission to buy property, the General Court denied her this right. Instead she was sentenced to be fastened to the tail of a cart, stripped to the waist, and whipped through the towns of Cambridge, Roxbury, Dedham, Salisbury, and Dover, her daughter suffering the same punishment by her side. She remained in New England, nevertheless, until 1665, then returned to England where she was again imprisoned for her beliefs. In 1671 she set out with George Fox on a third mission to the American colonies, intending to visit New England, but she became ill on the island of Jamaica and died there at the age of seventy-two.

Meanwhile, Mary Fisher had returned to England. In 1657 she joined a group of Quakers traveling to the Near East. The English consul at Smyrna sent them back to Venice. Mary Fisher went on alone, traveling over six hundred miles to Turkey to interview the sultan. She managed to gain an audience and presented herself as an ambassador of "the Most High God." The sultan received her message gravely and treated her kindly, a sharp contrast to her reception by the Christians of both England and New England.

Mary Fisher returned to England and married a Quaker sea captain, William Bayly, and with him had three children. After Bayly was lost at sea, she married John Cross and migrated with him to Charleston, South Carolina, in 1682. Here she died in 1698. A granddaughter, Sophia Hume, became a noted Quaker preacher and a pioneer woman author.

About the same time that Mary Fisher and Ann Austin landed in Boston in 1656, or possibly a few months earlier, another woman, Elizabeth Harris, traveled to Virginia to preach the Quaker message. She evidently did not meet persecution but was instead "gladly received." Elizabeth Harris is today regarded as the mother of Quakerism in Maryland and Virginia, and perhaps the first American Quaker pioneer. Returning to England, she later conducted a traveling ministry in Europe.

Despite Elizabeth Harris's friendly reception, most Quakers in the New World encountered widespread fear. Two men who followed in Elizabeth Harris's footsteps in Virginia in 1658, Josiah Coale and Thomas Thurston, were imprisoned, and in 1660 the colony of Virginia passed an act suppressing the Quakers. Maryland also reacted with alarm. New York, where a group of Quakers had landed in 1656, passed an anti-Quaker Act in 1658. Only in Rhode Island under Roger Williams, in enclaves on Long Island, and on Shelter Island, bought as a haven for Quakers, were members of the Society of Friends free to practice their beliefs.

Though persecution of Quakers was widespread in the American colonies, it reached its most savage heights in New England. The Puritan reverence for order and the disorder they perceived in Quakerism contributed to their hostility. So did the Puritan emphasis on male authority as contrasted with the Quaker practice of equality between men and women. Some of the anti-Quaker literature published in Boston attempted to link Quakerism to witchcraft (itself based on a fear of the power of women) and to warn Puritan magistrates "to save their nurselings from the poison of the destroyer." Although Quaker women were not singled out in this literature, the fear that Quakerism would introduce gender equality must certainly have frightened the Puritans. Since Puritan values, including the idea of the male as the sole authority figure in each household, came to dominate the American culture, this early encounter between Quakerism and Puritanism is particularly relevant.[4]

Quakers in the New World needed a colony of their own to ensure protection from widespread persecution. For this reason William Penn secured land from his friend Charles II and in 1681 established Pennsylvania as a colony which he called a "Holy Experiment." Brought up in the British upper class, William Penn retained some ambivalent attitudes toward the role of women, despite his statement that in souls there is no sex. Nevertheless, in his Laws Agreed Upon in England (a code of laws which accompanied his charter for the new colony), William Penn stated several times that religious liberty must be available to persons, "whatever his or her Conscientious Persuasion." Women were allowed to plead their own cases in court. While property laws and the punishment for adultery were unfavorable to women in Pennsylvania, there is some evidence that women served on juries in the early days of the colony. At the only witch trial ever to be held in Pennsylvania, William Penn is supposed to have asked the woman, "Art thou a witch? hast thou ridden through the air on a broomstick?" When she answered yes he commented that he knew of no law against it. The woman was found guilty of "the common fame of a witch," but not of being one, and she was freed on her husband's recognizance.[5]

The Call to Ministry

The small Quaker communities struggling to survive in the New World were nurtured by visits from traveling Quaker ministers, many of whom were women. Of the first eighty-seven ministers to visit New England from 1656 to 1700 according to one calculation, twenty-nine, or approximately thirty-three percent, were women. This does not include those who traveled with their husbands.[6]

Generally two women traveled together, as did Mary Fisher and Anne Austin or Elizabeth Hooten and Joan Brocksopp. The pairing of a young woman and an older woman was encouraged. Friends were concerned about the propriety of their min-

Mary Dyer. Permission from Earlham College. Photo by Susan Castator.

isters, and some felt that ministers ought to practice celibacy, at least while traveling. Thus when two young people, Thomas Holme and Elizabeth Leavens (the same young woman who was whipped at Oxford), traveled together during early Quakerism, fell in love, and married, they encountered some opposition from Quaker leaders. Elizabeth had a baby, and although she worked as a seamstress to support herself and the child when not preaching, Margaret Fell felt that she had become a burden to the Society of Friends and seemed annoyed with her. Behind Margaret Fell's uncharacteristic attitude evidently lurked the feeling that the baby was a too patent proof that the ministers had been sexually engaged with one another. When Joseph and Jane Nicholson of Cumberland, England, were imprisoned in Boston in 1660, three Quakers from Salem also under sentence refused to join in fellowship with them because Jane was with child. Joseph Nicholson wrote to Margaret Fell that he teased the other Quakers about it:

I had and have much peace in plaguing of them, as I ame moved of the lord. For that spirit did vex mee much after I came from london till I found it out, and many times did much over power mee . . . it was the sorest thing that ever befell mee in my life time before I found it out . . . for often times it did much cowll my afection towards my wife and alsoe towards my children . . . as my wife knows right well.[7]

Friends learned that it was important to distinguish between religious exultation and sexual attraction. In the eighteenth century Catherine Phillips, a traveling English Friend, wrote to young single traveling women ministers about their bearing toward young unmarried men. She cautioned them to avoid too familiar behavior, but not on the other hand to be too austere. They must also guard their own minds, "lest they admit of any pleasing imagination, and stamp it with the awful name of revelation."[8]

Journals kept by the traveling women ministers give us some knowledge of the prejudice they encountered as women "out of their place," and also the difficulty they had in ridding themselves of the feeling that they were inferior. Jane Fenn, a young woman who migrated to Philadelphia in 1712 and became in time a traveling Quaker minister of note, describes sitting in meeting one day and hearing an inner voice declare that she had been chosen for the ministry:

Yet I must confess, this awful word of Divine command shocked me exceedingly, my soul and all within me trembled at the hearing of it; yea my outward tabernacle shook insomuch that many present observed the deep exercise I was under. I cried in spirit, "Lord I am weak and altogether incapable of such a task, I hope thou wilt spare me from such a mortification; besides I have spoken much against women appearing in that manner."[9]

For six or seven months, Jane Fenn continued to resist the command to speak in meeting, until she could withstand the pressure no longer. She stood up to utter a few broken words and returned home rejoicing. Nevertheless, for many years thereafter, she continued to struggle with her own sense of inadequacy when confronted with the growing demands of the Spirit that she not only preach to local meetings, but also travel through the colonies and eventually back to England.

Often women resisted the command to preach and listened instead to the voice of evil, which they called "the Reasoner." The Reasoner told them that they were mistaken, that they were inadequate, or that they were unfit. Listening to the Reasoner and resisting the divine command led to a period of dryness and depression, sometimes even physical illness. When these women finally decided to be obedient to the inner voice, they often spoke of "giving up." It was a surrender not only of their will and pride, but also of their right to plan their own lives. God might require that they leave their husbands and children and travel in the ministry for years at a time. They risked death at sea or in the wilderness. Yet such was the spiritual reward of the surrender that they counted the world well lost.

Elizabeth Webb, a British Friend who settled in Chester County, Pennsylvania, in 1703 and returned to England to travel in the ministry in 1712, wrote a letter to William Boehm, a religious leader who served as chaplain to Prince George of Denmark, the consort to Queen Anne of Great Britain. In the letter she described many years of struggle that preceded a decision to obey the Spirit. Following a meeting in which she at last uttered a brief prayer, she was so uplifted that she felt herself to be "in love with the whole creation of God. . . . So everything began to preach to me; the very fragrant herbs, and beautiful innocent flowers had a speaking voice in them to my soul, and things seemed to have another relish with them than before."[10]

The battle was never wholly won, and many of the Quaker journalists—male and female—describe seasons of dryness, of being shut up as though in prison, and again listening to the Reasoner. Periods of suffering, which Friends called deep inner baptisms, led to further spiritual growth. They used the language of being nurtured by God, of "receiving a fresh supply of bread from the heavenly table," and of being supported by the "nursing Father." Since Friends regarded themselves as channels of the Holy Spirit, they never recorded in their journals what they spoke in meeting. Rather, they used such circumlocutions as "we had a favored meeting" or a "precious meeting," or "Truth prevailed."

Adventuring Overseas

Although the traveling Quaker ministers followed the leading of the Spirit in determining where to go and how long to stay, they were regulated by their home meetings through certain mechanisms. The first and most important was the traveling minute. The person who felt compelled to travel in the ministry had to appear before the ministry committee of her own monthly meeting, which would then discuss her request in light of her health, her family duties, and the strength and soundness of her ministry. If the local meeting felt all was well, the quarterly and then the yearly meeting had to be consulted.

This took time but prevented men and women from wandering about, preaching doctrines not in accordance with Friends' beliefs. It also tested the strength of the minister's original sense of mission.

Once a minister had been provided with a minute to travel in the ministry, her home meetings were responsible for her expenses. The meetings she visited were expected to provide hospitality and money for the return voyage. Refusal to provide this funding was another form of control.

Friends who were not ministers sometimes traveled on business, of course. They did not have to have a traveling minute, but they sought one if they intended to visit any Friends' meetings. This was a different minute, more like a letter of introduction. Only recognized ministers with minutes authorizing them to travel *in the ministry* were allowed to preach in other meetings. Such persons were called Public Friends.

One of the favorite exercises of Quaker scholars and scribes in the late eighteenth and early nineteenth centuries was the compiling of lists of Public Friends, who visited the American colonies during the first one hundred years or so of the Quaker movement. Because Quakerism was born in England, London Yearly Meeting was always looked upon as the parent body, and the visits of British Public Friends to this country were the most frequently cataloged. There was, however, a vigorous flow of American Friends to Great Britain, starting shortly after the establishment of Pennsylvania in 1681. The trips of these American Public Friends were also compiled. A particularly useful and clear list, *Ministering Friends of America who have visited foreign parts in Truth's Service*, is to be found in the Quaker Collection of the Haverford College Library.

According to this record, 103 Public Friends visited Great Britain between the years 1700 and 1800. (Some of the ministers, such as Susanna Morris and Samuel Emlen, made more than one trip in this period. The number includes only one trip for each minister.) Of this number, 42, or almost half, were women. Since Quaker history until recent decades focused on the lives of its most prominent members—George Fox, William Penn, Stephen Grellet, John Woolman, Job Scott, Thomas Scattergood, Elizabeth Fry, Lucretia Mott, and others—little attention has been paid to these traveling women ministers and the contribution they made to the growing respect for women within the Society of Friends and ultimately within the larger society.

Although the majority of the 42 were married, seven made the trip as single women. Barbara Bevan, a young member of Radnor Meeting in Pennsylvania who had become a minister at sixteen, traveled to Great Britain at age twenty and later died there. Ann Chapman of Wrightstown Meeting Pennsylvania was a single woman of thirty in 1711 when she made the first of two trips. Jane Fenn, mentioned above, traveled to Barbados in 1726 and to Great Britain in 1727, returning to Pennsylvania three years later, before she married. Elizabeth Hudson was twenty-seven when she set sail in 1748. Ann Chapman, Jane Fenn, and Elizabeth Hudson all married later in their thirties and forties. Elizabeth Whartenby came to Philadelphia as a widow in 1713 and supported herself by keeping a small shop. When she applied to her meeting for a certificate to travel in the ministry to Great Britain and Ireland in 1727, it was noted that she was to receive permission because of her "orderly conduct and freedom from marriage engagement." Margaret Ellis, originally from Wales, migrated to Pennsylvania against her father's objections and became a member of Radnor Meeting in 1730. She made the return trip in 1752, still a single woman. Rebecca Jones, who made an impact not only on Philadelphia Yearly Meeting but also London Yearly Meeting, was a teacher and minister who never married and shared her home and life with a beloved woman companion.

Most of the married women who traveled were beyond the childbearing years, but there were exceptions. Elizabeth Coggeshall was a young mother of twenty-eight when she traveled to Great Britain for three years in 1798. Margaret Lewis was approximately forty and the mother of nine children ranging in age from twenty to two years of age when she set out with Margaret Ellis in 1752. Although there is good evidence that Quaker women had some rudimentary knowledge of birth control, Margaret Lewis miscalculated. Seven and a half months after leaving Philadelphia she gave birth to a baby boy near the city of Bristol.[11] Up until two months before this birth, she kept up a rigorous schedule of riding from town to town, generally by horseback, and preaching at two or three meetings each day, as well as meeting with Quaker families for prayer and Bible reading.

Sometimes a woman's travels began before the oldest children were grown. Charity Cook, a minister from North Carolina who visited not only Great Britain but also the continent, began her travels in the ministry in 1776 with a trip to Georgia at age thirty-one. She left behind seven children with her husband, Isaac. The oldest was a son of twelve; the youngest, a baby of three months. Sarah, a ten-year-old daughter, undoubtedly helped her father, and friends and neighbors probably assisted, but Isaac is thought to have borne the chief responsibility of caring for the family.[12]

Patience Brayton, a Rhode Island Friend, traveled to the southern colonies in 1771 when she was thirty-eight, leaving a large family behind for her husband, Preserved Brayton, to care for. Several months after departing, she received a letter telling her that one of her children had died. Although she was grieved, she did not feel free to disobey her leading and abandon her mission, and she continued to travel for many months. Returning to Philadelphia, she began to long for home, since she was worried about her family. Twice she set out for Rhode Island and twice she felt she must return to Philadelphia. Finally it came to her that she had failed to speak in meeting in Philadelphia because of her fear of appearing inadequate before "great men." Acknowledging this fear seemed to be required of her by the Lord. Once she had admitted it, she felt that the Holy Spirit "took the word for the deed" and released her. On her return home she found her husband ill and one child near death from a prevalent fever. After this she remained at home for twelve years before feeling called to travel abroad.[13]

Many of the traveling women ministers set out with full knowledge that they might never see their families again, since illness and fevers were widespread during the eighteenth century. Three of the traveling ministers died in Ireland. A fourth marrried a man in Bristol and died four years later of smallpox. Ann Dilworth, who made the trip from Pennsylvania to Great Britain in 1700, left before her husband was given a traveling minute. He contracted yellow fever and died before he could set out to join her.[14]

Travel in the eighteenth century was both arduous and perilous. Susanna Morris of Richland Monthly Meeting in Bucks County, Pennsylvania, made three trips to England and several to the other American colonies. She was shipwrecked three times, once in Chesapeake Bay, once off the coast of Great Britain, and once in the Irish Sea. In each case she felt the Lord told her what to do, so that she and the crew would be saved. Patience Brayton described being lost in the woods, sleeping on the ground, crossing mountains in a snowstorm, and swimming with her horse over great rivers. Charity Cook, Sarah Harrison, and Mary Swett were imprisoned in Friedberg, Germany, in 1798, for attempting to hold a Quaker meeting. Finally released, they were sent under guard to the next town. Mary Swett recorded in her diary that she thought the guards were puzzled. "The officers after being with us several times were asked by Sarah Harrison if they believed that they were spies & they answered no. I believe it was the truth but they did not know what to do with us or what to make of us three such old women from America."[15]

Occasionally the adventures of the traveling ministers were of a less perilous but more embarrassing nature. Elizabeth Hudson, an adventurous young woman of twenty-seven from Philadelphia, arrived in Edinburgh one dark night just before nine o'clock. This was the time the city gates would be locked and the inhabitants of the tall houses would dump the day's accumulation of slop down on the street below. In her eagerness to find shelter for herself and her companion before this rain of filth occurred, Elizabeth Hudson inquired for a nearby inn and stopped there, only to discover she had somehow entered a brothel. With great presence of mind she dispatched a note to a local Quaker, who came and rescued them from this awkward situation. Later Eizabeth Hudson was captured by a highwayman while out on the lonely moors, but she persuaded him finally to release her.[16] Other women wrote of being asked to sleep in a room where men were also spending the night, or putting up in taverns where the drunken revels kept them awake to all hours.

Husbands were supposed to seek the agreement of wives, and wives, husbands, before making trips in the ministry. If, however, the spouse did not agree and the other partner continued to feel under divine pressure to make the trip, the meeting would sometimes intervene on the would-be traveler's behalf. In 1699 Jane Biles told her husband, William, that she felt a concern to visit Great Britain, the land of her birth. William, however, felt that her health was too poor to make the trip. Jane did not agree with his decision and informed the General Meeting of Ministering Friends of the situation in the tenth month of 1699. Again two months later she informed the meeting that she still felt she should go, even though William could not agree. The two were told to wait "for further assurance of mind of the Lord in it." Six months later the situation remained the same, and the meeting told Jane that she was at liberty to go, since the members were not satisfied with her husband's objections. The very next day William announced that he was now satisfied to "give up" Jane to her mission and that in fact he thought of accompanying her. Thinking that he had come around too readily, the meeting was not prepared to give him a traveling minute until another six months had passed. Jane decided to wait for him, and the two sailed together in the spring of 1701. Ironically, the nineteenth-century scribe who recorded this trip titled it as that of "William Biles and wife."[17]

Having left their families and braved the perils of shipwreck, the traveling Quaker women ministers who arrived in Great Britain during the eighteenth century were a spirited lot. Elizabeth Hudson felt it her duty to call a public meeting for the residents of a small town in northern England. The local Quakers objected, saying that "the Town never came to meetings, or was it usual to invite them they being a low, careless people." Elizabeth Hudson nevertheless insisted that an invitation be sent out, and to the surprise of her Quaker hosts, great crowds came and the meetinghouse was filled. Later she embarrassed another group of local Friends by calling for a public meeting and then not speaking, because she did not feel an opening to do so.[18]

The appearance of the American Quaker women, some of whom smoked pipes on the public streets, further embarrassed the British Friends, while the Americans found the growing wealth and social conservatism of their British cousins distressing. Part of the tension between the two groups arose over the fact that British women Friends were not permitted to hold a London Yearly Meeting of Women Friends. As early as 1753, American women began to protest this state of affairs. Susanna Morris, on her third trip to Great Britain at age seventy-one, raised a concern for a duly constituted women's yearly meeting at the male London Yearly Meeting, in cooperation with British women Friends. She was told that there could not be two heads to one body. The matter continued to concern American women until 1784, when a group of four American women—Rebecca Wright, Patience Brayton, Mehetabel Jenkins, and Rebecca Jones—attended the London Yearly Meeting. They supported their British sisters in a deputation to the men's meeting to once more request a women's yearly meeting. This time the proposal found favor, although the male Friends hastened to amend their decision by stating that the Yearly Meeting of Women

Friends held in London was not to be "so far considered a meeting of discipline as to make rules, nor yet alter the Queries, without the concurrence of this meeting."[19]

Before a minister was given permission to travel in the ministry by the granting of a traveling minute, the ministers of her monthly, quarterly, and yearly meeting had to be sure that her ministry was sound. This was especially true toward the end of the eighteenth century, when doctrinal differences were beginning to emerge. Hannah Jenkins Barnard, a Quaker minister born on Nantucket but living in Hudson, New York, came to Great Britain in 1798 with another New York minister, Elizabeth Coggeshall. Hannah Barnard found the British Friends in a "low state," with tensions between the wealthy and poor Friends and power concentrated in the hands of the wealthy, many of them elders in London Yearly Meeting.

Traveling to Ireland, Hannah Barnard met a group of Quakers who had been disowned for advocating reliance on the inner Light rather than the evangelical doctrines beginning to take hold of the Society. The leader of the Irish rebels, Abraham Shackleton, emphasized that the Bible must be interpreted through the inspiration of the Light within and that biblical passages that apparently conflicted with one's own experience of God need not be accepted.

Hannah Barnard, already of an inquiring mind, was emboldened by this encounter to state that she could not believe that the Almighty commanded the Israelites to make war upon other nations. She was evidently discreet in her announcement, because she left Ireland with the entire support of all Irish Quakers. However, when she applied to London Yearly Meeting for a certificate to travel in the ministry to Germany, her request was denied. A long dispute followed, and she was sent home and eventually disowned (the Quaker term for excommunicated) by her own monthly meeting. The fact that the heretic was a woman seemed to make the case more upsetting to the elders both in London and the United States.

In general, however, the traveling Quaker women were supported and encouraged wherever they went. Money was discreetly raised to pay for their passage both from the American colonies to Great Britain and back again, and they were provided with hospitality, horses, and at times nursing care. At home their monthly meetings oversaw the family and stepped in to help if help were needed. For instance, Comfort Hoag, a New Hampshire Friend, left her husband and children to travel in the ministry in the American colonies. Hearing from Samuel Fothergill, a traveling British Friend, that Comfort Hoag's husband and children were in difficult straits, Israel Pemberton of Philadelphia wrote to Zaccheus Collins of New Hampshire, asking him to aid the family without letting them know where the money was coming from.[20] A few years later, Comfort set off for Great Britain with Sarah Barney, but after the vessel sprang a leak and returned to port she told her companion that she believed that the Lord had "taken the will for the deed," and that she need not be away from her family. Her husband died shortly thereafter and she married Zaccheus Collins. She is mentioned in Quaker records for having lived to the age of 101.

From Mary Fisher to Hannah Barnard, the traveling Quaker women ministers were an adventurous lot. One cannot question that they felt themselves to be under divine orders, and that they experienced a marvelous confidence and release of energy to deal with whatever problems or obstacles appeared in their way. The stories of their adventures with the perils of sea and land were told again and again, and the retelling increased the respect that members of their communities came to feel toward any female called to the ministry. Particularly in the early years of the Quaker movement, a joyousness and a sense of living fully in the presence of the Holy Spirit pervaded the journals and letters of these women. Although they gave up many comforts, they achieved a joy and a sense of liberation that is rare indeed.

3. Development of the Women's Business Meetings, 1670–1800

When the traveling women ministers were not engaged in adventures abroad, they joined their sisters at home in an enterprise of a different nature: the establishment of separate women's business meetings. Since this was the first instance of Protestant women's participation in church business, theirs was a pioneering task. While the work of the traveling Quaker women ministers was perhaps more exciting, it was in the developing meetings for business that Quaker women learned to rely on their own strength and to develop their own talents together. In the nineteenth century, when observers began to note that many Quaker women took leadership in the women's rights movement, they credited the women's training in business meetings with providing the necessary experience.

Having no models to follow, women Friends in the new American colonies carefully read the epistles addressed to them by George Fox and by the Lancashire Women's Meeting, and they tried to develop their organizations exactly as suggested. Like the men, the women were supposed to organize meetings on four different levels: the preparative meeting, made up of Friends in an immediate neighborhood; the monthly meeting, consisting usually of five or six preparative meetings in a given geographic area; the quarterly meetings, representing groups of monthly meetings in a county; and a yearly meeting, covering a regional area. Philadelphia Yearly Meeting covered Pennsylvania, Delaware, New Jersey, and parts of Maryland, while New England covered the present states of Maine, Vermont, New Hampshire, Massachusetts, Rhode Island, and parts of Connecticut. There was also a select meeting of ministers on the local, county, and regional level. In these select meetings, men and women were supposed to meet together, although here and there Quaker men were slow to grant Quaker women equal status.

There was, and is today, no hierarchy within Quakerism. Each monthly meeting is self-governing. The yearly meeting exercises authority by developing the disciplines, codified into a book of discipline, under which the local meeting is supposed to regulate its activities and those of its members. In the early days, meetings that were persistently disobedient could be punished by being "laid down," or terminated. The yearly meeting also granted permission to travel to ministers wishing to venture into the territory of other yearly meetings. Thus it could prevent the spread of heresy by denying a traveling minute to a suspect minister.

Particularly in the colonial period when travel was difficult, the vitality of the Quaker movement lay in the monthly meetings. Since the Friends had no pastors, the principal concern of those meetings was the pastoral care of members. The women's meeting from the first played an active and necessary role in this work. The chief duties of the Quaker women were to watch over the "conversation" or moral behavior of their members, particularly the young; to speak to those who strayed; to provide for the poor and the ill; and to provide for the education of children.

The women's meeting was also responsible for examining young couples' "clearness" or readiness for marriage, looking into the questions of whether they had any other entanglements, had received permission from their parents, and were in good standing in the meeting. The couple had to appear twice before the women's meeting and then twice before the men's meeting, before permission was granted. This procedure could be rather intimidating. In 1725 the women of the Radnor Monthly Meeting, in Delaware County outside Philadelphia, admonished young members against taking large groups of supporters with them when they appeared before the men's meeting.[1] Once the marriage was approved, the men's and women's meeting both sent representatives to make sure it was conducted in an orderly and seemly fashion.

In theory—that is, according to the rules of discipline—the women's monthly meeting did not have the final authority either in cases of discipline or in clearness for marriage. The men's monthly meeting published papers of disownment and finally approved a marriage. In principle the men's meeting could overrule the women. In practice, this bit of male authority was not always exercised, especially in colonial times and in frontier settlements.

In the eighteenth-century Blackwater Monthly Meeting, Surry County, Virginia, for example, women apparently had exclusive control over marriage. Once a couple had been cleared by the women's meeting, they were pronounced "at liberty to marry when they please." This meeting also disciplined its own members, drawing up its own "instruments of disownment," apparently without consulting the men's meeting. The women of Cane Creek Monthly Meeting in North Carolina also showed the same independent spirit. They handled sixteen disownments of members between 1751 and 1761 before consulting the men's meeting.[2]

One of the first tasks of a women's meeting was to purchase a book for recording the minutes of the meeting and keeping accounts. Quakers always prided themselves on their careful and conscientious record keeping, and the women were particularly scrupulous. Since Quaker marriages without benefit of clergy were at first considered illegal in Great Britain, and births were not recorded in a parish church, careful membership records were a vital matter to the young society. Most of the women's meetings raised money, which they called "a stock," to respond to the needs of the poor and the widowed in their midst. Some meetings evidently received their stock from the men's meeting, but others gathered and recorded small sums at each session of monthly meeting. Those who collected their own funds appeared to gain strength from handling their own accounts.

In 1686 Radnor Monthly Meeting contributed funds toward "bilding a chimne for Margaret James" and for giving to the family of "Ellis ap Hugh two bushels of Wheat." Showing the cosmopolitan concerns of this pioneer meeting, it also sent funds to England for the relief of "Friends held captive at Maquenos under the Emperor of Morock," a reference to a group of traveling ministers captured and held in slavery by Moslem pirates.[3]

The early monthly meetings were training grounds for women who became strong in the ministry and the business of the Society of Friends. In turn, these budding leaders drew strength from other independent and self-respecting Quaker women. In 1708 a Nantucket women's monthly meeting was set up under the leadership of one such woman, Mary Starbuck. Daughter of Tristam Coffin, one of the pioneer settlers on Nantucket, and married to Nathaniel Starbuck, a partner in the purchase of the island, Mary Starbuck and her eldest son are credited with converting many of the residents of the island to a pre-Quaker form of religion, and later, after the arrival of some traveling Quaker ministers, to the sect itself. When Friends on Nantucket decided to form a meeting, she was one of four women, who, along with four men, applied to the New England Yearly Meeting. Permission was received for the men's meeting, but not the women's. The first monthly meeting held on the island was consequently for men only, while the women met separately for worship. After the men's meeting broke, the women announced that the Holy Spirit had instructed them to set up "their own monthly meeting."

The minutes of Nantucket Monthly Meeting for Women, meticulously kept, reveal how active the Nantucket women were in concern for education, the poor, and local morals. Nantucket, with its isolation and the frequent absence of husbands and fathers on whaling trips, became a training ground for the development of strong Quaker women: Lucretia Coffin Mott, Martha Coffin Wright, Phebe Hanaford, Maria Mitchell, and many other pioneer feminists came from Nantucket. Mary Starbuck herself lived to a ripe old age and played a role in the public life of the island as well as the meeting, earning herself the title "the Great Woman." According to local legend, she would often introduce her views by saying, "My husband and I think . . ." Whether or not Nathaniel agreed, he did not interrupt.

In Flushing, Long Island, meetings were originally held in the home of John Bowne, and it was here that the "Flushing Remonstrance" asking for freedom of religion on the island had been written. In the Flushing Monthly Meeting members of the Bowne family, first Grace and then Margaret, played a leading role. In Westbury, another early Long Island meeting, Phoebe Willets Mott Dodge visited families and wrote the epistles. Phoebe had at first felt called to travel to England in 1728, but her mother objected, and the meeting would not consent. So Phoebe stayed home, married Adam Mott in 1731, and had several children. One of them, Adam, was the grandfather of James Mott, Lucretia's husband. After her husband died, Phoebe made her long-postponed trip to Great Britain in 1752 and remained for a year, writing long letters back to her Long Island family. Following her return she married Tristam Dodge and continued to play a vital role in her meeting for another thirty years.

Grace Lloyd, the friend and protector of Jane Fenn Hoskens, was often clerk of Chester Monthly Meeting, and later became clerk of the Philadelphia Yearly Meeting. Her strength and motherly interest in the younger women of the meeting lent stability to Chester.

One measure of the strength of the American women's monthly meetings was the place accorded them in the design of American meetinghouses. Whereas in England the early meetinghouses often had a small loft or separate shed for the women's meetings, in the American colonies the meetinghouses were constructed from the beginning with more or less equal space for women. An ingenious system of movable shutters divided a large room into a men's side and women's side. During meeting for worship the shutters were raised, and the two sets of ministers sat on the front benches facing the body of the meeting, the female ministers facing the women, and the male, the men. Below them sat the elders, male and female, in the same order. Spoken ministry was thus heard by both the men and the women. During meeting for business, however, the shutters were lowered, and the men and women were able to meet separately. Men and women were appointed to carry messages to the opposite meeting whenever necessary.

Early Regional Meetings

The quarterly meeting met once every three months, using one of the meetinghouses within its jurisdiction. Men and women appointed by their monthly meetings met together for worship and separately for business with the shutters closed. This meeting served principally as a communication center, appointing representatives to the yearly meeting and receiving epistles and advices to be distributed to the monthly meetings within its area. It was also an arbiter of disputes. A man or woman who had been disciplined and wanted to appeal the decision of the monthly meeting could bring it to the quarterly meeting. Disputes between monthly meetings were sometimes addressed.

The quarterly meeting was one step removed from the real business of Quaker women—overseeing local membership matters—and therefore was sometimes a rather perfunctory affair. Women who wielded power at the local level sometimes deferred to their brothers at this level of formality. On the other hand, the women's quarterly meeting sometimes played the role of a yearly meeting when women possessed no such structure.

Quaker Woman preaching. Permission from the Friends General Conference.

The Rhode Island Women's Quarterly Meeting was organized in 1704, sixty years before a New England Women's Yearly Meeting was established in 1764. It exchanged epistles with several yearly meetings of women Friends and received reports from constituent monthly meetings. Under the leadership of Susanna Freeborn and others, this group nurtured a strong tradition of independence. Once the Rhode Island Men's Quarterly Meeting, having decided to hold the gathering every three months in different locations, met in January in Newport, forgetting to tell their sister meeting of the change. The women, gathering in East Greenwich, prepared a frosty formal complaint of this inconsiderate treatment. When the men apologized, the women received their paper huffily, remarking that they regarded themselves as "part of that body [the church of Christ] which admits of no division."[4]

In Virginia and North Carolina, where no women's yearly meeting existed until 1763, quarterly meetings played a somewhat expanded role. Not infrequently, a center of Quakerism, such as Flushing on Long Island and New Garden, North Carolina, became the headquarters of both a monthly and quarterly meeting, with the same women playing leading roles.

The first women's yearly meeting in the New World was organized in Maryland. It was actually a half-yearly meeting, alternating between the eastern and western shores of the Chesapeake Bay. (Later the eastern shore meetings were joined to Philadelphia.) On April 4, 1677, Maryland women agreed to hold a regular "general" meeting and to raise a stock of money to meet the needs of poor Friends. Margaret Berry, a source of strength to this meeting until 1688, was appointed to take care of the stock. The women also discussed the need for a school for the children. They began a correspondence with the women Friends of London, sending along two hogsheads of tobacco as a mark of their esteem.

We having Rseaved many Episels from our dear friends in London and of late a Prcell of Boocks as a token of true love to our women's Meeting here in Maryland, it is agreed upon at this our gnerall Meeting to wright a Lettr from ye womens Meeting hear in Maryland to ye Womens Meeting in London and to send it with two hhd. of tobacco . . .[5]

In the same year the women Friends expressed a concern that the children of Friends be educated in regard to the justice for "Affricans and their posterity formerly in slavery."

After this promising beginning, the Maryland Yearly Meeting of Women Friends continued strong. It soon received reports from representatives from the constituent meetings and dealt with the care of the poor and matters of discipline usually reserved for the men.

The New York Women's Yearly Meeting first met at Flushing in 1729, the third such body to meet in the New World. The minutes of the yearly, quarterly, and monthly meeting were kept in the same minute book until 1752, and apparently the same women were involved. Like other yearly meetings, the group at Flushing heard reports on the state of the Society in member groups, as the first record of the first meeting testifies:

At a yearly meeting held 1729 at Flushing where accounts were brought to us by the friends concerned in that service from the several meetings that friends were in love and unity and their meetings kept up and also the visitors of families gave us an account of that service to the satisfaction of the meeting. Also several faithful testimonies were borne and good counsel and advice given forth on the truth.[6]

The women Friends of Flushing Yearly Meeting, as it was first called, were soon exchanging epistles with London, Philadelphia (which had been organized in 1681), and "Road Island" and receiving reports from the Friends in Oblong Quarterly Meeting "on the Main," as the New York Yearly Meeting became less closely bound to Long Island.

In the middle of the eighteenth century, American Quakerism experienced a reformation and a tightening of its discipline. One recommendation made by the reformers was that women's meetings must be developed everywhere. In several areas of the country, where strong monthly and quarterly meetings had been apparently sufficient to meet the needs of the women, women's yearly meetings were now at last developed. These were New England, North Carolina, and Virginia.

Women of the Holy Experiment

William Penn, the founder of Pennsylvania, shared George Fox's vision of employing women's energies in the work of the Society, at least those aspects for which he thought women particularly fitted:

But it is asked why should women meet apart? We think for a very good reason. The church increaseth, which increaseth the business of the church, and women, whose bashfulness will not permit them to say or do much, as to church affairs before men, when by themselves, may exercise their gift of wisdom and understanding, in a direct care of their own sex, at least, which makes up not the least part of the business of the church, and this, while the men are about their own proper business, also, as men and women make up the church, men and women make up the business of the church.[7]

The encouragement of Penn, the sturdy self-reliance of the women Quakers, and the fact that Quakers were soon concentrated in Pennsylvania and New Jersey made the Philadelphia Women's Yearly Meeting particularly strong. At the first general meeting held in 1681 to establish Philadelphia Yearly Meeting, it was agreed that a women's meeting should be held. This body continued to meet annually thereafter, one year in Pennsylvania and one year in New Jersey until 1760, and in Philadelphia thereafter. During a bitter controversy that tore the Society apart in the first years, the minutes for the women's yearly meeting from 1682 to 1690 were unfortunately lost. This worried the Philadelphia women for many years, since the careful keeping of records was a matter on which they prided themselves.

At the women's meeting in 1691, a system of reports from the various quarterly meetings was begun, and each monthly meeting was admonished to answer the query as to whether members were "clear" or innocent of giving liquor to the Indians. The women also suggested that the monthly meetings take up a collection to send as a token of love to Friends in London.

In 1694 the Yearly Meeting developed a petition addressed to the inhabitants of the colony of Pennsylvania, objecting to the rudeness and wildness of the youth and children and advising parents to keep their offspring away from the "world's rude language, manners & vain needless Things & Fashions in apparel." Published and distributed, this petition bore the names of two Quaker women, an unusual public act for the day.[8]

Though the Philadelphia Women's Yearly Meeting sessions were carefully recorded, business at first appears to have been scanty. "Friends in Burlington have nothing to report but send their love," was a typical entry. The task of reading and answering epistles became an important part of each session. At first the women corresponded with London, later adding Maryland, Flushing, Rhode Island, Virginia, and North Carolina. In 1705 the women's yearly meeting decided to raise its own stock, if they could do so with the concurrence of men Friends. After the men's yearly meeting passed a minute "condescending" to this request, the women sent their funds to the "dear friends and sisters in East New England who are suffering great distress." Later they set aside these funds to aid those who traveled overseas in the ministry, including many of their own number.

At first the names of the women who clerked the meetings were not recorded in the minutes, but by 1726 a procedure was initiated whereby the representatives of the various quarters proposed the name of the presiding and recording clerk for each session. The clerks were women of stature in the Quaker community: Hannah Hill of the Philadelphia Monthly Meeting, a granddaughter of Thomas Lloyd, early governor of the colony; Grace Lloyd, the influential member of Chester Meeting; Mary Pemberton, wife of Israel Pemberton, clerk of the men's meeting; Hannah Cathrall, for many years the companion of traveling minister Rebecca Jones.

In 1756 at the time of reformation, the women's meeting read and answered the new queries developed by the men but decided to appoint a committee of their own to revise them and to "contract them by omitting such parts as appear calculated principally for the service of men Friends." The men, however, told the women to read the queries as written, omitting the word "brethren" and inserting "followers of Christ," when appropriate. Despite this snub to women's initiative, the men invited the women's meeting to appoint several of their number to the new committee in charge of discipline, "with a single eye to the exaltation of Truth and the exaltation of the church."

One result of the period of reformation was the decision on the part of the women's meeting to copy the epistle they received from London and share it with constituent quarterly meetings. They suggested that the London women do the same. When they learned that the London women did not have a properly constituted yearly meeting of their own, they sent a delegation to the men's yearly meeting to ask that some proposal for helping the London women might be suggested. The men, however, were not prepared to challenge the home meeting:

The friends appointed to attend the Men's Meeting with the above Minute returned with an answer in writing signifying they received a proposal of a Yearly Meeting for Women Friends in London as a matter of weight, and should give it due consideration . . . that they truly sympathized with the present circumstances of our Friends in England, and that they had appointed a committee to consider the affair, and who upon solidly deliberating they agreed to report that it was their sense and judgment that Friends here should abide under the weight of the concern and exercise, until a more convenient time offered to move thereon, especially as they had been informed that Friends in England had lately endeavored to bring about such a work, without the desired result.[9]

A more convenient time never came for this concern to be acted upon officially by Philadelphia Yearly Meeting, but the women continued to keep alive their interest in helping their British sisters achieve more control of their own affairs. When Rebecca Jones and her three American colleagues supported the move for a British women's yearly meeting in 1784, they had the full if informal support of the Philadelphia Women's Meeting.

Aside from the effort to enlist the men in their concern for London Yearly Meeting, the women's meeting remained in general rather docile until a problem of meetinghouse space arose. From 1760 on, the women held their yearly meeting in the Great Meetinghouse near Market Street in Philadelphia. On market days, which were every day but First day, the stalls along Market Street were in full cry, and the women found it difficult to hear one another. The women appointed a committee to contact the men with a concern for a new building.

The men's meeting did not see the necessity, but the women persevered and after eight years were able to report that the men had concurred, and a new building would be erected.[10]

Over the years, the minutes of the women's meetings reveal a slowly increasing confidence on the part of these Quaker women that made it possible for them to assert themselves, especially on matters concerning either their own space or the welfare of other women. As the years passed the minutes grew longer and more complete, and a spirit of independence emerged. After the reformation, more and more women served on joint committees with men. Slowly the full meaning of the belief that "in souls there is no sex" was beginning to take hold. And if some of the functions of the early Quaker women seem conventional—care of the children, the poor, and the sick—it must be remembered that the Society of Friends as a whole was concerned with these matters. The women's meetings were at the very heart of preserving and developing the androgynous values that had set aside from the very beginning the Children of Light.

4. Quaker Women in Colonial America

One of the early families to take up land in Penn's new colony was that of John and Barbara Bevan of Treverigg, Glamorganshire, Wales. John was a devoted Welshman, but Barbara thought it would be better to raise their children in a Quaker community and prevent their corruption by the loose behavior of youth and the bad example of many aged persons in their native village. "As I was sensible her aim was an upright one, on account of our children, I was willing to weigh the matter in true balance," John later wrote. He agreed in 1683 to emigrate to Pennsylvania. They spent twenty-one years in the new colony and saw four of their children married and settled there before John decided he would like to die in his beloved Wales.[1] Their daughter Barbara had become a minister at age sixteen. She returned with them to a land she had never seen, traveled in the ministry, and died at twenty-two.

The Bevans' story illustrates the central position the early Friends gave both to childraising and to the role of women in family decision making. Early minutes of advice by women's meetings constantly referred to the importance of parents setting a good example as the prime means of raising children properly. Although naughty children were sometimes whipped, and disobedient youth were threatened with disinheritance, Quaker parents emphasized reasoning and persuasion. John Woolman recorded in his journal that at age twelve he had made an "undutiful" reply to his mother. His father brought the matter up when they were riding home from meeting, and John felt such shame and confusion that he never again "spoke unhandsomely to either of my parents."[2]

Young Quakers were free to choose their own mates, and although parents might exercise a veto, the meeting could over-rule them if a committee found the reasons for parental objections were arbitrary. Young men and women sought divine guidance in their choice of mates, but in most cases this was a matter of seeking sanction for the choice of their affections. John Smith, a devout Quaker minister who felt led to court Hannah Logan, wrote to her in 1747 that "a man in love was the silliest creature in the universe." Dr. Richard Hill told his daughter Rachel in 1758 that he believed the happiness of a marriage depended "principally on a mutual and well grounded affection," so that he would never persuade a child to marry anyone for whom such affection was not felt.[3]

Once married, husband and wife were to live together as helpsmeet, with "no rule but love between them," according to the advice of London Yearly Meeting. The two should exercise authority over children and servants, but this authority should be tempered by sweetness. Although in matters of business and politics—matters outside the home—the husband was generally in charge, within family boundaries decision making was shared. Fox's many epistles on the subject of marriage stressed the concept that marriages made under the leading of the Light were "honorable, and the marriage bed was not defiled." Quaker wives were not to be viewed as descendants of Eve, seducing their husbands to the sin of sex, but as equal partners, at least in the enterprise of raising children. The Quaker marriage ceremony, in which the man and the woman took each other on equal terms, neither one promising obedience (a ceremony that has continued untouched to this day), also attests to the respect felt for women within the Society of Friends. While the status of Quaker women in colonial America was certainly not equal to that of the men, it was considerably higher than that of women of other sects.

Because of the scrupulous care with which Quakers recorded marriages, births, and deaths, Friends have extensive and complete demographic records from colonial times. Studies made from these records reveal that the high status of Quaker women affected the composition of colonial families. The stereotype of colonial marriage in which the wife married young, had many children, died early, and was in turn replaced by another young wife, does not prove true in the case of the Quakers. Quaker women born before 1730 married at the average age of 22.8 years, while comparable males married at 26.5 years. Most couples were close in age, and marriages between older women and younger men were not uncommon. The average span of these marriages was 30.8 years, and the couples produced 6.7 children. Women were more likely to outlive their husbands than vice versa. Remarriages after the death of a mate were accepted, although Friends tried to insist that they not take place for at least a year.[4] Of the traveling Quaker ministers, fifteen of the thirty-eight who married were widowed; of these, four married a second time, and two a third time.

As the decades passed, Quaker women married later and had fewer children. Studies indicate that after 1760 they must have used some form of birth control to limit their families. Those who married early were able to space their later children and to stop producing before the end of the childbearing years, while those who married late and desired children had them up until the age of menopause.[5]

Quaker mothers generally nursed their babies, although the wealthier families occasionally employed a wet nurse, preferably at home but occasionally at the home of the nurse. Mary Pemberton, the second wife of Israel Pemberton, wrote her brother-in-law that "after much fatigue with nurses, have plac'd our Little boy abroad, with a honest Reputable woman, in an airey part of the town, much to our satisfaction, and he thrives well."[6] Younger mothers, however, preferred to nurse because breastfeeding was considered a means of birth control. Also, Quaker women ministers preached against the practice of employing a wet nurse, claiming that it was motivated by selfishness and deprived the infant of tender care and "a close sympathy" between mother and child.

One reason most Quaker parents in colonial America desired a large family was that probably some children would die before they grew up. The death of infants or toddlers was a part of life for all colonial families. One estimate suggests that one out of every three children died before the age of five. Puritans dealt with the possibility of children's death by baptizing them and zealously supervising their moral development, lest any be consigned to hell. Quakers, however, were quite sure that children of parents who had received the Light would not be so punished. Margaret Hill Morris, a young Philadelphia matron, lost one twin son in 1760 and recorded a prayer on the occasion of his death:

O thou, whose bounteous hand has given me many sweet and delightful cups to drink, be pleased, I pray thee, to sanctify to my soul this which appears at present to be a bitter one. . . . My darling first-born child thou hast pleased to take from me; and as thy wisdom saw fit not accept of him as servant, I thank thee that thou art pleased to accept him as a saint, spotless and innocent as I received him from thee. Oh that he may be as acceptable an offering as Abraham's only son in thy sight! Great God! I pray thee to pardon me if at times nature—fond nature—should so far prevail as to make me wish it had been thy will to spare him to me. . . .[7]

Elizabeth Collins, a minister in Evesham, New Jersey, recorded in her journal in 1793 at the time of a yellow fever epidemic that she heard an inner voice saying, "A great sacrifice will be required of thee." Shortly thereafter she lost three children in a row. Sitting at the bedside of one dying child the day after burying another, she again heard a voice that said, "Just entering the city whose walls are salvation and her gates praise." This comforted her sufficiently to endure the loss.[8]

Miscarriages were frequent and also produced a sense of loss and depression. Martha Cooper Allinson, a New Jersey minister, was the mother of seven children, but she had a series of miscarriages in her later childbearing years. She wrote in 1790 that she had just suffered a painful miscarriage but had found that a "distressed tossed & not comforted mind is more afflicting & hard to bear than any Bodily pain."[9]

Many Quaker women in the colonial period never married and still retained a respected position in the Quaker community. The fact that they could travel in the ministry or teach school or support themselves by other means prevented their being seen as a burden on the households of their male relatives. Of daughters born to Quaker families before 1786, 9.8 percent of those who lived to age fifty never married. After 1786, the figure jumped to 23.5 percent. In Philadelphia in the second half of the nineteenth century, 40 percent of all Quaker women were single, though this was probably a special case and would not hold true of Quaker women in the Midwest.[10] It was not unusual for two single Quaker women to share a home and a warm devotion to one another, as in the case of Rebecca Jones and Hannah Cathrall.

Educating Daughters

Although Quaker girls were taught household skills in colonial America, they were also given some degree of education. George Fox had been interested in the education of both boys and girls and had recommended the founding of a school at Shacklewell, England, "for instructing girls and young maidens in whatsoever things are civil and useful in the creation." George Fox also wrote a primer for the instruction of Quaker children of either sex. Shortly after he established Philadelphia, William Penn granted a charter to Philadelphia Monthly Meeting to conduct a school designed "to teach the rich at moderate rates and the poor to be maintained and schooled for nothing." Under this charter, the Quakers ran schools in Philadelphia for Quakers and non-Quakers and blacks and whites of both sexes until the time of the American Revolution.

These schools not only provided education for girls, but also jobs for young Quaker women. The first schoolteacher mentioned in the Philadelphia Monthly Meeting minutes was a

Margaret Morris. Permission
from the Quaker Collection,
Haverford College Library,
Haverford, PA. Photo by Ted
Hetzel.

Hannah Penn. Permission from
the Historical Society of
Pennsylvania.

woman, Olive Songhurst, who asked for an increase in salary
in 1702. In subsequent minutes many women were mentioned
as conducting schools under the care of the meeting, primarily
those run for the poor and for blacks.

Epistles from London Yearly Meeting during the colonial period regularly urged parents to oversee their children's education. The women's meetings for business in the various
colonies devoted time to this issue. Ideally, each monthly meeting was to conduct a grammar school in order to teach children
in the area to read and write. These early schools, however,
tended to be transitory affairs. A local Friend might be engaged
to teach school for a period, but when he or she moved on to
other things, the school was neglected. Studies made in Virginia, North Carolina, Maryland, and New England indicate
that there were no stable schools until the beginning of the
nineteenth century. Rhode Island founded a school early in the
eighteenth century, but it was never continuously staffed. Even

Nantucket, with its concern for the education of girls as well as boys, did not have a stable school until 1797. Only in Pennsylvania and New Jersey, with their comparative density of Quaker population, were schools maintained regularly, and most of these were within the Philadelphia area itself. Abington Monthly Meeting established a school in 1697, which is still in existence. Radnor Monthly Meeting may have opened a school as early as 1731, but it had closed by the nineteenth century.

Nevertheless, Quaker children of both sexes received at least rudimentary education, either from their parents, aunts, and uncles, or from "dame schools" in the neighborhood. By studying signatures on marriage certificates and noting how many persons signed with a mark, one historian was able to develop some idea of literacy rates for colonial American Quakers. Although more women than men were illiterate, the group as a whole was far more literate than the non-Quaker population in England at the same time.[11]

Quaker fathers, particularly those of some wealth and leisure, took an interest in the education of their daughters. In 1723 James Logan wrote of his daughters' education to his brother, William:

Hannah [age 3] is a very hearty child, spelling in her Primer. . . . Sally [9], besides her needle, has been learning French and this last week, has been very busy in the dairy at the plantation, in which she delights as well in spinning, but is this moment at the table beside me (being first-day afternoon and her mother abroad), reading the 34th psalm in Hebrew, the letters of which she learned very perfectly in less than two hours' time, an experiment I made of her capacity only for my diversion, though I never design to give her that or any other learned languages, unless French can be accounted as such.[12]

Despite the apparent slur to women's education in this letter, Logan insisted his daughters read Milton, Pope, and Dryden as well as translations of Lucan, Homer, Juvenal, Horace, Seneca, Pythagoras, Epictitus, and Xenophon. They were allowed full access to his magnificent library. Isaac Norris also encouraged his daughters to read widely. Elizabeth Hudson recalled in her journal that while staying with Elizabeth Norris at Fairhill she "had also the opportunity of their liberary in which was a good collection of books that at times I Entertained myself with having some lust of books and indeed in time found had too high a relish for them, they being very Ingrossing both of our time."[13]

Dr. Richard Hill was a Maryland Friend who moved with his wife Deborah to the island of Madeira in 1739 because of some financial difficulties. The Hills left six children in Philadelphia under the care of their newly married daughter, Hannah Moore, herself just sixteen. Both parents wrote many letters home suggesting ideas for the instruction of these distant children. Deborah wrote to Hannah that she approved of Hannah's decision to educate her little sisters at home. They ought to write a copy or two every day, and also do needlework, she advised. Richard wrote to the older daughters suggesting that they improve their minds by reading good and instructive books, write many letters in order to develop their handwriting, and look into a spelling book or dictionary whenever they were not sure of the spelling of a word. At a time when spelling was still haphazard, this was good advice indeed. Several of the Hill daughters later became proficient journal keepers.

For Philadelphia families interested in the education of daughters, the decision of Philadelphia Monthly Meeting to establish a girls' school in 1754 under the tutelage of a famous educator and abolitionist, Anthony Benezet, solved the problem of finding a good tutor to come to the home. Benezet taught French, Latin, and the classics, insisted that his pupils learn to compose short literary pieces, and provided opportunity for gymnastic exercises. Among his students were Deborah Norris, later Logan, the first woman historian; Rebecca Jones, teacher and traveling minister; Sally Wister, journalist; and Anne Emlen, a clerk of Philadelphia Women's Yearly Meeting. Poor girls were also educated at this school, which has been called the first public school for girls in the American colonies.

Public Figures

Although the young Quaker girl in colonial America might aspire to be a teacher or a traveling minister, other role models existed also. In New Jersey lived Elizabeth Estaugh, who as Elizabeth Haddon, a young woman of twenty, had come to the American colonies in 1701 to manage some large tracts of land bought by her father in the county of Gloucester near the site of the present town of Haddonfield. John Haddon had originally planned to emigrate, but his business responsibilities and growing health problems had prevented it. When Elizabeth told her parents that she felt divinely led to go in his place, to establish a home in the wilderness for traveling Quaker ministers and to serve as a physician to the colonists and the Indians, they were at first very unwilling to give their permission, thinking her very young to manage a plantation. She agreed to wait three months and spent the time studying herbal medicine. Seeing that she was determined and evidently sure of her leading, her parents then consented, providing her with a female companion and two male servants to travel with her.

After a brief stay in Philadelphia, Elizabeth Haddon and her company settled in, planted a crop of corn and rye, and enlarged the house already standing on the land. Four months after her arrival, Elizabeth was ready to entertain traveling ministers. Among the first to stop was John Estaugh, whom Elizabeth had first seen when he preached in London Yearly Meeting. According to a legend perpetuated by the poet Henry Wadsworth Longfellow and the journalist Lydia Maria Child, Elizabeth felt a leading that John was to become her husband and told him, "I have received from the Lord a charge to love thee, John." John was at first unprepared for this news but evidently later received a corresponding charge, for in December of 1702 they were married.

Although John became legal head of the Haddon plantations after their marriage, he continued to travel in the ministry, not only in the colonies but also in England and Ireland and the

West Indies. He was also frequently ill. Elizabeth therefore continued to manage the estates. In 1713 she moved to the present site of Haddonfield. She also continued to develop her healing skills. A salve she invented was still being used in the area one hundred years after her death.

The Estaughs had no children, so a nephew, Ebenezer Hopkins, inherited the lands. Despite the lack of a family, so highly valued in colonial times, their married life was regarded as idyllic. "I will venture to say few if any in the married state ever lived in sweeter harmony than we did," Elizabeth wrote in memorial. John died of a fever on Tortola Island, in the Caribbean, in 1742. Elizabeth outlived him by twenty years, and as a widow again managed the plantation. She donated the land on which the Haddonfield Monthly Meeting was built and served as clerk of its women's meeting for many years.[14]

Another colonial woman who served as proprietor was Hannah Penn, William's second wife. Originally, William's attitude toward marriage had reflected the class in which he was raised. He urged men to look for a wife who would be "a companion, a friend, a second self" and admired the educated young woman, Gulielma Springett, whom he married in 1672. Yet he expected Guli to devote herself to the home and children and did not give her any responsibility for his estates when he traveled to Pennsylvania in 1682. Instead he made a disastrous choice, turning his affairs over to Philip Ford, a man who later defrauded him.

After Guli's death, William looked for a second wife with the capacity to aid him, and he chose Hannah for her common sense and her business acumen. In 1699 Hannah Penn accompanied William to Philadelphia, where he intended to settle at Pennsbury on the Delaware. They had to return to England in 1701 to take care of pressing matters relating to Penn's colony. During the intervening months, Hannah was occupied with the birth of a son and with overseeing the new plantation while William was busy with his colonists. Nevertheless, she won respect for her common sense, prudence, and dignity. Such men as James Logan, Penn's agent, and Isaac Norris spoke highly of her.

William and Hannah never returned to Philadelphia. In 1712 William was incapacitated by a series of crippling strokes, and Hannah took over the management of the colony of Pennsylvania from their home in Ruscombe, England. In correspondence with James Logan, she guided the colony and protected it from Penn's son by his first marriage, William Junior, who was endeavoring to exploit it for his own gain. At first in favor of surrendering the colony to the crown in order to clear William Penn of debts, she came to feel that it was her responsibility to keep it under the management of the Penns in order to keep the promises William had made to his colonists. After William Penn died in 1718, she managed all his estates as well as those of her deceased parents. By 1726, when she died, she had the satisfaction of seeing William Penn's will settled. For the young women of colonial Pennsylvania she presented a legendary and powerful role model. She illustrated the capacity of a woman to manage affairs in the world of business, still so much relegated to men.[15]

A much more visible woman of affairs was Susanna Wright, who lived on the frontier of Pennsylvania in Chester County on the Susquehanna River, the present site of Columbia. A single woman, Susanna Wright was widely read, wrote poetry, was fluent in French and conversant in Italian and Latin, and maintained a lively interest in natural sciences. After the death of her mother, she managed her father's household for twenty years, then assumed responsibility for her brother James's family, living in a house she inherited from another pioneer. In addition to managing these plantations, she experimented with raising silkworms and producing silk from her own mulberry trees. Benjamin Franklin, one of her correspondents, presented a court dress made of her silk to Queen Charlotte of England. She was interested in her frontier neighbors, often helping them by writing their wills and other legal documents and prescribing simple herbal remedies for their ills. She was a friend of the local Conestoga Indians, and she came to their defense when they were attacked by frontier hoodlums in 1763.

As she grew older, Susanna Wright became a well-known figure in Philadelphia. Deborah Norris Logan, the first American woman historian, in later years vividly remembered Susanna Wright's visits to her father's country home and the impression she made on all she met. Despite her worldly learning, she continued to dress very plainly and observe Quaker practices.

Other colonies also contained prominent Quaker women. Sophia Hume, the granddaughter of Mary Fisher, grew up in South Carolina. After she became a widow she left the Episcopal church and returned to the Quakerism of her ancestry. Although she moved to England, she traveled frequently in the southern colonies. Her book decrying luxury, *An Exhortation to the Inhabitants of the Province of South Carolina*, published in 1748, was widely read by Friends and non-Friends alike. A second book, *A Caution to Such as Observe Days and Times*, besides defending Quaker practice, offered remarks on theological and social topics. Paradoxically, she brought from her Anglican background the belief that a woman should lead a secluded life devoted to home and church, while she herself was fond of erudition and of public life.

Everyday Colonial Life

It is not easy to form a clear picture of the life of ordinary colonial Quaker women. Those who kept journals devoted their writing almost exclusively to their travels or religious experiences and said very little about their families or their communities. One exception is the journal of Ann Cooper Whitall from New Jersey, the ancestor of a long line of Quaker feminists including Hannah Whitall Smith and M. Carey Thomas. In a small book written with a spelling style all her own, Ann Whitall mixed acerbic observations of her husband and her neighbors with pious exhortations to herself and others.

Born in 1716 in Haddonfield, Ann Cooper married James Whitall in 1739 and moved with him to a farm in Red Bank, New Jersey, on the banks of the Delaware River. The two had nine children. Ann Whitall was a pious and gloomy Friend, but her husband was fond of "gadding about," she claimed, and he rarely went to meeting with her. (This charge must be weighed against the minutes of Haddonfield Quarterly Meeting, which show him to have been a Friend in good standing, frequently appointed to committees.) When the fish were running in the Delaware, the men gathered in fishing parties, drinking hard cider and carousing.

3-16-1760. firs day to meeting a poor dad condition some of the time oh this enimy of our sols & this ant all the trublel I have for if the children & I am at hom thare father wont stay at hom (not three firs days in the hol year if he can help it: I often think if I run gadding about so as he dus what sort of a house shud we ceep. . . .

10-4-1760 I am ful of sorrow & indeed I always am in fishing tim for I think thare is so much drinking & play & prating that there cant be much gud in there heds I hant sol tham any sider yet I have most pees to sell them non at all. . . . When Nese Lord was here she did believe it never was harder to bring up children to be good in any age of the world then it is now & if she was here in fishing time I shuld have won to help me, I believe.

Shortly after Ann Whitall uttered these lamentations, James Whitall nearly died. He was cutting a piece of cedar to make a spill to draw the cider, and the knife slipped and pierced his breast, going through his thick clothes and just missing his heart. Ann nursed him and rejoiced in his narrow escape, concluding that though they disagreed on many matters, it would be "a hundred fold wose if I was alone with such a pasal of children."[16]

Ann Whitall almost never mentioned her daily chores of keeping the house and tending the children. That men and women both worked from morning to night was taken for granted. One Quaker husband, however, took time to enumerate the tasks of his wife:

To do her that justice which her services deserve by entering them minutely would take up most of my time, for this genuine reason that, from early in the morning till late at night, she is constantly employed in the affairs of the family which for some months has been very large, for besides the addition to our family in the house is a constant resort of comers and goers who seldom go away with dry lips or hungry bellies. This calls for her constant attendance not only to provide, but also to attend at getting prepared in the kitchen, baking our own bread and pies, meat &., but also on the table. Her cleanliness about the house, her attendance in the orchard, cutting and drying apples, of which several bushels have been procured, add to which her making of cider without tools, for the constant drink of the family, her seeing all our washing done, and her fine clothes and my shirts, all which are all smoothed by her, add to this her making of twenty large cheese, and that from one cow, and daily using milk and cream besides her sewing, knitting & . . . she also stretches out her hand to needy friends and neighbors.[17]

The wife described came from a comparatively well-to-do home that employed servants. In the country and on the frontier, life was much harder and servants were scarce. When Rachel and John Wright, the parents of Charity Wright Cook, arrived in Cane Creek Valley, North Carolina, in 1748, with seven children between the ages of three months and ten years, they had to build a house and clear the land and raise enough food to feed the family. Each child, no matter how young, had to be given some task to perform. Yet Rachel was a traveling minister, and she put the needs of the Quaker meeting first. In 1751 she and her neighbor, Abigail Pike, the mother of nine, volunteered to ride two hundred miles through the wilderness to attend Quarterly Meeting at Little River in Perquimans County, in order to ask that Cane Creek be allowed as a monthly meeting. No one seemed to think that this was an unusual service for two busy mothers to undertake. They returned safely, having accomplished their mission, and the meeting was set up on June 30, 1751. Both continued to be traveling ministers, leaving their growing broods with their husbands and older children. They were extremely pious women, but it is likely that getting away from the rigors of family life promised both relief and adventure. Perhaps their motives were innocently mixed.

5. Reformation and Revolution

In the American colonies, and especially in Pennsylvania, the Quakers prospered. Their industrious habits and their reputation for honest dealings made them successful merchants and bankers. Some became wealthy, owning summer plantations as well as city residences. Some invested in real estate and in mines. Both in England and in America a class of Quaker grandees emerged, famous for keeping a good table and for dressing in "the best, but plain." Some went beyond this and were called gay, or fast Friends.

As a result of their growing wealth and power, the leading Philadelphia Quaker families formed a virtual establishment. The children of these families—Norrises, Pembertons, Logans, Drinkers, Emlens, and Fishers—intermarried. Generations of Quaker merchants served in the Pennsylvania Assembly and as weighty members of Philadelphia Yearly Meeting. Their wives and daughters too were prominent. Marriages took place with leading British Friends, and transatlantic visits and correspondence were frequent. Many of the wealthy families paid frequent social visits to one another.

Anne Head Warder, a young British matron, came to Philadelphia in 1786 to visit her husband's family, and she kept a journal for the amusement of her sister, Elizabeth, recording the strange ways of the Americans. Her clothes were regarded as too worldly by the Philadelphians. She in turn felt the American women's use of brown and drab was ugly, although she noted that they took pains with their costume. The custom of paying constant visits among friends and relations was time consuming, she thought. It was impossible to keep up with one's mending, and if one slighted a cousin or other connection, they were sure to complain.

I darned a place in my light calico gown torn some weeks ago, have had no time before to darn it, in which situation I have now a great heap of work that decreases very slowly through gossiping about, which is unavoidable without giving my kind friends offense, for the great number I have got once around renders it necessary to begin again. . . . It is a custom to visit here more than with us, and they destroy the social freedom of it by too much dressing.[1]

Sarah Logan Fisher, the wife of a Philadelphia merchant, wrote regularly to an English cousin, giving news of the American branch of the family. She revealed the strong Anglophile attitudes of the wealthy American Quakers of the time, asking this cousin to help members of the firm visiting London to pick out articles of clothing for the children, "handsome and gentell" such as Friends children in England might wear. Her brother, George Logan, had married an "amiable and accomplished young woman, & one who even would be admired in England for the Beauty of her person and the elegance of her manners." This bride was Deborah Norris Logan, the historian.[2]

To a lesser degree, the same trends were developing in other metropolitan centers where Quakers were prominent—New York City, Providence, and Baltimore. The urban Friends were thus becoming wealthy and worldly, with resulting changes in the daily lives of Quaker women. Rural Friends, on the other hand, continually struggled to educate the young people in Quaker disciplines and to prevent them from marrying out of meeting and converting to Anglican or Presbyterian churches. Without the stirring spirit of the early Friends, the quiet meetings were too often used for sleeping. Discipline was lax, and ministry lacked fervor. It began to seem as though the Society of Friends was about to lose its identity and its members to become merged with "the world's people."

In addition to these problems of discipline, common throughout the colonies, the Pennsylvania Quakers were struggling to maintain their pacifism while controlling the governing body of the colony, the Assembly. Subject to the Crown of England, they were regularly called on to provide funds for the British army. Taking a position that Friends should pay taxes unless they were specifically for purposes that violated their consciences, the Quakers in government regularly voted money to "the King's use," without facing the obvious fact that the funds were used to buy guns and ammunition. This bothered some consciences, but it seemed a necessary compromise in order to keep the colony under Quaker rule.

In time this problem became even more complex. By the middle of the eighteenth century Friends had become a minority in their own colony, since their policy of toleration had attracted many settlers of other persuasions. Frontier settlers who had no tradition of pacifism were in direct contact with the Indians. Through seizing Indian lands, these settlers came into frequent conflict with their neighbors and demanded more defense against the Indians from the Quaker Assembly.

This developing conflict reached a head during the French and Indian War. The British were demanding large sums in order to protect the colonists, including those of Pennsylvania. The proprietors of the colony, Anglican descendants of William Penn and their Pennsylvania allies, were eager to oust the Friends from government. They reported in London that the Quakers were irresponsible pacifists and urged the crown to bar them from seats in the Assembly. London Yearly Meeting lobbied to prevent this defeat for Quakerism from taking place, but the best compromise they could reach demanded that the Pennsylvania Friends voluntarily withdraw from their seat of authority. It soon became clear that the Friends could not continue in government without seriously jeopardizing their consciences. In 1755 they began to withdraw from the Assembly and other public posts.

The loss of control of the colony that had been formed as a haven for Friends was a blow to the self-confidence of the Pennsylvania Quakers, and it affected Quakers in other colonies as well. Male and female ministers from both England and America who had been preaching against the worldliness and extravagance prevalent in the Society took this loss as a sign that reformation was needed. In September of 1755, at the Philadelphia Yearly Meeting, changes were put into effect. A reformation was launched that spread throughout the American colonies and ultimately affected the status of Quaker women and the value system of all Friends.

In the years from 1755 to 1775, Quaker discipline was tightened, queries—questions for regular self-examination by individuals and by the group regarding beliefs and practices—were developed to be read and answered by monthly meetings, delinquents were disowned, education was strengthened, and humanitarian concerns, such as the abolition of slavery, were undertaken. Friends withdrew from public life into a period of quietism, which prevailed for almost one hundred years. It was not a static situation, however. Behind the walls that Friends erected between themselves and the rest of the world, new trends developed. The increased emphasis on education and reform movements was a step away from preoccupation with power, a step toward shared concerns for men and women.

Scruples Against War

The Quaker reformation, with its increased emphasis on the peace testimony, was in full swing by the time the American Revolution began. Friends believed not only that they ought to keep out of all armed conflict, but that they ought to be loyal to established government, so long as that government did not impose on their consciences. Although many Friends had objected to the Stamp Act and had joined in the nonviolent resistance to the importation of British tea, they felt they could have no part in the preparations for armed revolution. They therefore refused to serve in the militia and were reluctant to use the continental currency because it supported both the war and the revolution. Anne Emlen, a young Philadelphia reformer, wondered in 1780 if she ought to leave her mother's house, since her mother would not forsake the use of the congressional currency. She later turned down a marriage proposal from a man whose estate was collected with the aid of such currency, and she refused to accept interest, "or at least as high interest as customary," on her patrimony, because it would mean accepting the currency. In 1781 she asked to address the men's Yearly Meeting in regard to her scruples on this matter, but she was not admitted to the meeting because she came as an individual without the approval of the women's yearly meeting.[3]

Friends felt they should remain quiet in the tumult of war surrounding them. They tried to maintain normal lives in the face of the conflict as a way of witnessing to a way of life which if universal, would take away all "occasion," or reason for war. The minutes of the women's yearly meetings for the period make almost no mention of the conflict. The New York Yearly Meeting for women commented in 1777 that they had not received an epistle from Philadelphia, "which we rather impute to the difficulty of conveyance." The next year the same meeting observed it had had no report from "Friends on the Main due to difficulties attending passing to this place occasioned by the commotions now prevailing." New England mentioned in 1779 that their last epistle had failed to reach Philadelphia. The Philadelphia women casually spoke of "the current time of tryal and outward commotion."

When Ann Moore, an elderly Friend from Gunpowder, Maryland, felt drawn to visit Friends in New York in 1778, she and her companions traveled up through Pennsylvania and into New Jersey without running into trouble. In Rahway, New Jersey, they decided to see General Anthony Wayne and show him their traveling certificates. With his permission they attempted to cross into Manhattan, held by the British, but they were forbidden to do so by British troops. Several of the party, though not Ann Moore herself, went so far as to see a colonel on Staten Island and ask for a pass. With this in hand, they crossed the war zone peacefully and continued their journey, concluding it without further trouble.

Phebe Yarnall, a Chester County Friend, felt "drawings in my mind to visit Friends eastward" in 1776. Paying no attention to the war, she traveled to Philadelphia, crossed the river to New Jersey, and drove to Woodbury, Greenwich, and Salem with Rebecca Wright, another traveling minister. They heard the cannon roar, saw men marching, and heard that English men-of-war were on the river. Phebe wrote her husband that they might not meet again, but she hoped he would stand fast and seek divine guidance if soldiers came to his farm to ask for provisions. She and her companion then set forth for New York and New England, quite impervious to the war.

In 1777 a battle was fought on the farm of James and Ann Cooper Whitall at Red Bank, New Jersey. The American patriots had seized part of the farm and built a fort in the orchard on the banks of the Delaware. British gunboats from the river and a company of Hessian soldiers together attempted to seize this fort. James took shelter in the basement, but Ann, believing that she should not recognize the warfare in this fashion, sat at her spinning wheel in a second-floor window. When a spent cannon ball landed at her feet, she recalled that pride was one of her vices and decided to join her husband in the basement. After the battle she cared for the wounded, mainly Hessian soldiers, while scolding them for "coming to this country to butcher people."

Further up the river, at Burlington, Margaret Hill Morris stayed in her riverside home, watching the American gondolas on the water and hearing reports of engagements up and down the river. As the daughter of Dr. Richard Hill, she had some medical knowledge, and when the patriots on the barges and their wives were taken ill she nursed them. In return, one of the bargemen offered to carry supplies to her family in Philadelphia.

The wealthy Quaker families in Philadelphia were regarded as having Tory sympathies. In late August of 1777, when a

British attack on the city seemed imminent, the executive Council of Pennsylvania ordered the arrest of forty-one persons whose loyalty was in question—twenty-six of them Quakers—and demanded they swear an oath of allegiance. The Friends refused since they had conscientious scruples against taking oaths, and on September 2, a number of them were arrested and transported the next week to Winchester, Virginia. Henry Drinker was one of those arrested, and Elizabeth Drinker, a forty-two-year-old mother of five, managed her household alone while the British took the city. Her house was looted, and a major, his servants, and his horses were quartered in her home. In April of 1778, she set out with Mary Pemberton, Molly Pleasants, and Susannah Jones, all prominent Quaker women, to see General George Washington at headquarters in Valley Forge. They were ushered instead into the presence of his wife, "a sociable, pretty kind of woman," and although the general joined them for dinner and "discoursed with them freely," he left after the meal, saying he could do nothing for them but to grant them a pass to Lancaster. Accordingly they set out the next day through pouring rain and spent several weeks visiting the various council members and lobbying for their husbands' release. Whether due to their efforts or not, they were told by Council Secretary Timothy Matlack that the exiles were to be released and returned to Shippensburg later that month. The women waited for them, and together they made their way through the lines to Philadelphia.[4]

Many younger Quaker women found the war exciting. Sally Wister, age sixteen, joined her family in taking refuge at the Foulke's farm in North Wales. Here she enjoyed a series of flirtations with American army officers who were quartered nearby, about which she wrote extensively to her best friend, Deborah Norris. Her parents were evidently patient with these encounters with non-Quakers, and they came to nothing. Sally grew up to be a very pious Friend, cared for her mother, never married, and was listed under "heads of households" in the 1790 census.

Turn Toward Philanthropy

While Friends held themselves aloof from the conflict they were not unaware of the sufferings of their fellow human beings. Several meetinghouses, including Radnor in Pennsylvania and Flushing on Long Island, were used as hospitals for the wounded. When word spread that the siege of Boston was causing hunger among its civilian citizens, Friends in Philadelphia, New York, and the British Isles raised large sums for the New England Yearly Meeting to distribute throughout the city "without distinction to sects or parties." Moses Brown of Rhode Island was one of a party who rode on horseback in the dead of winter to distribute food and fuel to those suffering in the outlying towns.

Later, when the scene of war shifted, relief was also given to non-Quaker civilians living in the Hudson Valley. At the same time, considerable aid was raised for Quaker war sufferers on Nantucket Island, where neutral ships and goods were seized by both patriots and the British, and in South Carolina and Georgia, where Friends in the outlying settlements had suffered the ravages of war.

Historians have seen this effort as the beginning of the long tradition of Quaker relief work. It helped move the Society as a whole into the field of philanthropy, a field generally designated as women's work. Although the gathering and distribution of large sums during the Revolutionary War was accomplished by the men's yearly meetings, a precedent was set. Hereafter the chief business of the Society of Friends would reflect humanitarian concerns.

Another result of the Quaker reforms during the Revolutionary War period was increased opposition to owning slaves. Friends in Germantown, Pennsylvania, had spoken out against slavery as early as 1688, and in such communities as Chester, Nantucket, and Flushing, the question of keeping slaves was hotly debated early in the eighteenth century. It was not until the 1770s and 1780s, however, that the yearly meetings, influenced by reformers such as John Woolman, began to make it a disownable offense for any Quaker to own slaves.

Women's journals of the period reflect this change. Elizabeth Drinker recorded in 1807 that she had been visited by a slave she and Henry had sold fifty-one years ago, in 1756. "When we sold her, there was nothing said against keeping or selling negroes. . . . Some time after, we were more settled in our minds and were very sorry we had sold the child to be a slave for life." The Drinkers tried to repurchase her at a higher price in order to set her free, but the new owner refused to part with her. Later she was sold again, and Henry Drinker called on the new owner and tried to persuade him to liberate the young woman. He did not "see the matter in the same light as we did," Elizabeth wrote, "but at his death, he left her free."[5]

Writing in 1761, Ann Cooper Whitall recalled how her grandfather, Benjamin Clark, wrote and spoke against owning slaves. At that time he found few who agreed with him. "I often thinks of him now there is so many books put out against ceeping of them both frinds and others has wrote a del, how glad wod he a bin to rad them & have had the company of these frinds that is appointed to go to those that ceps slaves among frinds."[6]

Although the Quakers of the northern states were the first to rid themselves of slaveholding, the southern Friends were not far behind, even though they suffered ostracism and economic loss as a result. Aiding individual Quaker families to make the hard decision to release their slaves became the goal of a new generation of traveling ministers. Sarah Harrison, a Philadelphia minister and mother of ten (one of the old women arrested for preaching Quakerism in Germany in 1798), traveled through the southern states in 1788 visiting Quakers and urging them to give up their slaves. She is credited with the freeing of two hundred slaves. In the area of Blackwater Monthly Meeting, Virginia, she prayed with the owners of some fifty slaves until they were persuaded to set them free. Five years later the Blackwater women's meeting was able to state that "we know of none that hold slaves that have it in their power to release them."[7]

Friends also lobbied against slavery in state governments and in the new American Congress. In Philadelphia a society was organized largely by Friends to lobby and to protect people of color. The Pennsylvania Society for the Abolition of Slavery, the Relief of Negroes Unlawfully Held in Bondage, and for Improving the Conditions of the African Race first met in April 1775, numbering among its members Benjamin Franklin. It nurtured infant abolition societies in many other states, both south and north. The fact that its members were all male was accepted at the time, but later it was challenged by the abolitionist feminists of the nineteenth century.

A second Quaker move into the field of philanthropy was the organization of the Society for Alleviating the Miseries of the Public Prisons, in Philadelphia in 1787. The first effort of this society was to try to convert the Walnut Street prison into a penitentiary, a place where prisoners had the opportunity to meditate upon their sins and repent, while being given moral instruction by a group of friendly visitors. While this group also was originally for men only, it was entering a field in which Quaker women had been active since Elizabeth Hooten first wrote to the king to protest prison conditions in 1655. Twenty-five years after the organization of the Pennsylvania Prison Society, as it came to be called, Elizabeth Fry of England became the pioneer woman prison reformer, and she influenced her American sisters to become involved in the prison reform movement.

Pennsylvania Quakers for many years pride themselves on keeping peace with the Indians. Although this peace was broken during the French and Indian War and the Quaker withdrawal from government, the Indians continued to believe that the Quakers were their friends and to ask them to represent their interests when they made treaties with the new American government. Thus in 1794 four Quakers went to Canandaigua,

New York, to see that the Six Nations were treated fairly in a new treaty with the United States, and that the Indians were not given liquor before they were asked to sign. Shortly thereafter the various yearly meetings began to develop Indian Affairs committees, acting as watchdogs for the Indians' interests, and establishing centers where farming and other skills were taught to Indians on reservations. In the nineteenth century, women began to serve on some of the Indian committees.

Influenced by the spirit of reform, and barred by custom from serving with men on the new benevolent associations, the Quaker women began to develop such societies of their own. In 1795 Ann Parrish, a young single woman of twenty-five, gathered a group of twenty-three friends at her home in Philadelphia and organized a committee called the Friendly Circle, and later known formally as the Female Society of Philadelphia for the Relief and Employment of the Poor, the first charity organized by women and for women in the United States.[8] Within a few years of the founding, the Female Society developed a House of Industry where women were employed to spin flax and wool. They decided to employ a few older women to watch the children of the spinners, thus establishing perhaps the first day care center in the country. Ann Parrish also organized a school for poor children, the Aimwell School, which continued into the twentieth century. In 1798 a group of Quaker women meeting in New York at the home of Catherine Bowne Murray established a Female Association for the Relief of the Sick Poor, and for the Education of Such Female Children as Do not Belong to, or Are Not Provided for by Any Religious Society. The schools this group developed included 750 pupils when they were taken over by the New York Public School Society in 1845,[9] and became the public schools.

The increased involvement of Quaker men in philanthropy, beginning at the time of the Revolution, led in the long run to the sharing of tasks between Quaker men and women and the increased status of women in the Society. At the beginning, however, Quaker men tended to take over the women's sphere

REBECCA JONES
DRAWN BY SARAH HUSTLER AT UNDERCLIFF,
FROM HER SHADOW, 1787

Rebecca Jones. Permission from
the Quaker Collection,
Haverford College Library.
Photo by Ted Hetzel.

of philanthropy, just as men who first entered the fields of
education and social work tended to assume administrative responsibility. Denied the exercise of power in government,
Quaker men seemed at first more concerned than ever to be
the dominant group within the Society. The penchant of
Quaker men for appearing at the women's meeting to exhort
them to proper action became more pronounced during the
reformation. It would take another sixty years before some
women began to point out the incongruities of the situation.[10]

Coeducational Academies

As a result of the reformation, Quakers began to pay more
attention to the education of their children. They established
meeting schools on a more regular and permanent basis. They
began to feel that they needed academies, or high schools, to
train their young people to teach in the lower schools, or to

prepare for professions without contact with the people of other religious faiths, "the people of the world."

When Rebecca Jones, a Philadelphia schoolteacher, went to England in 1784, one of her purposes was to visit Ackworth, a boarding school established in 1779 for children of nonaffluent Quaker families. Both boys and girls were educated at Ackworth, although in separate classes, and the atmosphere of the school was that of a family, with a married couple serving as mother and father at the head of the school. Children were expected to leave their own families and become part of the school family. There were no vacations to look forward to, children were only allowed to go home four times a year, and the visits of family members were curtailed.

Despite the Spartan rules, Ackworth was an immediate success and the American Quakers, eager to improve education for Quaker children, were interested in setting up similar schools under yearly meeting auspices. In the same year as Rebecca Jones's trip, New England Friends established a Friends Boarding School in Portsmouth, Rhode Island, modeled in some respects after Ackworth. This school eventually closed, but it reopened in 1819 in Providence and became known as the Moses Brown School. In 1796 the New York Friends founded Nine Partners near Poughkeepsie, while in 1799 Philadelphia established Westtown School twenty-five miles west of the city.

Returning from her visit to England, Rebecca Jones served on the yearly meeting committee that established Westtown. Like Ackworth in many respects, Westtown did not take poor children only but accepted also those whose parents were able to pay for their education. Its goal was to provide a religiously guarded education for young men and women who would become Quaker teachers. Children of all ages were admitted. Rebecca Budd, one of the first scholars, was old enough to be asked to become a teacher eight months after entering the school.

Life at the Quaker boarding schools was stern. At Westtown, students rose at 6 A.M. and went to bed at 8:30 P.M. They were expected to study before breakfast and to walk to and from the dining room two by two in perfect silence. Although boys ate at one end of the dining room and girls at the other, there were to be no glances back and forth. Breakfast consisted of coffee, bread and butter, and occasionally salt fish. Classes continued until the break for dinner—soup, salt pork, potatoes, bread, and custard—and then through the afternoon until it was time for a supper of mush and, once a week, pie. On First Day and Fifth Day there was meeting, and occasionally in the evening a lecture from some pious visiting Quaker minister. The segregation of boys and girls was a principal concern of the Quaker couple who ran the school. Once every two weeks at Westtown, brothers and sisters were allowed to meet in the central hall under supervision. These occasions became an opportunity for boys and girls to pass notes, and many flirtations flourished under the very eyes of the chaperones. Nor were scholars the only culprits; Rebecca Budd and John Comly, both teachers, carried on a brisk courtship before their marriage by slipping a tiny book back and forth while waiting for the children to come to the dining room.

Despite the separation of the sexes, educational opportunities were remarkably similar for girls and boys in the Quaker schools. Girls did not study Latin, nor Greek when it was offered, and boys did not share in the classes of needlework, but both had grammar, penmanship, arithmetic, and scientific studies. These included botany, ornithology, collecting minerals, and even experiments with electricity. Ann Cope described such an experiment in a letter home: "Last Second-day we had electricity and fine fun. The girls stood on what is called the insulating stool and took a hold of a chain that passed from the electrical machine and conveyed the electricity to the person who held it, and when they are touched the electricity will fly off in sparks and hurt a little."[11]

In one important respect, however, the Quakers did not treat the sexes equally in their schools. At Nine Partners, Lucretia Coffin (later Mott) graduated from the role of student to unpaid assistant teacher, earning room, board, and tuition for a younger sister. Since she was only sixteen this seemed fair to her, until she discovered that her male colleague, James Mott, was being paid twice as much as the mature older woman Lucretia Coffin was assisting. She resolved on the spot to "claim for myself all that an impartial Creator had bestowed."[12] At least one hundred fifty years passed, however, before Quakers began to pay women teachers on the same scale as the men.

The Quaker boarding schools had been in session for about twenty-five years when Jonathon Dymond, a Quaker moralist and essayist, wrote about them in 1825:

There does not appear any reason why the education of women should differ in its essentials from that of men. The education which is good for human nature is good for them. They are part—and they ought to be in a much greater degree than they are, a part—of the effective contributors to the welfare and intelligence of the human family.

Within the last twenty-five years the public have had many opportunities of observing the intellectual condition of Quaker women. The public have not been dazzled:—who would wish it? but they have seen intelligence, sound sense, considerateness, discretion. They have seen these qualities in a degree, and with an approach to universal diffusion, that is not found in any other class of women as a class.[13]

As a traveling minister, as well as educator, Rebecca Jones had played a vital role in all aspects of the reformation of the Society. By 1796 she was fifty-seven and considered herself old and tired. The yearly meeting that September was busy with philanthropic concerns. It heard a report from the school committee that had bought the land for Westtown; it appointed a committee to raise funds for the Indians in Northern New York State; and in answer to a query from a quarterly meeting, it decided that blacks could be accepted as members. (A number of concerned women Friends served on a committee to discuss the admission of blacks and were influential in the decision, according to a traveling British minister, Martha Routh.) The meeting also discussed the proposal brought by the women's yearly meeting that a new meetinghouse be built in Philadelphia. Writing to the son of a beloved English Friend about all these ventures, Rebecca Jones said:

I expect thou hast accounts of our great works which are in contemplation—such as attempting to civilize the inhabitants of the wilderness, and to establish a Boarding school after the manner of your Ackworth; build a large meeting house, after your example to accommodate both sexes at the Yearly Meeting; admit black people into society fellowship, &, &. Well, my heart wishes well to every great, noble, and virtuous undertaking; but such is my declining state of health, advanced age and dimness of sight, that I have no expectation that these things will be so perfected as that I may adopt the language of good old Simeon thereon. . . .[14]

Rebecca Jones underestimated herself. She lived another twenty-two years and saw all the reforms come to pass. She continued to care about the role of women within the Quaker society. In 1802 she wrote to a woman minister in England, urging that the women's Yearly Meeting decide for themselves in regard to the case of Hannah Barnard, the New York traveling minister disciplined for liberal views in London in 1801, remembering that the church "is composed of females as well as males, who alike have need to move under a sense of their own weakness."[15]

6. The Nineteenth Century: Expansion and Change

Although Friends in the South had cleared their consciences by giving up slaveholding in the 1780s, their problems seemed only to multiply. The slaves they freed were often caught by unscrupulous traders and sold back into bondage. Laws were passed making it illegal to educate blacks, even though this is what the discipline required of Friends. In an economy based on slavery, the Quakers forced to hire help found survival difficult.

When the Northwest Territory opened in 1787 as a land forever free from slavery, it must have seemed to southern Friends like an answer to prayer. The ordinance establishing the territory also guaranteed freedom of religion and called for a just and peaceful relationship with the Indians. The land was fertile and cheap, enticing large Quaker families who wanted to settle sons and daughters on adjoining farms. As a result, whole families and at times whole meeting communities migrated from Georgia, the Carolinas, Virginia, and Maryland. Other Friends from the Middle Atlantic and the New England states joined the exodus, providing settlers for the new states soon to be carved out of the territory: Ohio, Indiana, Michigan, Illinois, and Wisconsin.

In 1805 a twelve-year-old Quaker girl, Rebecca Wright, traveled from Baltimore to Waynesville, Ohio, as a part of a family group of twenty-one members. In her journal she described crossing the Alleghenies by moonlight. "We sometimes had to drive late to reach our destination. Then the wagons would seem to pitch from rock to rock and the descent was so steep that, should we pitch over it would be hard telling where we should land."

They had hoped to reach Cincinnati by flatboat, but the river was low, so they set off overland in wagons, leaving Rebecca's older sister, Rachel Wright Farquhar, with her husband, Benjamin Farquhar, and their six children to stay with Farquhar relatives in Wheeling, West Virginia. The remaining thirteen members of the Wright party crossed the state of Ohio through wilderness territory. Sometimes they shared crude dwellings with pioneer families and sometimes they slept in the wagon or under a tent. When they finally reached Waynesville in southwestern Ohio, they found no place to stay; the one-room dwelling of a relative was already occupied by a large family. Rebecca's father rented a little cabin where the entire family spent the winter, and in the spring they moved to a three-hundred-acre farm with a one-room dwelling.

Rebecca's brothers kept the family supplied with food by hunting game until the farm could be made to produce. Rebecca, the youngest, was sometimes left alone at home. On one such occasion, she was visited by three Indians "with their knives bloody from the chase," who made signs that they wanted something to smoke. Misunderstanding and frightened, Rebecca started to prepare food, until one of the Indians managed to say "pipe."

The Wrights thrived in their new setting. Two years later they could write to relatives saying that one sister was teaching school, that a new sawmill was about to be put into operation, that one brother was establishing a store, and that two new monthly meetings had been set up. To one of these, Caesars Creek, the venerable Charity Cook of North Carolina had just moved her membership, along with a large number of her immediate family.[1]

Life on the frontier was dangerous and often fraught with tragedy. It demanded a special kind of courage. In 1807 Sarah Foulke, a twenty-year-old Quaker woman from New Jersey, moved to Wheeling, West Virginia, to join her father and his third wife. One disaster followed another for this family. A baby born to the stepmother died a few days after birth. The father, deeply in debt, set off down the river to escape his creditors and to recoup his fortunes, only to be murdered by his boathands for the cargo. Sarah and her stepmother decided to support themselves by opening a small school in Mount Pleasant, Ohio, in 1808, but this was evidently not successful enough to support them both, for Sarah Foulke soon moved on to teach in another school at nearby Smithfield.

While at Smithfield, Sarah Foulke was courted by and eventually married William Farquhar, a relative by marriage of the Wright family. After her years of loneliness, she was very happy, and the birth of a little son ten months later filled her cup to overflowing. But within a few months her husband fell ill and died of a brain fever, and the baby soon followed him. In 1811 Sarah, a widow and a grieving mother at just twenty-five, made the long trip back to Philadelphia to teach at the new Westtown School.

After a long period of deep depression, Sarah felt compelled to speak in meeting, and thereafter she became a traveling minister. In 1816 she married James Emlen, also a minister. The two took turns staying home with the farm and the children and had a relatively serene life, but Sarah remained subject to periods of depression that seemed to date from her frontier experiences.[2]

As the decades passed, new settlements in the old Northwest Territory became established, and the frontier expanded westward. In 1837 Rachel Way Joy emigrated with her parents from Henry County, Indiana, to a budding Quaker community in Salem, Iowa. Here she married John Fisher and had four children, three of whom died in an epidemic. John, Rachel, and the living child, Angelina, started out over the plains to Oregon in the spring of 1847 in a covered wagon. During this disastrous trip both John and Angelina died, and Rachel reached the Washington territory alone. Although she married again and had six children, of whom five survived, she remained lonely all her life for the Quaker community she had left behind.[3]

Frontier Schooling

Isolation was a very real problem for the frontier Friends. The maintenance of the Quaker subculture, a complete society living in but not of the world, depended on the reinforcement of a community of those with common values. Density of Quaker population had always played a role in the success with which meetings and schools were maintained. The first concern of the migrating Quakers, therefore, was to establish new monthly, quarterly, and yearly meetings to meet the needs of their developing communities.

Schools to serve these communities were of primary importance. Colonial experience had made it clear that it would be difficult to keep the children in the Quaker faith if they were permitted to go to school with the children of the "world's people." Also, in Ohio and Indiana, the early public district schools and seminaries were supported by fines imposed on Quakers and others for refusing to serve in the militia, so that Friends were advised by their yearly meetings not to participate in the institutions so supported.[4] As a result, both elementary and secondary schools were established by Friends and flourished throughout much of the nineteenth century in Tennessee, Ohio, Indiana, Kansas, and Iowa. In 1850 ninety-six elementary schools reported to the Indiana Yearly Meeting, while twenty academies were added in the second half of the century. Although many of these institutions were ultimately absorbed by the local public school systems, others became permanent boarding schools, such as the one at Friendsville, Tennessee, and Barnesville, Ohio, and some evolved into small colleges, all of them coeducational.[5]

Quaker girls and women on the frontier, therefore, continued to have the opportunity to study and to teach. In the earliest

Indiana Yearly Meeting of Friends, 1844. Permission from the
Friends Historical Library, Swarthmore College, Swarthmore, PA.

frontier days many communities looked for a male teacher to
manage the one-room log schoolhouses because of the physical
tasks involved: splitting wood, shoveling snow, repairing the
roof. Also, frontier neighbors remarked that "wimmin ain't fit-
tin' to be schoolmasters."[6] Often Quaker women taught only a
summer term, as did Sarah Foulke Farquhar Emlen. But as conditions grew a little easier, the numbers of male and female
teachers employed equalized, although the men continued to
be paid far more than the women.

Expansion and Schism

Despite their success in establishing the Quaker schools and
meetings as they moved westward, Friends found it difficult to
maintain their old fervor or support a living ministry in the

rigors of frontier life. Working days were long and hard, the distance to the nearest meeting was great, and their non-Quaker neighbors were unsympathetic. In addition, all of Quakerism in the nineteenth century was shaken by a series of schisms that arose in the older eastern communities but had their most profound effect on the midwestern and western meetings. While the story of these troubles is a complicated one, some summary is necessary to understand the role of Quaker women in the nineteenth century.

The disownment of Hannah Barnard in 1802 for her liberal interpretation of the Bible was a foretaste of troubles to come. Influenced by John Wesley and the evangelical movement, a number of British Friends and their American followers became concerned that the concept of the inner Light was leading some Friends away from the authority of the Scriptures and belief in the atonement of Christ as the road to salvation. While George Fox had always emphasized the primacy of the direct relationship between souls and their Creator, he had never questioned that the Bible was divinely inspired in all its particulars, nor that the historical Christ was also the risen Christ to whom men and women had direct access. Thus there had been room from the birth of Quakerism for both an evangelical and a liberal theology. Though the evangelicals of his own day had regarded Fox as a heretic, every generation following his had included both evangelical and mystic, or prophetic, Friends.

Quakers have always been able to live comfortably with this ambiguity, since they did not require members to subscribe to a creed. In periods of strength and of creative growth, members have been bound together by a sense of a living testimony, a spiritual unity of purpose behind apparent diversity. In less creative periods, however, when persecution has ceased and no overwhelming sense of task or mission pulls members together, tensions over doctrinal differences have come to the surface. This was the situation at the end of the eighteenth and the beginning of the nineteenth century. Although the effort to impose uniformity of belief seems to have begun with the

London Yearly Meeting, it had its most tragic effects in the United States.

In Philadelphia Yearly Meeting, where the trouble began, the wealthy and somewhat worldly urban Friends were the first to become concerned about doctrinal orthodoxy. They attempted to impose their views on rural meetings, which clung to the quietism introduced by the reformers of the 1750s and 1760s. Rural Friends resented this intrusion, viewing freedom of expression in meeting as a precious right and regarding the effort to discipline or disown members whose ministry was considered unsound as striking at the very roots of the Quaker message.

The controversy came to a head around the figure of Elias Hicks, an old-fashioned country quietist from Long Island and a strong opponent of slavery and of the new evangelicalism. He insisted on the primacy of the Christ within the believer over the Christ of the Bible, and he downplayed the importance of the crucifixion. Hicks was a preacher who traveled up and down the eastern seaboard, wearing unbleached linen to avoid the use of slave products. With his piercing black eyes, long white hair, and vibrant message, he influenced the young Walt Whitman and the young Lucretia Coffin as well as James Mott. Later, after the Motts were married and living in Philadelphia, they accompanied Hicks on his visits to meetings in the Philadelphia area.

The elders of Philadelphia Yearly Meeting feared Hick's heresy and tried to prevent him from speaking. This offended the rural Friends, who united behind the leadership of John Comly of Byberry, the former Westtown teacher, to defend Hicks's right to speak, a separate issue from their endorsement of his views. Some did, but many did not, agree with him. The struggle was complicated by the efforts of English Friends to intervene on behalf of the evangelicals. Finally in 1827, Comly and his party, which was in the majority, withdrew from a tense yearly meeting session. With much pain and bitterness, the Society of Friends separated into two factions, the Orthodox and the Hicksite. Families were divided, the ownership of meetinghouses and schools contested, lawsuits commenced. The Quakers, whose discipline required regularly answering the query "are love and unity maintained among you?" fought for almost one hundred years.

The schism in Philadelphia was only the beginning. The next year Friends in New York, New England, Maryland, and Ohio Yearly Meetings were faced with the dilemma of responding to the epistles of either the Hicksite or the Orthodox group in Pennsylvania. Like a widening fissure, the separation spread through much of American Quakerism.

Born in the midst of anguish, the Hicksite branch of Friends remained strong in Pennsylvania, Ohio, New York, Maryland, and later Indiana, Illinois, and Canada for more than one hundred years, contributing leadership to many of the contemporary reform movements. This was particularly true of women's rights. Lucretia Mott, Susan B. Anthony, Florence Kelley, and Alice Paul were all Hicksite Friends; Jane Addams was associated with the Hicksites although she was not one herself.

The minutes of the Hicksite Women's Yearly Meeting in Philadelphia after the schism reveal a new spirit of liberation. The Hicksite women became more assertive, initiating actions and undertaking concerns without waiting for the approval of the men. The corresponding Orthodox women's minutes show no such change; in fact, there was more tendency to defer to the "brethren" for decisions.[7]

The Orthodox branch did produce some outstanding feminists. The Whitall and Thomas women belonged to this group, and many of the evangelical Quaker women of the Midwest were leaders in suffrage and women's rights. But the wealthy, urban Quaker men who dominated the Orthodox appear to have absorbed from their non-Quaker business colleagues the nineteenth-century concept of the special sphere of woman. The rural Hicksites, continuing to share responsibilities between husband and wife on the farm or in the small shop, were less influenced by the new ideas of separate roles for men and women and more loyal to the older Quaker tradition. Wealth and power, it seems, always tended to undercut gender equality within Quakerism.

Yet the Hicksites were by no means united. Quietism remained strong, and members were discouraged from mingling with outsiders in the reform movements. Several prominent Friends were disowned for taking part in the antislavery movement, and small groups of antislavery Friends separated from the main Hicksite meetings in Michigan, New York, Ohio, Indiana, and Pennsylvania, forming the Progressive Friends or Congregational Friends or Friends of Human Progress. These radical Hicksite Friends also questioned the authority of the ministers and elders and the inequality between men and women. Liberty of conscience was their major theme. Nicholas Hallock, member of a small separatist group from Milton, New York, preached the motto that Lucretia Mott heard and made famous: Truth for authority, not authority for truth.[8]

The Orthodox also suffered a schism over the slavery issue in Indiana in 1842, and later a smaller one in Iowa. These troubles, however, paled to insignificance as Orthodox Friends of the 1840s and 1850s became involved in another bitter battle over creed. In 1837 Joseph John Gurney, a handsome, wealthy, and magnetic British Evangelical Friend, came to the United States to tour the Orthodox meetings, preaching the centrality of the atonement, more emphasis on Bible study, and increasing attention to education. He wanted to end the isolation that years of quietism had brought. His visit was generally regarded as a great success, bringing religious revival to some of the rural meetings that had been stagnating.

To some older and more conservative Friends, however, his progressive message struck at the very roots of Quakerism and sounded to them very much like an Episcopalian creed. While rejecting the Hicksite liberalism, these Friends cherished the silent meeting and relied on the guidance of the inner Light. From Rhode Island a spokesman, John Wilbur, arose to oppose the changes that Gurney seemed to be bringing to Quakerism.

A separation between the Gurneyites and the Wilburites took place in New England Yearly Meeting in 1845 and spread to Ohio and North Carolina. Philadelphia Yearly Meeting, torn between the two groups, decided to cut off all correspondence with other yearly meetings rather than face a second division.

Joseph Gurney was very much a Victorian gentleman, and he viewed the role of Quaker women with ambivalence. On the one hand he defended their right to preach under the direct leading of the spirit. On the other he warned that they must not usurp authority over men, as the apostle Paul had said. He observed that many Quaker women ministers in England understood the distinction. "For we well know that there are no women among us, more generally distinguished for modesty, gentleness, order, and a right submission to their brethren, than those who have been called by their Divine Master into the exercise of the Christian ministry."

Joseph Gurney noted with some alarm that there were more women than men in the ministry, and he thought the balance ought to be rectified since "the stronger sex" ought to fight the battles of the Lord, and not leave them to women "whose physical weakness and delicacy have an obvious *tendency* to render them less fit for combat."[9]

During his American tour, Joseph Gurney was in Philadelphia in May of 1838 when the advocacy of women's rights led to the burning of Pennsylvania Hall. Later, touring New England, he reacted to the fact that the Grimké sisters were speaking to audiences composed of both women and men. In his letters to his family in England he made it clear what he thought of all this:

Some of the talented *women* in this country are making a grand effort to obtain the same political rights and privileges as the man. They are aiming to be voters, orators . . . etc. etc. What shall we all come to?

I do not approve of ladies speaking in public, even in the antislavery cause, except under the immediate influences of the Holy Spirit. Then, and then only all is safe. Should my dear ladies have to speak in this way, I have no objection.[10]

Joseph John Gurney probably did not so much initiate as reflect a current attitude toward women among the evangelical branch of the Society of Friends. Even his famous sister, Elizabeth Gurney Fry, the prison reformer, had mixed feelings about women carrying out public roles and often wished she could be more retiring. She did not approve of Lucretia Mott and made every effort not to meet her face to face when the latter was in London. Nevertheless, Gurney's influence had repercussions on American Quakerism.

After the Civil War the Gurneyite meetings, especially in the Midwest, were swept by a series of revivals complete with altar calls and mourners' benches, quite foreign to any previous Quaker practice. A former Methodist, Esther Frame, who became a Quaker in order to preach, led these revivals along with a number of Quakers allied with the Holiness Movement. Many Friends saw these revivals as a return to the early spiritual ecstasies of the seventeenth-century Quakers. Others were appalled and tried to call their coreligionists to their senses.

The revivals had a lasting effect on the nature of the Gurneyite worship service. As the first fervor of the revival experience faded, meetings began to feel they could not go back to the old sleepy ways but must have a hired pastor and a more organized service for worship, with prayer, music, a sermon, and Bible reading. The worst fears of the Wilburites seemed realized, as pastoral Friends churches developed services not unlike their Methodist or Baptist neighbors. A second phase of the Wilburite separation took place, therefore, in the late 1870s and 1880s, as conservative Friends, alarmed by these innovations, withdrew to form new Conservative Yearly Meetings in Indiana, Iowa, Canada, Kansas, and later, North Carolina.

As conservers of Quaker values of an earlier day, the Wilburite or Conservative Friends have kept alive the concept of the spiritual equality of women and men. Indeed, Wilburite women have continued to travel in the ministry well into the twentieth century. In their schools the Wilburites have continued to emphasize coeducation and to provide roles for women as teachers. Two of these boarding schools, Olney in Ohio and Scattergood in Iowa, have played a vital role in the modern Society of Friends. But the Wilburites have resisted social change and the application of spiritual equality to the temporal world. They objected to higher education for women, played no role in the women's rights struggle, and were the last to grant the women's business meeting true equality.

The new Gurneyite pastoral Friends churches, as they came to be called, preserved many Quaker traditions including that of a lay ministry. Men and women in the church who felt led to the ministry and whose gifts were recognized were recorded as ministers in accord with long Quaker tradition. Women with such gifts helped in the First Day School or with missionary activities or in visiting the sick. But when the meeting hired a full-time pastor, they frequently sought someone with biblical training, which few women could offer. The pastoral churches also began to hire a secretary to coordinate church work within a given yearly meeting, and this position was almost always filled by a man. Women wanting to exercise ministerial gifts sometimes took special training or prepared for missionary service overseas. Though men eventually predominated in the pastoral meetings, the old tradition of women's ministry was never entirely lost.

Quaker Colleges

The schisms of the nineteenth century had one good effect upon the Society of Friends: they further encouraged the development of higher education. The need to develop a duplicate set of schools, one for the Orthodox and one for the Hicksites, created a demand for more trained Quaker teachers. The evangelicals within the Orthodox fold, later to become Gurneyites, were more interested in a rational approach to theology than had been their quietist ancestors, and at the same time they were eager to raise their children in a protected

Quaker environment. The liberals within the Hicksites move-ment also supported education.

In 1833 the first Quaker college was established at Haverford, Pennsylvania, although it did not grant degrees until 1856. Un-like Westtown, Nine Partners, and Friends Boarding School of Providence, it was for men only, serving the sons of well-to-do Quakers who might otherwise have gone to Harvard or Yale. Joseph John Gurney, who visited it in 1838 after stopping first at Westtown, described it as established for the education of "an older and more opulent class of lads."[11] Since young men, rather than their sisters, were sent to college at the time, no justification for the exclusion of women was offered in the minutes of the Board of Managers establishing Haverford. In 1857 one descendant of Ann Cooper Whitall, Hannah Whitall Smith, decided to prepare herself to enter the junior class at Haverford. What might have happened as a result of this chal-lenge to the all-male policy we do not know, for Hannah Smith had to abandon her plans because of the demands of her chil-dren. In 1870 the Haverford faculty, influenced no doubt by the Hicksite founding of coeducational Swarthmore, recom-mended unanimously that women be admitted to the college, in order to improve the "moral earnestness of all."[12] The Board of Managers responded by totally ignoring the recommenda-tion. As a result, in 1885 a group of Gurneyite Quakers estab-lished Bryn Mawr College for women a few miles away. Haverford did not become coeducational until 1979.

M. Carey Thomas, a strong Quaker feminist and niece of Hannah Whitall Smith, became president of Bryn Mawr in 1894 and struggled to prove that women were at least equal to, if not superior to men intellectually. The Bryn Mawr faculty re-garded Haverford as not quite rigorous enough, and the re-lationships between the two schools remained cool until the mid-twentieth century.

More in keeping with the older Quaker tradition of coedu-cation was the establishment of New Garden Boarding School in Greensboro, North Carolina, in 1837. Here boys and girls were taught separately, as at Westtown, until after the Civil War. Dr. Nereus Mendenhall who then became president believed that a girl's education ought to be on the same level as a boy's, and he integrated the classes. In 1889 New Garden became Guilford College under Mendenhall's son-in-law, Louis Hobbs. His wife, Mary Mendenhall Hobbs, a strong advocate of equal education for women, made it possible for more Quaker girls to earn the money to attend New Garden Boarding School by establishing a study and work program. Later she turned her energies into promoting a public state normal school for the young women of North Carolina. In the early twentieth century, Mary Hobbs became a famous advocate of woman suffrage.[13]

Ten years after the New Garden Boarding School was begun, Indiana Yearly Meeting Friends started the Friends Boarding School of Richmond, Indiana. In 1859 it became Earlham College. Coeducational from the start, it thus became the first Friends college to educate men and women equally (Oberlin College in Ohio had become coeducational in 1833 and Antioch, also in Ohio, in 1852). It was also the first to pay an equal salary to women teachers. As a student Mahalah Jay had transferred from Oberlin to Antioch because women were not allowed to read their own papers at commencement. She and her husband, Eli Jay, both Quakers, joined the staff at Earlham on condition that they receive the same salary. This was achieved by reducing Eli's. Mahalah continued to urge equal pay for women until she was appointed head of Earlham's preparatory department, a lingering vestige of the earlier boarding school, at the same pay as a full professor. She was finally named Earlham's first woman teacher, in charge of rhetoric and composition. Rhoda Coffin, a midwestern prison reformer and minister, supported Mahalah's crusade, and many women in the Earlham community rejoiced at her victory.[14]

Soon after the Hicksite-Orthodox separation, the Philadelphia Hicksite Women's Yearly Meeting under the leadership of Lucretia Mott undertook an extensive survey of Hicksite schools. Many Hicksite children were forced to remain at West-town, it was discovered, because there was no alternative school for them. Not until 1893 was a Hicksite boarding school, the George School in Bucks County, created. However, a committee of Friends from Philadelphia and Baltimore began to meet to discuss other options, and as a result Swarthmore College was founded in 1864 and began to hold classes in 1869. Anna Mott Hopper, Lucretia Mott's daughter, served on the Board of Managers. Mott's early influence was still felt at the college when Alice Paul became a student in 1901.

Other small Quaker colleges were established toward the end of the nineteenth century. These included Wilmington College in Wilmington, Ohio, 1870; William Penn College in Oskaloosa, Iowa, 1873; George Fox College, Newberg, Oregon, 1885; Whittier College, Whittier, California, 1891; and Friends University in Wichita, Kansas, 1898. While representing very different points of view theologically, these schools maintained two basic Quaker testimonies: a devotion to peace and coeducation.

In addition to their own schools, Quakers helped endow and develop such institutions as Cornell and Johns Hopkins, and they insisted on the eventual admission of women. In 1850 a group of Quaker businessmen opened the Female Medical College of Pennsylvania, the first such institution in the United States.

Scattered by the western migrations, and shattered and decimated by schisms and disownments, the Society of Friends in the nineteenth century nevertheless provided a cultural seedbed from which developed a number of strong feminists and feminist initiatives. The institutionalization of the traveling ministry, the separate women's business meeting, and the concept of equal educational opportunities for women had laid the groundwork for the strides Quaker women were to make in reforms and professions in the decades ahead.

7. Pioneers in Antislavery and Women's Rights

In 1806 Alice Jackson Lewis of Chester County, Pennsylvania, spoke in the Philadelphia Women's Yearly Meeting urging members to avoid the use of cotton, sugar, and other products of slave labor. While a few of the early Quaker reformers, such as John Woolman and Warner Mifflin, had themselves abstained from using such products, it had been regarded until now as an individual matter. Alice Lewis was the first in a series of Quaker women to urge her sisters to use their buying power to boycott slave products. It was not only a matter of principle, it was also one of the very few avenues open to women to express their opposition to slavery.[1]

Barred by custom from participating in the various abolition societies of the day, Quaker women continued to conduct schools for poor and black children and sewing rooms for poor mothers, and to read antislavery tracts by Thomas Clarkson, Woolman, Hicks, and others. In 1824 a British Quaker woman, Elizabeth Heydrick, published a pamphlet titled *Immediate, Not Gradual Emancipation*, which many thought influenced the changes in public opinion leading to Great Britain's abolition of slavery in 1833. In 1826 a young Quaker woman from Delaware, Elizabeth Margaret Chandler, began to publish antislavery poetry and essays in Benjamin Lundy's newspaper, *Genius of Universal Emancipation*. She consistently reminded her sisters that to abstain from buying slave products was their most effective action against slavery.[2]

The prohibition against women speaking in public was universally enforced and accepted in the early nineteenth century. Thus when the Scottish radical Frances Wright toured the eastern United States in 1829 and addressed mixed audiences with a message combining antislavery with anticlerical attitudes, the shock was great. Some Wilmington Friends were disciplined and threatened with disownment for allowing their children to hear "that woman." The case was appealed to Philadelphia Yearly Meeting where Lucretia Mott, then a young mother and recently recognized minister, campaigned for the rights of the families being thus criticized. She herself was spoken to by the elders of her meeting for this intervention—the first, but by no means the last time she felt the weight of Quaker displeasure for her liberal views.[3]

In 1830 James and Lucretia Mott were visited by William Lloyd Garrison, a young journalist who worked on the *Genius of Universal Emancipation* and had just spent seven weeks in prison as the result of an intemperate editorial he had written about a slave owner. Lundy and the *Genius* supported the Colonization Society, a scheme to buy slaves and send them back to Africa, regarded as a moderate way to end slavery. Garrison had made a number of black friends in Baltimore, and they convinced him to oppose colonization and support a more radical approach. His jail sentence had also confirmed his belief that the "Slave Power," an oligarchy of business and public men who benefited from slavery, was in control of the country and must be fought more aggressively. After leaving the Motts, with whom he formed a lifelong bond, he returned to Boston and began to publish *The Liberator*, a newspaper that called for immediate emancipation. He began to advocate other radical reforms as well, including the rights of women. He also urged the formation of female antislavery societies, first in New England and later nationwide.[4]

Prudence Crandall, a Quaker schoolteacher in Connecticut, was influenced by Garrison and the *Liberator* and announced that she intended to admit a few "young colored Ladies and Misses" to her school. When one black pupil applied and was admitted, the rest of the students were withdrawn. Prudence Crandall had to close her school temporarily, but she reopened it as a school for black girls. Incensed, the townspeople persuaded the Connecticut legislature to pass a law prohibiting the education of out-of-state blacks. Prudence fought this law with the aid of the leading abolitionists, and though she was jailed three times, her conviction was finally reversed. Unable to get rid of the school by legal means, Prudence Crandall's opponents organized a boycott among the town merchants so that she could buy no supplies, filled her well with manure, and set the school on fire. After almost a year of battle, she gave up and moved away. Not until more than fifty years later did the Connecticut legislature apologize. Her story, reported in *Liberator*, was followed eagerly. Quaker women abolitionists had found their first hero and martyr.[5]

In 1833 Garrison decided to form a national antislavery organization. At a meeting held in Philadelphia in December, a few women were invited to attend but not to participate in the deliberations. One of the onlookers was Lucretia Mott, who made a few suggestions from her seat in the balcony. Four days later she joined with other women, black and white, Quaker and non-Quaker, in organizing the Philadelphia Female Anti-Slavery Society. At their first session they asked a black minister, James McCrummel, to preside, since none of the women had conducted such a meeting. Thereafter, they elected their own officers and became stronger and more confident with each passing year.

Although not the first such group to be organized, the Philadelphia Female Anti-Slavery Society was the strongest and the longest lived, and it became the center of a web of such societies. In 1837 its leaders helped to organize the first Anti-Slavery Convention of American Women, which met in New York City and pledged itself to a giant petition campaign to eliminate slavery in the District of Columbia and the new territories. Among its members were Lydia White and Sydney Ann Lewis, Hicksite Quaker women who ran stores where only free produce was sold; Sarah Pugh, a Hicksite schoolteacher; Charlotte, Marguerite, and Sarah Forten, daughters of a

Burning of Pennsylvania Hall. Permission from the Quaker
Collection, Haverford College Library, Haverford, PA. Photo by
Norman Wilson.

wealthy black Philadelphia family; Harriet Forten Purvis, wife
of Robert Purvis, a wealthy black who became a leader in the
antislavery movement; Grace and her daughter Sarah Douglass, black Quaker abolitionists and feminists; Alba Alcott, wife
of transcendentalist Bronson and mother of Louisa May Alcott.
Most of Lucretia Mott's female relatives were present, all Quakers, as well as a sprinkling of Unitarian and Presbyterian
women.[6]

"The Woman Question"

Joining the Philadelphia Female Anti-Slavery Society in 1835
were two sisters from South Carolina, Angelina and Sarah
Grimké. The daughters of a wealthy slaveowning family, they
had been influenced by their older brother Thomas, an abolitionist and a nonresister, and had decided to move north and
become Quakers in order to enlist in the antislavery cause.

Their personal experience with slavery made them eloquent speakers and writers against the institution, especially Angelina, the younger of the two.

By the time they joined the Female Anti-Slavery Society, the Grimkés were questioning their relationship to the Society of Friends. The meeting they had joined and the friends they had made within the Society were Orthodox and did not approve of Lucretia Mott and the antislavery agitation. There was a special bench in the back of the meetinghouse where black members were supposed to sit. Angelina and Sarah Grimké protested this discrimination by sitting on the bench in question, but they were eldered for this action. Sarah, attempting to preach against slavery from the floor of the meeting, was publicly silenced and rebuked.

In 1836 Angelina published a pamphlet, *An Appeal to the Christian Women of the South*, which became a sensation. The following year she was asked to lecture for the American Antislavery Society to women's audiences in New England. So great was her appeal, however, that men began to slip into the back of the room to hear her. Soon she was speaking to mixed or "promiscuous" audiences, as they were called, and the clergy was outraged. The Council of Congregational Ministers of Massachusetts issued a pastoral letter warning ministers and their congregations against the danger inherent in "females who itinerate." Wherever the sisters spoke, mobs collected to throw rotten eggs and stones.

Aroused by this abuse of her younger sister, Sarah Grimké wrote a series of *Letters on the Equality of the Sexes and the Condition of Women*, which served as a clarion call to the coming struggle. She based her argument, she said, not on the Quaker testimony on the equality of the sexes, but on the grounds of human rights:

I ask no favors of my sex. I surrender not our claim to equality. All I ask of our brethren is that they will take their feet from off our necks, and permit us to stand upright on the ground which God has designed for us to occupy.[7]

While many within the antislavery cause responded to the courage of the Grimkés, others feared that introducing the "woman question" along with the slavery issue would cause the whole movement to collapse. Among the critics of the Grimké sisters were John Greenleaf Whittier, an Orthodox Friend, and Theodore Weld, a Presbyterian minister turned full-time abolitionist, who was by now engaged to marry Angelina. Not surprisingly, she found his opposition hard to bear, and shortly after her marriage to him in May of 1838, ill health compelled her to retire from speaking.

The Weld-Grimké marriage, for which Angelina and Sarah were disowned by the Friends meeting from which they were already estranged, occurred on the eve of a climactic series of meetings at Pennsylvania Hall in Philadelphia. The hall was a newly erected structure to house abolitionist and other reform groups, paid for in part with money raised by the Philadelphia Female Anti-Slavery Society. The hall was opened with ceremonies on Monday, May 14, and a series of reform meetings was scheduled. There were meetings on temperance, Indian rights, physical education for children, and colonization. There was also a meeting of the American Convention of Anti-Slavery Women.

A hostile mob, alarmed at the fact that blacks and whites were meeting together, soon formed around the hall. The crowd grew on Wednesday, after a series of posters appeared all over town urging citizens to interfere, "forcibly if they must," with the convention. On Wednesday night, men and women met together in an unofficial antislavery meeting. This was necessary because some members of the female antislavery societies still objected to men and women meeting together. "Let us hope," Lucretia Mott said, "that such false notions of delicacy and propriety do not long obtain in this enlightened country." But these notions were held by the mob outside, which feared intermarriage or "amalgamation of the races" might result from such mingling. They tried to drown out the speakers, throwing bricks and stones. Against the tumult, Angelina Grimké Weld delivered an impassioned antislavery speech that proved to be her swan song. She was followed by a new recruit, Abby Kelley, a young Quaker teacher from Lynn, Massachusetts, whose fiery speech led Theodore Weld to tell her that if she didn't devote full time to the antislavery circuit, "God will smite you."[8]

The next day the mayor suggested that black and white women cease meeting together in order to reduce tensions in the city. When they refused, the mayor threw up his hands and went home, and in the evening the mob burst into the empty hall and burned it to the ground. They then started for the Motts but were deflected and instead burned several buildings in Philadelphia's black community. Undeterred, the next morning the Anti-slavery Convention of American Women met in Sarah Pugh's schoolhouse.[9]

These experiences confirmed Lucretia Mott, Abby Kelley, Sarah Pugh, and others in believing that the issues of equal rights for blacks and for women were joined. There could be no retreat from an effort to establish women's right to serve on an equal basis within the antislavery movement, nor from the need for blacks and whites to meet together socially as well as in the antislavery cause. The Pennsylvania Anti-Slavery Society was by now composed of both men and women, and Lucretia Mott soon was named an officer. In the summer of 1838, Abby Kelley was appointed to a committee on the New England Anti-Slavery Society, and in 1839 she played a key role in efforts by the Garrisonians to add women to full membership in the American Anti-Slavery Society. In 1840 she and a Quaker minister from Nantucket, Eliza Barney, were both placed on a committee of the AASS. The more conservative and clerical wing promptly withdrew and thereafter called their organization the American and Foreign Anti-Slavery Society.

The culmination of the women's struggle to play an equal role in the antislavery movement came in the summer of 1840 in London, where a World's Anti-Slavery Convention took place. Women were not invited as delegates, but the New En-

gland and Pennsylvania Anti-Slavery Societies sent women representatives anyway. In addition to Lucretia and James Mott,
the Pennsylvania delegation included four young women: Mary
Grew, Abby Kimber, Elizabeth Neall, and Sarah Pugh. The latter three were Quakers. While they were at sea, the American
Anti-Slavery Society, having split, chose Lucretia Mott as a national delegate. When this group reached London, however,
they were told they could not be accepted as members of the
convention but must sit as onlookers. Despite a vigorous floor
fight, this rule was not reversed. The Motts discovered that the
British Quakers, alarmed by their Hicksite deviation, were
among their most powerful opponents.

Having been warned in advance that she might not be
seated, Lucretia Mott accepted the situation, but not without
a vigorous attempt to change the minds of those in charge of
the convention and to meet with British antislavery women.
She also preached in several London churches. Elizabeth Cady
Stanton, present at the convention as the bride of Edwin Stanton, a delegate of the American and Foreign Anti-Slavery Society, was so impressed by her strength and composure that
she adopted her as a role model as well as lifelong friend. "Mrs.
Mott was to me an entirely new revelation of womanhood,"
she later wrote.[10] Lucretia Mott spoke of the theories of Mary
Wollstonecraft, of the need to read the Bible in the light of the
inner teacher, and of the relationship of religion to reform. On
their last day together, Lucretia and Elizabeth promised each
other that after they returned to the United States they would
hold a convention to advocate the rights of women.

The Struggle Begins

The result of this pledge, the Seneca Falls Convention of
1848, is regarded as the birth of the women's rights movement
in this country. But in the intervening eight years Abby Kelley
and Lucretia Mott, with a number of recruits and disciples,
crisscrossed New England, New York, Pennsylvania, and Ohio,

Abby Kelley Foster. Courtesy of
the American Antiquarian
Society.

advocating antislavery and the rights of women. In Michigan
the young poet Elizabeth Chandler had joined a Quaker neighbor, Laura Haviland, in establishing an antislavery society in
1832. In the 1840s, such groups were formed in Illinois and
Wisconsin. Indiana had a particularly strong Female Antislavery Society, made up largely of Quaker women. Thus long
before the famous Seneca Falls meeting, there had been established a network of women ready to respond to the wom-
en's rights message.

Other such networks included those of churchwomen involved in the American Female Moral Reform Society and similar philanthropic concerns. The evangelical movement brought
many churchwomen into the reforms taking place at the time.
Nevertheless, most serious students of the women's rights
movement feel it cannot be understood without comprehend-
ing its relationships to the antislavery pioneers.

Abby Kelley, surely the most dramatic of those forerunners,
sought divine guidance in her decision to enter the antislavery
field, and all her long life she continued to dress and speak as
a Friend. Nevertheless, she became increasingly impatient with
New England Yearly Meeting's refusal to allow meetinghouses

to be used for antislavery meetings. In 1841 she decided she must resign from the Society, which had disowned several antislavery Friends and was, she felt, betraying its own testimonies. Her meeting, Uxbridge, Massachusetts, in turn decided to disown her for publishing criticisms of the Society in such papers as the *Liberator*.

In 1845 Abby married Stephen Symonds Foster, a Garrisonian radical. The two had one daughter and took turns farming and caring for Alla while they went on the lecture circuit.

Abby Kelley Foster was the target of attacks from clergy, who liked to call her a "Jezebel." She often took Margaret Pryor, a saintly looking Quaker woman from New York, along as her chaperone, but this did not improve her image. Abby Foster was especially controversial in the "burned-over" regions of New York (so called because of an explosive series of revivals that swept the area). Like other Garrisonians, Abby attacked the churches for supporting slavery and the Slave Power; the evangelicals then dominant in the area reacted to her anticlerical attitudes. In 1843 she spoke in the village of Seneca Falls, and being denied the use of a church, she preached from the porch of a local supporter to a crowd gathered outside. The Seneca Falls Presbyterians were so angered by her radical views that they conducted a lengthy trial of several of their members who attended her lecture.[11] Later, when she attempted to speak at Oberlin College in Ohio, her anticlerical views won her the hostility of the faculty. She was carried out bodily from the Orthodox Ohio Yearly Meeting when she tried to preach against slavery from the floor in 1845.

Yet her radical views attracted disciples. Jane Elizabeth Hitchcock from New York traveled with Abby Foster, settled in Salem, Ohio, there married a Quaker, Benjamin Jones, and with him edited the *Anti-Slavery Bugle*, an antislavery newspaper. Jane Jones became a popular lecturer and helped to make Salem a center for both antislavery and women's rights agitation. While still a teacher at Lynn, Foster had influenced a local Quaker woman, Lydia Estes (later the famous female healer Lydia Pinkham) to join the Lynn Female Anti-Slavery Society. Elizabeth Buffum Chace was a Rhode Island Quaker colleague of Abby's who also resigned from the Society over what she perceived to be its antislavery conservatism. Abby was an inspiration as well to Amy Post of Rochester and Mary Ann McClintock of Waterloo, both radical Hicksites. Among her other recruits were Pauline Wright Davis and Lucy Stone. She persuaded Susan B. Anthony to be a paid antislavery lecturer.

In contrast with Abby Kelley Foster's resignation from the Society of Friends, Lucretia Mott, who traveled almost as extensively as Abby during this period, always perceived herself as a traveling Quaker minister. She rarely kept a journal, but her letters and her sermons reveal that she experienced much the same struggle to "give way," to give up personal goals and be obedient to the divine command, much the same dependence on divine guidance, and much the same need to be obedient for the sake of the peace of soul it brought to her, as did her predecessors in the seventeenth and eighteenth centuries. She sought a traveling minute before setting forth, visited Quaker meetings for worship as well as yearly meetings, and she was careful to include pastoral visits to prisons and mental hospitals on her travels. Nevertheless, her sermons almost always touched on the problems of slavery and women's rights. The elders of the Hicksite meetings were alarmed by the controversy she caused. They tried to silence her by eldering her from the floor, and sometimes her own meeting would not give her a traveling minute. She maintained her membership in the Society of Friends precariously, and as a result she profoundly affected its direction.

Drawing strength from her spiritual depths and from an unusual ability to create and sustain supportive relationships— with her husband, children, extended family, and a large group of friends—Lucretia Mott was able to withstand a great deal of abuse from the newspapers and from society at large as well as from the Society of Friends. She had an enormous amount of energy and she poured it into several different causes. Narrowness of purpose was impossible, she believed, if one were truly open to the leading of the Light, for all human rights were bound up in one by the indwelling Spirit.

James Mott was also a strong women's rights advocate, supporting Lucretia and all the other activists in their circle. Less articulate than his gifted wife, he found great satisfaction in accompanying her on her travels and listening to her talks. When she spoke she expressed his feelings. It was a symbiotic relationship. She leaned on him for support when she was under attack; he, in turn, chaired many antislavery, women's rights, and peace meetings. The two were inseparable.

An advocate of equality in marriage, Lucretia Mott developed a maxim that she often repeated at weddings: "In the true marriage relationship, the independence of the husband and wife is equal, their dependence mutual, and their obligations reciprocal."

During the eight years between the London Convention and Seneca Falls, Lucretia Mott supported many aspects of reform. She spoke in Boston on women's rights, visited the legislatures of Delaware, New Jersey, and Pennsylvania to ask for stronger action against slavery, addressed Congress, called on President John Tyler, toured the South, and laid the groundwork for a new Philadelphia charity, the Northern Association for the Relief of Poor Women (the old Female Society was under the control of the Orthodox Quakers). She also organized correspondence between the women of Bristol, England, and the women of Philadelphia promising to work together to avert the threat of war in 1846 over the territory of Oregon, and she supported some Irish handloom workers in a strike for higher wages. Serving on the Yearly Meeting Indian committee, she raised a lone voice against "civilizing" the Senecas by converting them to white ways. Some suggested prevailing upon the women to give up farming and devote themselves to home. Lucretia responded that a council of squaws ought to be called before Quakers attempted to interfere in the domestic arrangements of the tribes involved. Her suggestion met with scorn.

Both Abby Kelley and Lucretia Mott joined the New England Non-Resistance Society, organized in 1839 by William Lloyd Garrison and others dissatisfied with the moderate American Peace Society, to explore the concept of Christian nonresistance. Evils such as slavery must be resisted, William Garrison argued, but might they not be resisted with the tools of truth and of love?[12]

Although the nonresisters drew most of their case material from Quaker experiences in resisting persecution, refusing to serve in the military or pay military tax, and keeping peace with the Indians, most Quakers distrusted the nonresistance movement. Friends believed that they must be obedient to civil authority unless they were directly guided to resist. The nonresisters, on the other hand, were much attracted to a form of Christian anarchy then being expounded by John Noyes. While a few radical Quakers, chiefly the Motts and their circle, embraced nonresistance as a logical outcome of earlier Quaker testimonies (as most Quakers believe today), the majority opposed it and thought of it as one more example of the schemes of "Wm. Lloyd Garrison & Jas. Mott, two madcaps of the antislavery school," as a wealthy Quaker merchant, Thomas Pym Cope, once described them.[13]

Whatever the intellectual origins of nineteenth-century nonresistance, the Quaker women who became part of the movement used the methods in practice. In 1838 Lucretia Mott had led a group of women, two by two, out of Pennsylvania Hall and safely through the angry mob, in the best traditions of nonresistance. (Modern Quakers would call it nonviolence.) The next year she refused Philadelphia police protection for the Third Annual Convention of Anti-Slavery Women, claiming convention attenders would protect themselves by moral means alone. An experience in Delaware, in which she was able to save an elderly cousin from a lynch mob by offering herself in his place, confirmed her belief in the efficacy of nonresistant practice. Later, at every antislavery and women's rights convention she chaired, she insisted on the use of nonresistant methods to protect the meeting from the usual mob violence.

Abby Kelley Foster also practiced nonresistant methods, on one occasion going limp and resisting arrest rather than obeying an unfair law. A few other women, such as Maria Chapman and Lydia Childs, occasionally practiced nonresistance, but it was the Quaker women who introduced nonresistant methods to the new women's rights movement. They continued to uphold them throughout the Civil War when pacifism was no longer fashionable among many abolitionists.

In the summer of 1848 Lucretia and James Mott journeyed to upper New York State to visit Lucretia's sister Martha Coffin Wright and her family in the small town of Auburn. They were present at the Genesee Yearly Meeting (New York) on June 9 when it was decided to terminate the Michigan Quarter, which was demanding more freedom to engage in the antislavery cause, less authority for the ministers and elders, and equality for women. In protest against this high-handed move, about two hundred members of Genesee walked out and later formed the Congregational Friends.

Some time after the close of this yearly meeting, Lucretia Mott and her sister Martha Coffin Wright were invited to tea at the home of Jane Hunt, one of the dissidents. Also present was Mary Ann McClintock, a relative of Jane's by marriage and the wife of Thomas McClintock, a leader of the liberal faction in the Michigan Quarter. Also present, perhaps at Lucretia Mott's suggestion, was Elizabeth Cady Stanton. This was of course the famous tea party where the Seneca Falls Convention was planned.

Although it was organized at short notice, the convention drew large crowds. Many of the attenders were the Progressive or Congregational Friends from nearby villages and a few from as far away as Rochester. Others were abolitionists involved in the Free Soil party. Besides Lucretia Mott and Elizabeth Cady

Stanton, the speakers included Frederick Douglass, an escaped slave who was an eloquent antislavery speaker and editor; Amy Post, a Quaker abolitionist and feminist from Rochester; and Thomas and Mary Ann McClintock. James Mott chaired one of the sessions and Thomas McClintock another. At the end one hundred persons, about two-thirds of them women, signed the Declaration of Sentiments. The contingent from Rochester decided to invite Lucretia and others to a second women's rights convention to be held two weeks later in their home town. At this convention the women were brave enough to preside over the mixed sessions. After this gathering, the Motts returned to Philadelphia, unaware that they had helped to make history.

Susan B. Anthony

In the thirteen years from Seneca Falls to the outbreak of the Civil War, the women's rights movement was loosely organized. Its principal promoter was Elizabeth Cady Stanton, who continued to plan strategy and write speeches throughout the period, although she was often confined at home with her growing family. Elizabeth Cady Stanton and Lucretia Mott maintained a lively correspondence, and Lucretia attended many of the women's rights conventions and chaired several. She was capable of dealing with hecklers in a manner that was forceful and yet never angry. She insisted that women speak up, as Quaker women had long been taught to do, and she resisted calling the police to deal with the near riots that often accompanied these meetings. She also argued for allowing all women the right to speak, whether or not they were voicing the majority view. When Eliza Farnham, author and prison reformer, advanced her argument that woman was the natural superior of man and should control him by denying him sex except for procreation, Lucretia Mott insisted that this view be heard, unpopular as it might prove. "Let each and all expound their own creed, and then let us judge."

She herself was quite clear that no special claims should be made for women, but that all barriers to their advance should be removed. Her *Discourse on Women*,[14] a speech she made in 1849 in response to Richard Henry Dana's attack on the women's movement, was a temperate but forceful statement for educational and professional equality. If some women continued to "hug their chains," as some slaves had done, it was the fault of the inequality they experienced and would be rectified by new law and custom.

She believed that equality was needed not only as a right, but for the sake of the androgynous values it would produce for society. She made this statement particularly well at a Cleveland Woman's Rights Convention in 1853:

It has sometimes been said that if women were associated with men in their efforts, there would not be as much immorality as now exists, in Congress, for instance, and other places. But we ought, I think, to claim no more for woman than for man, we ought to put woman on a par with man, not invest her with power, or claim her superiority over her brother. If we do she is just as likely to become a tyrant as man is; as with Catherine the Second. It is always unsafe to invest man with power over his fellow being. "Call no man master"—that is a true doctrine. But, be sure that there would be a better rule than now, the elements which belong to woman as such and to man as such would be beautifully and harmoniously blended. It is to be hoped that there would be less of war, injustice, and intolerance in the world than now.[15]

But while Lucretia Mott served as a mother and wise elder stateswoman to the new women's rights movement, and Elizabeth Cady Stanton wrote forceful articles and planned strategy, the movement needed someone with organizing skills and willingness to do the legwork to make the dream a reality. That someone was found when Susan B. Anthony, a Hicksite schoolteacher from Rochester, New York, met Elizabeth Cady Stanton in 1851.

Active first in the temperance cause, Susan B. Anthony became indignant when she was barred as a woman from speaking at an Albany temperance rally. Her reaction was to form a Woman's New York Temperance Society, with Elizabeth Cady Stanton as president. The next year, when she was refused an opportunity to speak from the floor at the World's Temperance Convention, she organized a Whole World's Temperance Convention. At the same time she demanded the right to speak at the New York State Teachers' Association. Thoroughly committed to women's rights by this time, she helped Elizabeth Cady Stanton organize a campaign in New York State for improvements in the Married Woman's Property Law. When Elizabeth Smith's simplified costume for women was introduced through the columns of *The Lily*, a reformist paper published in Seneca Falls by Amelia Bloomer, Susan B. Anthony wore bloomers regularly despite verbal abuse. A Garrisonian abolitionist, she took Lucy Stone's place as an antislavery lecturer from 1857 to 1861, working closely with Abby Kelley Foster.

Susan B. Anthony's father, Daniel, came from a long line of Quakers. It was said that a Rhode Island Anthony ancestor had been converted to Quakerism by Mary Dyer of Boston. Susan's mother was Baptist but had encouraged Daniel to raise the children in allegiance to the Quaker testimonies, including the equality of women. When the family moved to Rochester, New York, in 1846, they joined the local Hicksite meeting. After the Genesee split, Susan B. Anthony joined the newly formed Congregational Friends, or Friends of Human Progress as they were later called and once served as secretary of that group. She no longer attended the Hicksite meeting in Rochester after this split but went to the Unitarian church. However, she was never disowned, retaining her membership in the Hicksite Rochester Meeting to her death.

While she was annoyed with the slowness of the Society of Friends to take radical stands on women's rights and the abolition of slavery, Susan B. Anthony continued to dress with the Quaker simplicity and to express many typically Quaker attitudes. She was not impressed with the Victorian concept of the ennobling power of pure womanhood. Let us have equality, she urged. And with equal opportunities came equal responsibilities, as Lucretia Mott always said. Susan B. Anthony revered Lucretia Mott and went to meeting with the Motts when she was in Philadelphia. In her speeches, Susan often referred to the Quaker precedent for women speaking. Were Quaker women ministers, she asked rhetorically, "any less decorous in their manners, less affectionate in their natures, or less Christian in their daily lives . . . ?"[16]

Unlike Lucretia Mott, Angelina Grimké, or Abby Kelley Foster, Susan B. Anthony did not speak from inspiration. Public speaking was always a trial to her, not a source of refreshment. While her long years of devoted service to the ideals of equality and peace were inspiring to others, she did not seem to have the same access to spiritual resources as did the long procession of Quaker women who had gone before her. According to Elizabeth Cady Stanton, she became an agnostic, content to leave ultimate questions unanswered while she responded with religious fervor to the needs of the world. She once told an interviewer that she prayed every second of her life, but with her work, rather than on her knees.[17]

Susan B. Anthony and Elizabeth Cady Stanton had such complementary talents that they made an unusually effective team. With the advice of Lucretia Mott and the aid of Lucy Stone, Abby Kelley Foster, Paulina Davis, Ernestine Rose, Martha Coffin Wright, and a host of others, they kept the women's rights movement alive and growing in the days before the Civil War.

By keeping the network of women's rights conventions informal and allowing all points of view to share the platform, the pioneers avoided the sort of sectarian difficulties that had plagued the early antislavery movement and was still splintering the Society of Friends. While Lucretia Mott herself frequently used the Bible to defend women's equality, she advised that the women base their argument on the self-evident truth rather than Scripture, in order to avoid squabbles. But stresses and strains brewed below the surface. Some women put the abolition of slavery first, while others cared most about women's rights. Some believed nonresistance and pacifism were essential, while others began to feel that slavery must be brought to an end, if need be by the bayonet. Some believed that women had a special, purifying role to fulfill in society, and others thought that equality would bring its own rewards. After the dark days of the Civil War, these tensions bubbled over, and the new suffrage movement was born in the midst of divisions.

8. Quaker Women and the Early Suffrage Movement

For the Quaker abolitionists who had believed that slavery could be ended by nonresistant means or moral weapons, the outbreak of the Civil War posed a cruel dilemma. Now that the North as a whole supported the cause for which they had so long labored, should they not in fact find some way to help in the effort? Or must they stay true to their peace principles and their belief that warfare could win no lasting victory?

The supporters of women's rights faced an additional question. Should they suspend their conventions for the time being, while all the nation's interest was concentrated on the war, or should they keep up the pressure for women's rights? Susan B. Anthony, a pacifist, believed that the momentum gained should not be lost, but Martha Coffin Wright, Elizabeth Cady Stanton, and others reasoned that the women would increase the enmity against them if they continued to hold meetings. Elizabeth Cady Stanton supported the war and felt that some joint action by women was needed to demonstrate their loyalty and their strength. In the spring of 1863, she organized a Women's National Loyal League, the primary object of which was to collect three million signatures on a giant petition for a constitutional amendment ending slavery forever. Susan B. Anthony became the secretary for this group, reasoning that their efforts would be repaid in time by a second federal amendment giving the vote to women as well as to black men.

Lucretia Mott could not desert her Quaker principles to support the war. Instead, she continued to advocate nonresistance and to support the young Quakers and others who were conscientious objectors. Her son-in-law, Edward M. Davis, becoming a captain in the army, decided to lease his farm for the training of black soldiers. Lucretia Mott was a frequent visitor to the neighboring camp, somewhat incongruously named Camp William Penn. She conducted religious services and took the soldiers pies and turkeys, while still refusing to believe the resort to weapons could bring peace. She took part in a campaign to persuade the local transportation company to cease segregating the blacks who rode out to the camp to see their loved ones.

Sarah Pugh, longtime presiding clerk of the Philadelphia Female Anti-Slavery Society and officer of the Pennsylvania Anti-Slavery Society, also felt that the war confirmed her faith in the peace testimony of her Quaker ancestors. She therefore played no role in its support.

Critical of Lincoln for dragging his feet on emancipation and refusing to free the slaves in Union states, Abby Kelley Foster also took no part in the war beyond helping to circulate the petition for the Thirteenth Amendment. She was exhausted by years of campaigning and now discovered she was isolated from most of her old companions, who threw themselves enthusiastically into some form of war work.[1]

Many Quaker abolitionists, however, overcame their scruples against warfare and went to work as nurses or as aides to the newly freed slaves that began to gather in Washington and around army bases. One such was Laura Haviland, who had been active in the antislavery movement since 1832, when she and her husband along with the poet Elizabeth M. Chandler had organized the first Michigan antislavery society. In 1837 she had opened a school on her farm which became River Raisin Institute, an industrial and preparatory school open to all regardless of color. This made the institute a center for abolitionist activity. In 1844 the Havilands withdrew from the Society of Friends over attempts to limit their antislavery activities, and thereafter for many years they attended the Methodist church.

After losing her husband, both parents, a sister, and a child in an epidemic in 1845, Laura Haviland threw herself into the underground railroad, traveling through Ohio, Indiana, Kentucky, Arkansas, and Canada in her efforts to rescue escaping slaves. During the Civil War she visited hospital camps and freed slave settlements in Cairo, Illinois, and Memphis, Tennessee, and scolded the Union officers about camp living conditions. In 1864 she was made a paid agent of the Michigan Freedmen's Aid Commission, and she traveled in Mississippi and Louisiana, establishing aid stations and medical care for freed slaves.[2]

Elizabeth Comstock, a traveling Quaker minister of British birth and a Michigan neighbor of Laura Haviland, also spent the war years visiting army hospitals and camps for freed blacks in Maryland, Virginia, and Delaware, as well as the District of Columbia. On her second visit to Washington, she had an interview with President Abraham Lincoln, a session which began with a period of silence and ended with the president on his knees while Elizabeth Comstock conducted a "season of prayer."[3]

Lincoln had earlier received another Quaker visitor. Eliza Kirkbride Gurney, the widow of Joseph John Gurney, had felt led to seek an interview in 1862 and had both preached and prayed with him. A year later she received a request from the president that she write him a letter. She did so and within a year received an answer, to which she responded. There is a legend that her letter was found in his pocket when he was assassinated, but careful investigation makes this seem doubtful.[4]

Lincoln sought an interview with one young Quaker woman. Anna Elizabeth Dickinson of Philadelphia had become a fervent and much-admired lecturer against slavery in 1860 at the age of eighteen. Combining beauty and ardor, she became so popular as a speaker that the Republicans put her on the campaign trail in New Hampshire, Connecticut, and New York in 1863 and persuaded her to address Congress in early 1864. Although she had been critical of Lincoln's vacillation on freeing the slaves, she endorsed his reelection in the course of this speech. However, despite a private interview with Lincoln at his request, she withdrew her endorsement later in the year. She continued lecturing after the war and remained a stellar attraction for many years. Susan B. Anthony admired her and tried to persuade her to lecture for women, but Anna Dickinson replied that like any other Quaker woman she had to wait for a leading. Although she supported the rights of women, this leading never came.

Other Quaker women hurried to Washington during the war, if not to see the president, then to help the freed slaves. Emily Howland of Sherwood, New York, and Julia Wilbur of Rochester worked in a school for free black girls. Cornelia Hancock, a teacher from New Jersey who had volunteered to nurse the wounded at Gettysburg, spent a year nursing the freed blacks in Washington until she was called to be a regular army nurse. Abby Hopper Gibbons, a Hicksite prison reformer who had resigned her right of membership in the Society of Friends when the New York Yearly Meeting disowned her father, went to Washington with her daughter Sarah and her niece Maria Hopper (granddaughter of Lucretia Mott) and served as both volunteer nurse and aide to the contraband for over three years. Amanda Way, an Indiana Quaker and a strong supporter of women's rights, was also a Civil War nurse.

At the beginning of the war, the Union forces captured some of the Sea Islands off the coast of South Carolina. Here a band of earnest reformers, black and white, began preparing the former slaves for freedom. Miller McKim, secretary of the Port Royal Relief Committee, took his Quaker daughter Lucy with him to visit the islands in June of 1862. A trained musician, Lucy McKim was deeply impressed by the songs of the slaves and committed them to musical annotation. Her work led to the publication of a book, *Slave Songs of the United States* in 1867.[5]

The songs and the stories from the Sea Islands and from Gideon's Band, as the Port Royal reformers came to be known, influenced many. Emily Howland considered volunteering for service on the islands but decided instead to attempt to establish an ideal community, Arcadia, for newly freed slaves in northern Virginia. Cornelia Hancock, a New Jersey Hicksite and Civil War nurse, joined the Port Royal group at the end of the war under auspices of the Friends Association for the Aid and Elevation of the Freedmen, but she soon moved to Mount Pleasant, across the harbor from Charleston, where she started a school for black children. Ironically, it was eventually named not for Cornelia Hancock but for Henry Laing, the treasurer of the group that supported it, and it is today an integrated public middle school, the Laing School. Martha Schofield of Darby Meeting, Pennsylvania, who also worked as a Civil War nurse, volunteered to teach on the Sea Islands, but moved after several years to Aiken. Here she singlehandedly established a school, eventually named the Schofield School, which gave industrial as well as normal school education to black children and youth.[6]

In the Midwest, Indiana and Ohio Yearly Meetings established Committees to Aid the Freedmen and sent many couples south directly after the war to meet immediate needs and suggest long-range projects. Thus Elkanah and Irene Beard worked for freed slaves in Vicksburg and were asked to oversee schools for blacks in Mississippi and Louisiana. Ordered by a Union Army officer to provide an orphanage for some abandoned children, Elkanah Beard sent for a Quaker couple, Calvin and Alida Clark of Wayne County, Indiana. The Clarks opened a school in Arkansas, which became Southland College, an institution supported by British and Irish as well as American Friends. Alida Clark was "the moving spirit of the place" who ran the school and raised the money to keep it afloat. Her husband "ably and faithfully supported his wife in these endeavors," but for many years it was her school.[7]

Ohio Yearly Meeting at Mt. Pleasant also developed a Committee to Aid the Freedmen and ran a Colored School in Jackson, Mississippi, under the care of three women: Beulah Henderson, Hannah Binns, and Emma Jones. They reported to the yearly meeting session of 1874 that instruction in read-

Yᵉ MAY SESSION OF Yᵉ WOMAN'S RIGHTS CONVENTION—Yᵉ ORATOR OF Yᵉ DAY DENOUNCING Yᵉ LORDS OF CREATION.

Woman's Rights Convention. *Harpers Weekly,* June 11, 1859.
Courtesy of the New York Historical Society, New York.

ing, writing, arithmetic, and Bible study was in progress.[8] Apparently this committee continued to 1885. In its later years, Ohio's Freedmen Committee gave support to Elizabeth Comstock and Laura Haviland of Michigan, who went to Kansas to provide food, clothes, and shelter to the hungry and half-naked freed blacks pouring into that state following the withdrawal of federal troops from the South in 1877.

The Negro's Hour

The Thirteenth Amendment, for which so many abolitionist women's rights advocates had worked during the Civil War, was introduced into Congress in February of 1865 and ratified by December. Anticipating this development, William Lloyd Garrison had announced in 1864 that he considered the abolitionist struggle now over and felt the American Anti-Slavery Society should disband. More radical abolitionists were not as sanguine about the future of the blacks in the South. Women, meanwhile, remembered the promise they considered to have been implicit, that at the end of the war their comrades would join them in working for suffrage for both women and black men. The radicals and women together decided to keep the AASS going without Garrison's support.

By the summer of 1865, early drafts of the Fourteenth Amendment were circulated, revealing that the Republicans intended to work for suffrage for black men only. The insertion of the word *male* meant that a new constitutional amendment would be needed to enfranchise women. Alarmed by this development, Elizabeth Cady Stanton and Susan B. Anthony developed a new petition campaign, asking for the vote for both women and black men. To their surprise and dismay, many of their old comrades of both sexes objected to mixing the two issues. It was, as Wendell Phillips said, "The Negro's hour."

The feminists faced an agonizing dilemma. News from the South was not encouraging. The war was scarcely over before the southerners had begun to try to frighten or cajole their former slaves back into servitude. Women who had gone South to work among the freed slaves sounded the alarm and demanded that northern allies work quickly for the "shield of suffrage" to protect the blacks.

In May of 1866, a new organization, the American Equal Rights Association, was formed to work for both blacks and white women, with Lucretia Mott as president. But quarreling over the Fourteenth Amendment soon split the group into factions. Even Abby Kelley Foster, ardent supporter of the rights of women, felt that blacks needed the protection of the vote first. Angered by the desertion of her former comrades, Elizabeth Cady Stanton began to resort to racist and nativist arguments: "If all men are to vote—black and white, lettered and unlettered, washed and unwashed, then the safety of the nation, as well as the interest of women, demand that we outweigh this incoming tide of ignorance, poverty, and vice with the virtue, wealth, and education of the women of the country."[9]

In the fall of 1867, Kansas was scheduled to vote on a referendum on both black men's and women's suffrage. Elizabeth Cady Stanton and Susan B. Anthony hurried out to Kansas during the summer to campaign for women. There they met a wealthy eccentric Democrat, George Francis Train, who offered to support them if they would publish a paper advocating suffrage for women. A Copperhead (a northern Democrat opposed to abolition), Train was opposed to giving blacks the vote but believed that the country needed the vote of pure and educated women to counteract that of the uneducated former slaves. Financially desperate, the two women found Train's offer of support irresistible. In January they began to publish *The Revolution*.

For most of the veteran abolitionists, this apparent desertion of the black man's cause was the final straw. Even gentle Lucretia Mott lost her patience and wrote angrily to her sister Martha Wright, "*The Revolution* is unsatisfactory and I haven't the littlest notion of being a subscriber. . . . Elizabeth Cady Stanton's sympathy for Sambo [the black man] is very questionable." The next fall when Stanton and Anthony visited her in Philadelphia, she asked them bluntly how they could explain such disloyal affiliations.

The introduction of the Fifteenth Amendment, "The right of citizens of the United States to vote shall not be denied or abridged . . . on account of race, color, or previous condition of servitude," might have provided one more opportunity for women. Why could not the word *sex* be added? But once more the majority of the members of the Equal Rights Association favored black male rights. After the May 1869 meeting, Elizabeth Cady Stanton and Susan B. Anthony gave up the struggle and rather surreptitiously organized the National Woman Suffrage Association for women only, believing that the presence of men in the Equal Rights Association had led to their betrayal.

During the summer, Lucretia Mott and Theodore Tilton, a journalist committed to women's rights, worked together to try to resolve the differences between the two groups of women's rights advocates. Aged, newly widowed, and sick, Lucretia Mott visited Elizabeth Cady Stanton and Susan B. Anthony in New Jersey and Lucy Stone in Boston, trying to find common ground. Her own feelings were torn. She did not like Francis Train or the argument for "educated suffrage," but she was committed to women's rights and to the "old pioneers," of whom she was herself the oldest.

The peace efforts failed, and in November Lucy Stone, her husband, Henry Blackwell, Julia Ward Howe, and others established the American Woman's Suffrage Association. This was to be a representative group made up of delegates from state suffrage associations who would press for the vote for women, state by state. Shortly, it began to publish its own newspaper, *The Woman's Journal*. While the National Association under Elizabeth Cady Stanton and Susan B. Anthony sought allies everywhere—among working-class women and women in politics, such as Victoria Woodhull—the American Association became more and more middle-class and respectable.

For most of the Quaker women's rights activists, the split in the suffrage movement was extremely painful. As Abby Kelley Foster had said early in her career, "All the great family of mankind are bound up in one bundle. Rights are the same for one and all; when we aim a blow at our neighbors rights, our own rights are by the same blow destroyed."[10] To believe in "that of God in everyone," and then to make a deliberate, political choice in favor of any group over another, was impossible for one who actually tried to follow the leading of the Light. Until she died, Lucretia Mott did not give up her effort to heal the breach and to support both groups, although she gave most of her time and love to the National Association. Sarah Pugh refused to take sides at all but attended the meetings of both groups, as did Emily Howland. Phebe Coffin Hanaford, a

Quaker from Nantucket turned Unitarian minister, managed to keep on good terms with both groups while she worked for women's suffrage in New Jersey.

Martha Schofield, refusing to take sides, helped to organize the South Carolina branch of the American Association, but she accepted an invitation from Susan B. Anthony to speak at a National Convention in 1878. Other Quaker women put their energies into local suffrage work; Elizabeth Buffum Chace in Rhode Island; Elizabeth Jones in Ohio; Dr. Mary Frame Thomas and Amanda Way in Indiana; Ruth Dugdale, Mary Jane Coggeshall, Deborah Cattell, and Mary Coppoc Ralley in Iowa. Two of Mary Ralley's sons had joined John Brown in his ill-fated adventure at Harper's Ferry. Edwin had been hanged, but Barclay escaped, only to die on a Civil War battlefield. In writing to Susan B. Anthony to welcome *The Revolution*, Mary Ralley said that she rejoiced because this new *Revolution* was "a bloodless one."

Nonviolent Actions

Women soon took action to protest the fact that they were not allowed to vote. One method was to go ahead and vote anyway, a simple form of direct action in line with nonresistant principles. The first such demonstrations took place in New Jersey where women had voted sporadically until 1807. The state constitution, hastily adopted in 1776, had failed to disenfranchise women with property, and the error was not discovered for more than thirty years. Lucy Stone, living in Orange, New Jersey, was the president of the New Jersey Woman Suffrage Association, and she led a fight for women to challenge the state constitution by voting until she moved to Boston in 1870.

A dramatic voting demonstration occurred in Vineland, New Jersey, in 1868. The men customarily voted at a table at one end of Union Hall. On the day of the election, the women set up a table at the opposite end of the hall. One by one they tried to vote at the men's end and were rejected. They then carried out the complete voting procedures at their table in protest. Presiding as one of the women judges of election was eighty-four-year-old Margaret Pryor, Abby Kelley Foster's former traveling companion, wearing her Quaker bonnet and looking benign, while she watched younger members of this Quaker farming community come to vote. Altogether, 172 women, including four blacks, "voted" that day, and the demonstration inspired several others. On March 7, 1870, Angelina Grimké Weld and Sarah Grimké marched through a howling snowstorm in Hyde Park, Massachusetts, to the local polling place, where the judges of election had set up a special box to receive the token ballots of women.

Susan B. Anthony's hometown of Rochester had continued to be a hotbed of suffragist activity, and it was here that women made the most serious effort to vote, claiming that they had already been given the right of suffrage by the Fourteenth Amendment and could not be deprived of it by state law. In the fall of 1872, fifty women registered to vote in the presidential election and four days later, sixteen of the fifty actually voted in the eighth ward. Led by Susan B. Anthony herself, the group consisted of four Anthony relatives and eleven neighbors, several of them Quakers or former Quakers.

The administration in Washington, wishing to bring an end to these demonstrations, decided to make a test case of Susan B. Anthony. She was arrested, charged, and tried in a court of law for having "knowingly, wrongfully, and unlawfully voted for a representative to the Congress of the United States." In the weeks before her trial, Susan campaigned for women's rights throughout the county so thoroughly that the prosecution asked that the trial be moved to nearby Ontario County. When this was done, Susan and her friend and coworker Mathilda Joslyn Gage spoke in all the postal districts of that county. At the trial itself, the prosecution held that Susan was incompetent to testify, and the judge instructed the jury to find her guilty. Perhaps feeling slightly guilty himself, Justice Ward

Hunt then asked Susan B. Anthony if she had anything to say. Her response was a blistering attack on women's disenfranchisement:

Yes, your Honor, I have many things to say, for in your ordered verdict of guilt, you have trampled under foot every vital principle of our government. My natural rights, my civil rights, my political rights are all alike ignored. Robbed of the fundamental privilege of citizenship, I am degraded from the status of citizen to that of a subject, and not only myself individually but all of my sex are, by your Honor's verdict, doomed to political subjection under this so-called Republican government.[11]

The judge fined her $100, which she refused to pay. The judge deliberately refused to commit her to jail until the fine was paid, and he thus made it impossible for her to appeal the high-handed and improper methods of her trial.

Another form of direct action was to refuse to pay one's taxes. Dr. Harriot Hunt of Boston, a non-Quaker women's rights advocate and woman physician, began paying under protest in 1851. Lucy Stone refused to pay property taxes in 1858 and watched her household goods sold at auction as a result. They were bought by a friendly neighbor and returned to her. The author Lydia Maria Childs paid under protest, and two sisters in Glastonbury, Connecticut, Abby and Julia Smith, had their cows confiscated as the result of a similar refusal.

Naturally, the Quaker suffragists joined this campaign. In 1873 Abby Kelley and Stephen Foster decided to refuse to pay taxes on their farm. The city gave them a year, then seized the farm and sold it to the highest bidder, a spiteful neighbor. So many of the old reformers had backed the Fosters that the man relented and returned the deed. The Fosters then decided to call a convention on taxation without representation, while continuing to refuse to pay taxes. Asked what should be displayed at the woman's pavilion during the Centennial Fair of 1876 in Philadelphia, Elizabeth Cady Stanton suggested that the walls be adorned with "the papers issued by the city of Worcester for the forced sale of the house and lands of Abby Kelley Foster."[12] Worcester did not give up on collecting the back taxes, however, and the case dragged on until 1880, when the Fosters' daughter, Alla, encouraged them to arrive at a settlement, pointing out that they had made their case.

Another protester was Martha Schofield of Aiken, South Carolina. In 1876 a reporter from the *New York Tribune* sent to interview her about her stand on voting rights for blacks, wrote instead about her tax refusal: "She believes in what are commonly known as 'woman's rights' in so far as she denies the right of a government to impose taxes upon a woman who has no vote, and she has presented her views on the subject so forcibly to the officials of the State that her taxes have invariably been returned to her." The reporter was evidently carried away by his own eloquence, for there is no evidence that the state ever returned taxes to Martha, although she always wrote "paid under protest" on her tax checks.[13]

Yet another nonviolent demonstration for women's suffrage took place in 1876 at the time of the centennial celebrations in Philadelphia. Elizabeth Cady Stanton and Susan B. Anthony, with their usual flair, had conceived the idea of holding a National Woman's Suffrage Association convention at the same time as the official ceremonies were being planned to honor the one hundredth birthday of the Declaration of Independence. They asked the centennial commissioners to allow the aged Lucretia Mott to sit on the platform with the distinguished visitors and to present the vice-president with a copy of the women's declaration of independence. Lucretia Mott was to be accompanied by Elizabeth Cady Stanton. This permission was denied, but instead the officials offered the women five seats in Independence Hall. Lucretia Mott and Elizabeth Cady Stanton decided to forgo this dubious honor and concentrate instead on the women's convention at the nearby Unitarian church.

Susan B. Anthony, Matilda Joslyn Gage, and three other younger women, however, took the seats. On the morning of the fourth of July they attended the ceremonies, awaiting their chance. Just as Richard Henry Lee of Virginia, a descendant of one of the first signers, finished reading the original declaration, and the band was preparing to strike up the Brazilian national anthem in honor of the emperor of Brazil who sat on the dais, Susan B. Anthony arose and presented the women's declaration to Acting Vice-President Thomas Ferry. The five women then walked down the aisle distributing printed copies of the declaration to the right and to the left. Not quite sure what was going on, men stood on chairs to grab copies while the officials shouted for order. Outside the women climbed onto a bandstand erected for later entertainment, and Susan B. Anthony read the women's declaration to the crowd that had gathered to gawk at the dignitaries.[14]

Lucretia Mott, who had taken no part in this demonstration, chaired the National Woman's Suffrage Association Meeting at the nearby Unitarian church. A foreign visitor to Philadelphia commented in the press that her talk and her bearing were more exciting to him than the events at Independence Hall. However, neither Susan B. Anthony's action nor Lucretia Mott's speech were mentioned in the Quaker journals of the day, since both Orthodox and Hicksite groups continued to disapprove of such worldly activities.

A Narrowing Focus

As the years passed, the suffrage movement became more respectable and more middle-class. Other women's groups also were organized during the fourth quarter of the nineteenth century. Women who had graduated from college or had entered the professions set up women's clubs to help other women achieve the same goals. In Philadelphia a group of women who had participated in the centennial by organizing and running the women's pavilion, organized the New Century Club, with Sarah Hallowell as president and Eliza Sproat Turner as vice-president, both Quakers. Subsequently, Eliza Turner began to arrange evening classes for working women and girls, a development so enthusiastically received that it became a separate organization, the New Century Guild of Working Women. In New Jersey, Cornelia Collins Hussey, a Quaker with Nantucket ties, helped to organize the Women's Club of Orange, New Jersey, and used it as a platform to work for suffrage. Maria Mitchell, the Nantucket astronomer, was a founder of the Association for the Advancement of Women, and Phebe Hanaford served as vice-president. Hanaford was also a vice-president of the very popular New York–based women's organization, Sorosis.

The largest and most influential women's group to be organized at this time was the Women's Christian Temperance Union, which first met in Cleveland in 1874 with Frances Willard as its active and influential secretary. Willard also espoused women's suffrage and sought to join the two movements. The support of the WCTU was a mixed blessing to the suffrage movement, for it introduced a conservative element and helped to narrow the focus of the movement from women's rights to the vote alone. It also led the liquor interests to fear the women's movement and to fight it at every turn, a development that continued to have political repercussions for many years.

Quaker women had advocated temperance and worked in temperance societies since the 1840s. American Quakers—as opposed to their British cousins—were firmly opposed to the personal use of alcohol. They were also shocked into action by the oppression of wives by alcoholic husbands who confiscated joint property and beat their families. Some women, like Susan B. Anthony, found their way to the women's rights movement through the temperance movement. Others, like Abby Kelley Foster, always put abolition and women's rights first but campaigned for temperance in the 1870s.

Quaker women were active in various phases of the early temperance movement. In 1854 Amanda Way, a Quaker minister from Winchester, Indiana, organized a "Woman's Temperance Army," which attempted to close saloons. She was also a lecturer and organizer of a temperance lodge, the Independent Order of Good Templars, which her coworker in temperance and women's suffrage, Dr. Mary Frame Thomas, also joined. Both Laura Haviland and Elizabeth Comstock gave temperance lectures. Lydia Chace, who had followed Alida Clark as matron of Southland College, was the president of the Arkansas WCTU. Hannah Bailey of Maine established a department of Peace and Arbitration within the WCTU and became that organization's chief advocate of peace.

Mary Sibbitt of Wichita, Kansas, traveled throughout the country as a temperance lecturer, attending Friends yearly meetings and lecture series as she went and earning the reputation of being the "Kansas Cyclone" for her vehemence. Mary Whitall Thomas of Baltimore was president of the WCTU for Maryland, and her sister, the famous writer Hannah Whitall Smith, was an active supporter of temperance. A comparison of eighty-five Quaker women, and a random sample of eighty-five non-Quaker women, drawn from *The Dictionary of Notable American Women: 1607–1950*, shows that fifteen Quaker women, as opposed to seven non-Quaker women, were involved in temperance.[15]

In 1878 Susan B. Anthony managed to persuade a friendly congressman to introduce into Congress a new amendment: "The right of citizens of the United States to vote shall not be denied or abridged by the United States or any state on account of sex." Called the Susan B. Anthony amendment, this measure was introduced into Congress year after year for most of the rest of the century. Both the Senate and the House established select committees for women's suffrage, and both at first reported favorably on the measure. The western congressmen were sympathetic, but the eastern and southern representatives were opposed. Nothing was able to break the deadlock.

Meanwhile, the women continued to campaign state by state for the vote. Wyoming was the first victory in 1869. The women of Utah won the right to vote in 1870, but lost it again in 1887 when Congress outlawed plural marriage along with a bill that revoked women's suffrage. Colorado gave women the vote in

1893 and Oregon in 1896. In many other states women worked hard but lost the fight for the ballot.

Quaker women continued to campaign for suffrage, but few gave it their exclusive attention as did Susan B. Anthony. Many were now busy with campaigns against sweatshop labor and for women prisoners or immigrant women. Later still, their energies would be diverted to the peace movement. As suffrage became more and more a matter of political action, the earlier Quaker influence on the women's movement, with resulting emphasis on inclusiveness and nonviolence, became less prominent. The older pioneers were gone. Instead, Quaker women were turning their attention to breaking trails in the field of social reform.

9. One Reform and Another

The nineteenth century has been called the century of reform. The abolition movement and the temperance crusade flourished, along with a host of other causes aimed at personal and social improvement. For many middle-class American women hemmed in by the nineteenth century concept of woman's separate sphere, these reforms provided a legitimate means of self-expression. And everywhere Quaker women in their plain-colored dresses and white kerchiefs addressed public audiences with a poise that astonished their less liberated sisters. Thomas Woody, in his monumental two-volume study, *Women's Education in the United States*, commented on this phenomenon: "The freedom with which Quaker women preached—and more than that the freedom with which they entered the public platform in one reform and another—undoubtedly had a liberalizing effect on women's position in the nineteenth century."[1]

The sense that all reforms were intricately bound together was an aspect of Quaker perfectionism. Called to give expression to "living in that life and power that takes away the occasion for war," Friends felt they could not choose between the cause of, for instance, the slave and the prisoner. Both had to be pursued.

Commitment to social reform led nineteenth-century crusaders—both Quakers and non-Quakers—into widely diverging activities. Many were interested in moral reform, a euphemism for the abolition of prostitution. Others studied phrenology, a pseudoscience that explained human behavior by the shape of bumps on the skull and emphasized the importance of environment rather than heredity in understanding deviant behavior. Many advocated dress and food reform. They took up the natural foods diet being suggested by Sylvester Graham, and they tried cold water baths for the solution of almost all medical problems. A few of the more radical Quaker women dabbled in all these reforms. Abby Kelley Foster put her family on the Graham diet and plunged her daughter Alla into a cold bath every morning, much to the baby's surprise. Even Lucretia Mott, normally skeptical of such matters, was interested in phrenology and once pointed out that the heads of Nantucket women were larger than those of other women due to the opportunity they had had to exercise their brains!

But Quaker women possessed additional incentive for being involved in reforms. Their husbands, fathers, and brothers were increasingly making the abolition movement, the Indian rights movement, and the prison reform movement their domain for self-expression apart from business and meetinghouse. The Quaker withdrawal from government and acceptance of quietism had caused the whole Society to turn its attention to reforms, to education, and to philanthropy. Quaker couples were often partners in these enterprises. The comparison of Quaker with non-Quaker women, mentioned earlier, shows twenty-six Quaker women to five non-Quaker women sharing such work with their husbands. Moreover, it was not unusual to find the wife the stronger member of the team.

In some reforms, however, Quaker men had developed societies for men only in the eighteenth century. Not surprisingly, Quaker women were not content to be barred any longer from these concerns.

Prison Reform

In 1813, Elizabeth Gurney Fry paid her first visit to Newgate Prison in London and decided that something must be done about the conditions under which women prisoners and their babies survived—cold, naked, and hungry. In 1817 she decided to open a school for the women prisoners.

Word of Elizabeth Fry's accomplishments spread quickly through the transatlantic Quaker community. The fact that Eliz-

Abby Hopper Gibbons.
Permission from the Friends
Historical Library, Swarthmore
College, Swarthmore, PA.

abeth Fry was a member of the wealthy, evangelical Gurney
family made her particularly influential among the families of
the Philadelphia Quaker establishment, whose male members
served on the Board of Managers of the Prison Society. One
such family was that of Thomas and Mary Waln Wistar. The
parents of thirteen children, Thomas and Mary were also
Quaker leaders of some note. Thomas was a charter member
and officer of the Prison Society and an elder in his meeting.
Mary was a recorded minister in a Philadelphia monthly meeting. She was also the pioneer of women's prison reform in
America, although her story has remained buried.

Married in 1786 at twenty-one, Mary Waln Wistar was busy
with her large family for more than thirty years. But in 1819
her name appeared as correspondent for the Association of
Women Friends to Care for Poor Children. In 1823, inspired by
Elizabeth Fry, she organized the Female Prison Association of
Friends in Philadelphia and, with a few fellow members and
her husband as chaperone, paid a visit to the Arch Street
prison. This first meeting was devoted to prayer and the reading of Scripture to an assembled group of women. The visitors
were shocked at the condition in which they found the pris-

oners and wanted to supply them with clothing. Mary Waln Wistar wrote to her daughter Margaret, who was married to Roberts Vaux, the influential corresponding secretary of the Prison Society, about obtaining funds for this purpose. Vaux's answer to his mother-in-law reveals all too clearly the attitude of the men toward the women prisoners.

Vaux began his letter by explaining that the Prison Society did not provide articles of clothing to prisoners except in the case of extreme need during the winter. However, the Society was willing to bend to the women's wishes and buy the smallest number of articles mentioned in Mary Waln Wistar's letter. The Prison Society's caution was not due to stinginess but to the supposedly adverse effect of charity on the women prisoners themselves.

The unhappy females whom you visited yester-day form a circulating medium of poverty and vice, alternately to be found in the wards of the Alms House, & within the walls of the Prison.-They are known to almost every watch-man of the City, & their names are to be found on the docket of almost every magistrate.-Their habits have become chronic, & I fear in most instances past restoration.-If many of them were "arrayed in purple & fine linnen" by an unbounded charity, & set at liberty through the agency of a generous sympathy, such is the depravity of their minds, that in a few hours their garments would be surrendered as the price of some sensual appetite, the indulgence of which in a few more hours, would insure their return to Prison.— of consequence it follows, from the knowledge of these circumstances, that great caution be observed in administering assistance to habitual offenders, lest such be rendered more comfortable than those who subsist by honest industry, and thus unintentionally, tho in effect, offer a bounty for crime, and present a reward for vice.[2]

Despite such warnings, the Female Association soon began to visit the prisoners regularly, offering them instruction in sewing and writing, giving spiritual counsel, and trying to place discharged prisoners in homes or institutions. They also began to campaign for better conditions for their imprisoned sisters. The first crusade of Mary Waln Wistar's group worked

for the establishment of a House of Refuge for juvenile offenders. At first the Prison Society felt that this enterprise was
beyond their financial means, but by holding public meetings
and raising money, members gathered the necessary funds and
established the House of Refuge in 1828. The women next argued for a matron for the female prisoners at Arch Street Jail.
The first reaction again was negative, but several years later a
woman was appointed. In 1835 Moyamensing Prison was
opened in south Philadelphia and all the women prisoners
transferred there. This meant a considerable trip for the members of the Female Society, and they lobbied for and obtained
transportation funds from their male counterparts.

In 1846 in Baltimore, a group of Orthodox women from the
Baltimore Monthly Meeting organized a Women Friends Association for Visiting the Penitentiary, with a twenty-six-year-
old woman, Elizabeth King, as its leader. The group set about
teaching the women prisoners to read and write and felt that
this made such a difference that they organized a school and
a library. In 1847 Dorothea Dix, a famous crusader for prisoners
and the mentally ill, visited them and praised their efforts.
They took an interest in the placement of discharged prisoners,
suggested to the prison officials that the prisoners be classified
and separated, lobbied for a female matron, and established a
Sabbath school. By 1858, they had recruited from other denominations to work with them in the prisons.[3]

In New York City, Abby Hopper Gibbons had been working
with her father, Isaac Hopper, in establishing a Female Department to the New York Prison Association. After a period
of visiting prisons, Abby Gibbons and her colleagues decided
in 1846 to open a halfway house for discharged women prisoners, very likely the first such institution in the world. The
stay at the Home for Discharged Female Convicts was entirely
voluntary, and the regime was strict: rising at 5:30 A.M., worship at 6 A.M., breakfast at 6:30 A.M., and so on through a day
of classes in reading, writing, arithmetic, and sewing until retiring at 9 P.M. Any inmate showing up drunk was discharged.

At the end of eight years the home published a report on nine hundred former inmates, showing that three hundred of the women had remained in placements secured for them by the home, another 150 were in satisfactory situations, while the rest had not been heard from.

The Female Department became independent in 1853 and was called the Women's Prison Association and Home. Still under the leadership of the indomitable Abby Gibbons, it continued to operate the house—renamed the Isaac Hopper House—for many years and later crusaded for the hiring of female police matrons and for the establishment of a separate "reformatory" for women prisoners. Abby Gibbons, who was also an abolitionist, a Civil War nurse, and a pioneer in social work, made her last appearance before the New York legislature at the age of ninety-one to lobby for the women's prison, and she had the satisfaction of seeing it approved before she died.[4]

Encouraged by the success of the New York women, the Philadelphia Association proposed a halfway house to the Pennsylvania Prison Society. Unfortunately that organization remained committed to the idea of separating prisoners so that they would not have a bad effect upon each other. Some of the more doctrinaire members therefore objected to the halfway house as a violation of the principle of separation, since obviously the women would mingle. The men insisted that the home not be restricted to women prisoners, but opened also to other women needing protection from vice, and they earmarked their contribution so that it would not support the mixing of former women prisoners. The women finally decided to raise money independently, and in 1853 the Howard Institution for Discharged Women Prisoners was opened on Poplar Street and continued to operate with some degree of success until 1917, when it was returned over to the Society for Prevention of Cruelty to Children.[5]

Of the female pioneers in prison reform whose names have been preserved in history, about thirty percent were Quakers.

The most colorful of these pioneers was Eliza Farnham, writer and advocate of the superiority of women. In 1844 Eliza Farnham persuaded the authorities to appoint her matron of the women's branch of Sing Sing prison. Here the all-male, Quaker governing board, the New York Prison Society, had instituted the "silent system," their answer to the "separate system" in Pennsylvania. Prisoners were allowed to work together and to eat together, but never to speak to one another. The women prisoners had rebelled against this harsh rule, and there had been prison riots before Eliza's coming. She blithely disregarded the rule of silence and brought in a piano, encouraging the women to sing and read together. A believer in phrenology, she thought that environment could influence the development of character. She added curtains at the windows, flowers, and even dolls for the younger prisoners to play with, as part of an effort to make the prison more homelike. As a result, she was in constant conflict with other staff members and the prison chaplain, and with a change of administration in 1848, she was fired.

A group of midwestern Friends with evangelical leanings were also pioneers in prison reform. Elizabeth Comstock, the abolitionist, was sometimes called "The Elizabeth Fry of America." As a traveling Quaker minister, she visited prisons, hospitals, and asylums wherever she went and alerted lawmakers to the existing abuses. Sarah Smith, also a traveling minister and an abolitionist, felt called to a ministry among the prostitutes of Indianapolis, where she operated a Home for the Friendless. She so impressed the city officials that she was appointed to a newly created post, City Missionary. In this capacity she visited jails and prisons and became convinced that a separate facility was needed for women. She began a campaign with the help of other Friends, which resulted in the establishment of the Indiana Reformatory for Women and Girls. With her husband, James, she was appointed cosuperintendent of the new institution. James, who was older and not in good health, supported his wife while she played the major role and took much adverse criticism. According to her biographer, Rhoda Coffin, also a Quaker prison reformer, eighty percent of her prisoners did not return to crime.[6]

Elizabeth Buffum Chace, abolitionist and advocate of women's rights, also participated in prison reform. After the Civil War she began to work for better treatment of women prisoners by urging that women be appointed to serve on state penal boards. As a result, in 1870 Rhode Island appointed her to an advisory Board of Lady Visitors. Elizabeth Chace soon discovered that this board was created for appearance's sake and lacked influence. After six years of struggle, she resigned but accepted reappointment when some more power was given the Visitors.

Many of the Quaker women prison reformers were equally interested in mental hospitals or asylums, as they were then called. Reforming the care of the mentally ill was one of the concerns of the Society of Friends as a whole. At York Retreat in England, and at Friends Asylum at Frankford, near Philadelphia, Quakers had pioneered in humane treatment of the mentally ill and the use of occupational therapy. The traveling Quaker women ministers, such as Elizabeth Comstock, Lucretia Mott, and Sarah Smith, routinely visited asylums as well as prisons. Eliza Farnham spent a year as matron of the Female Department of Stockton Insane Asylum in California. Some of the first Quaker women doctors worked in mental hospitals.

Indian Rights

Throughout the nineteenth century, the traditional Quaker concern for Indian rights continued to involve both Quaker men and women. In the early part of the century, Quakers protested the action of the United States government in moving the Senecas and the Cherokees off their land. After the Civil War, President Ulysses Grant asked various Quaker groups to undertake the superintendencies of several large Indian reservations in the West. His goal was to pacify and civilize the

Indians, and since Quakers had a historic friendship with the Native Americans, Grant called the new experiment his Peace Policy.

The results of this enterprise were mixed. Making Quakers the agents of the government in an effort to enforce compliance to a policy of "pacification" removed them from their historic role as the advocates of native Americans. Many of the Friends themselves became increasingly uncomfortable in this role, while the commissioners of Indian affairs in Washington grew critical of the Friends for their too friendly administration. After ten years the project was abandoned.

Meanwhile, many evangelical Quaker churches were interested in developing a missionary outreach, converting Indians to membership in the Society of Friends. After the peace policy was abandoned, therefore, new missionary schools and settlements were established. Friends in the missions remained sensitive to the exploitation of the Indians and often aided them in making their complaints against local merchants or intruding white landowners to the government authorities.

Quaker couples often served together as matron and director of the Indian stations, but single women took assignments to teach school and housekeeping skills. Mary Sibbitt, the Kansas temperance lecturer called the "Kansas Cyclone," spent eight years with Asa and Esther Tuttle among the Modoc Indians before her marriage.

An ardent advocate of Indian rights was Helen Hunt Jackson. A girlhood friend of Emily Dickinson, Helen Hunt married as her second husband William Sharpless Jackson, a Quaker from West Chester, Pennsylvania, and she thereafter described herself as a Quaker, although she never joined meeting. Traveling with her husband, she heard the Ponco chief Standing Bear describe the wrongs done to his tribe and was overwhelmed by what she described as a "Quakerly concern" to fight for Indian rights. She wrote a book, *Century of Dishonor*, using government documents to indict the government for its conduct of Indian affairs. Published in 1881, the book earned her a commission to study the needs of the Mission Indians on the West Coast. Her report was blistering, but no action was taken. She then decided to copy the example of Harriet Beecher Stowe, whose *Uncle Tom's Cabin* had helped to sway public opinion against slavery. She therefore put her complaints in fiction form, which resulted in the very popular novel *Ramona*.

Housing Reform

Few of these early Quaker women reformers were aware that basic economic problems could lie behind poverty and exploitation. The current middle-class attitude was that vice, ignorance, and laziness produced poverty. A few women, however, took exception to this view. Ellen Collins, a niece of Phebe Collins Hussey, the New Jersey Quaker suffragist, became concerned about housing conditions in New York City after serving as a member of the New York State Board of Charities, and in this capacity visiting city almshouses, hospitals, and asylums. The more she saw of poverty, the more interested she became in attacking it at the source. One source seemed to be the rapidly deteriorating slums from which the inmates of many of the institutions came. The experience of Octavia Hill, a British woman, in rehabilitating slum dwellings was a source of inspiration to her. In 1880 she invested a large part of her inheritance in the purchase and repair of three New York City tenement houses. With the help of a resident manager she was able to maintain them, rent them at low rates to the poor, and still make a modest return on her investment.

Cornelia Hancock, Civil war nurse and founder of the Laing School in South Carolina, returned to Philadelphia in 1875 and helped to begin the Society for Organizing Charity, and later the Children's Aid Society. As a "friendly visitor" for the SOC, she too made the discovery that poor housing provided an environment in which it was very hard to escape from poverty. With a friend, Edith Wright, she moved to Wrightsville, a shantytown of some forty dwellings in south Philadelphia, near a factory owned by Edith's father. There she set about duplicating the experiment of Octavia Hill and Ellen Collins. She wrote and published a pamphlet about this interesting venture.[7]

The Settlement House Movement

In the latter half of the nineteenth century a new breed of Quaker women reformers began to appear. These were the more radical and dedicated pioneers of social work and social change who crusaded for an end to child labor, regulation of the sweatshop working conditions, and improvement in the welfare of immigrants. Many were associated at one time or another with Jane Addams of Hull House, the pioneer settlement house in Chicago.

Jane Addams herself was the daughter of self-styled Hicksite John Addams, whom she adored. Although never a member of a Quaker meeting, she maintained close ties with Quakers throughout her life. In September of 1889 she and her close friend Ellen Starr moved to Chicago and rented a house on Halsted Street in a crowded immigrant ward. This was Hull House, where she remained for the next forty-six years of her life, entering into campaign after campaign for justice and later for peace, and drawing to her many young women with a desire to identify themselves with the struggles of the poor.

One of the most interesting of Jane Addams's recruits was Florence Kelley, a descendant of the Quaker botanist John Bartram, and a great-niece of Sarah Pugh, the abolitionist. Her mother had grown up in the home of Sarah Pugh, and Florence Kelley was deeply impressed with this serene and committed great-aunt and her refusal to use slave products. She attended Friends Central School in Philadelphia and always said that Quaker values were very important to her, although she did not join a meeting until she was in her sixties.

In 1882 Florence Kelley graduated from Cornell University, which was by now coeducational, Emily Howland having convinced Ezra Cornell that as a Quaker he must make it so. But when she applied next year for the University of Pennsylvania Law School, she was turned down because she was a woman. After several months of teaching classes for working women at the New Century Guild, she decided to travel abroad with her brother.

In Zurich Florence Kelley met M. Carey Thomas of Baltimore, later to be the president of Bryn Mawr. M. Carey Thomas had also attended Cornell, been refused admission to the all-male Johns Hopkins, and had decided to get her Ph.D in Europe. Florence Kelley was likewise inspired to enroll at the University of Zurich. Here she met a group of young socialists and was converted for a time to socialism. She translated the works of Engels and Marx into English for publication in the United States and began a correspondence with Engels.

While in Switzerland, Florence Kelley met and married a young Russian medical student, and with him and their first child she moved back to the United States, settling in New York City. Two more children were born to the couple, but the marriage was not a success. In 1891 they separated, and Florence moved to Hull House, installing her mother and three children in an apartment nearby.

Perhaps in part because she was the mother of young children herself, Florence Kelley was deeply moved by the conditions under which children worked in the "sweating system" of the garment industry. Her investigations revealed that women, too, suffered under this system. Appointed chief factory inspector for the state of Illinois, she risked smallpox as well as bullets to gather evidence against the sweatshop operators. At the same time, she enrolled in evening classes at Northwestern Law School and earned her law degree in 1894.

Investigation was one thing; reform was another. Florence Kelley's attempt to introduce legislation to curb sweatshop abuse was ahead of its time, and although she got some regulations passed by the Illinois legislature, others were struck down. In 1897 she was dismissed. After another two years at

Hull House, she returned to New York City where she became the first general secretary of the newly formed National Consumers League, an effort to improve working conditions by organizing a consumer boycott of the products of sweatshop labor. She often referred to her aunt Sarah Pugh's boycott of slave products as a source of her inspiration. She continued to work with the NCL until her death, lobbying always for laws giving special protection to women and children. Why, she asked, are "seals, bears, reindeer, fish, wild game in the national parks, buffalo, migratory birds, all found suitable for federal protection, but not the children of our race and their mothers?"[8]

Florence Kelley died without seeing the passage of federal legislation protecting children. Her crusade was picked up by another Quaker reformer from Hull House, Grace Abbott. Twenty years younger than Jane Addams and Florence Kelley, Grace Abbott did not move to Hull House until 1908. Her first crusades were for women garment workers and for the immigrants pouring into Chicago and other American cities. She was also an ardent supporter of woman's suffrage. In 1917 she was invited to join the staff of the U.S. Children's Bureau, and in 1921 she became its head, a post she held for thirteen years. She worked continuously for the passage of a constitutional amendment prohibiting child labor. Although this never was ratified by a sufficient number of states, she was pleased when the 1938 Fair Labor Practice Act placed a partial ban on child labor. She died the next year and was buried as a Quaker.

The line of nineteenth-century Quaker reforms stretched from an evangelical missionary on an Indian station in the West, to a settlement house worker investigating sweatshop conditions. Quakerism in the nineteenth century was diverse, and the women reformers reflected that diversity. But they were alike in feeling that they were following their deepest leadings. The assurance which this sense of rightness gave them, combined with their experience in speaking in meeting, made them poised interpreters of the new reform movements and encouraged other women of other religious traditions to follow in their footsteps.

10. Pioneering the Professions

Whenever she spoke, Lucretia Mott urged women to take advantage of every opportunity to learn new skills and to enter the professions. This was woman's chance to advance in the "scale of being," she said, and to demonstrate that her abilities had been held in check. "A new generation of women is now upon the stage," she declared, "improving the increased opportunities furnished for the acquirement of knowledge."[1]

Suiting action to belief, Lucretia Mott herself put much of her energy into developing and supporting institutions that offered education to women. She served on the committee that established Swarthmore College and helped raise money for the Philadelphia Female School of Design. But most important, she supported the founding of the Female Medical College of Pennsylvania.

The same impulse that was carrying many of their sisters into the various reform movements was impelling some women in the middle of the nineteenth century to seek the study of medicine. Health care for women was so poor that many refused to seek medical assistance for serious conditions, preferring to take chances with herbal remedies. The concept of self-development that was part of the women's rights movement led many of the reformers to lecture on female physiology. Women had to learn to know and control their own bodies if they were to be free.

As early as 1835, Harriot Hunt of Boston had begun practicing medicine without a license. She applied several times for entrance into Harvard Medical School but was denied each time. Elizabeth Blackwell, the first American woman to be trained as a physician, had applied to many medical colleges with the backing of Quakers, before Geneva College in New

York made an exception in her case in 1847. Other women were studying privately with liberal physicians. The need for an institution that would give women medical training was becoming urgent when William Mullen, a Quaker businessman in Philadelphia, decided to see if something could be done.

The board of trustees that Mullen formed to found the Female Medical College of Pennsylvania in 1850 was composed of seventeen men. A number of them were Quakers with strong sympathies for women's rights, including James Mott. It apparently did not occur even to Lucretia Mott to suggest that women be included among the trustees, although she sat on the platform during the opening ceremonies.

Classes began in October 1850, with eight women, five of them Quakers, enrolled for the degree of doctor of medicine, and another thirty-two to attend the lectures as "listeners." At first the faculty was male, but by September of 1851, one of the students, Hannah Longshore, who had been tutored in medicine before enrollment, was selected as a demonstrator in anatomy, and she was listed as a faculty member. A classmate, Ann Preston, was appointed professor of hygiene and physiology in 1853 and became dean of the college in 1866.

Hannah E. Myers Longshore's career typifies that of other Quaker women pioneering in medicine. Born in 1819 in Sandy Spring, Maryland, she was the first child of a widowed schoolteacher and abolitionist, Samuel Myers, and his new wife, Paulina. Hannah had two older stepsisters, one of whom, Mary Myers Frame Thomas, also became a physician, as did a younger sister, Jane Viola Myers.

In 1833 the Myers family moved to New Lisbon, Ohio, to get away from slavery. Here Hannah went to the nearby New Lisbon Academy and began a lifelong interest in the study of science. And here in 1836 Hannah, Mary, and one other young Quaker woman held a "woman's rights" meeting under a tree in the Myers yard, and each agreed to write an article on the subject. Mary wrote on suffrage and was thereafter always a suffragist.[2]

Samuel Myers supported women's rights, and after Hannah finished school he encouraged her to give lectures on science and on women's rights and to aspire to study medicine. But the family was too poor to help her with further study, and in 1841 she married a teacher at New Lisbon, Thomas Ellwood Longshore, also a Quaker, an abolitionist, and an advocate of the rights of women. Thomas encouraged Hannah's ambitions but could do nothing to help financially. The young couple lived with the Myerses while their two children, Channing and Lucretia, both named for reformers, were born.

In 1845 Thomas was discharged from New Lisbon Academy for his antislavery views, and the couple moved to Bucks County, Pennsylvania. Here Thomas's brother Joseph practiced medicine in the little town that is now Langhorne. Dr. Joseph Longshore was an ardent believer that women should be permitted to enter medicine, and he gladly tutored Hannah. He was meeting with the committee that formed the Female Medical College at the time, and the speed with which Hannah learned encouraged him to take on other private women apprentices. When the college was opened in 1850, he brought five such pupils with him. In his enthusiasm for their skills he came to believe that women might be better qualified than men: "That woman, from the acuteness of her perceptions, correctness of her observations, her cautiousness, gentleness, kindness, endurance in emergencies, conscientiousness and faithfulness to duty, is not equally, nay by nature abundantly better qualified for most of the offices of the sick room, than man, very few will venture to contradict."[3]

After graduating from the Female Medical College, Hannah Longshore taught at the Female Medical College of Boston and later at the female department of the Penn Medical University. She then hung out her shingle, the first woman doctor in Pennsylvania and one of the first in the nation. Her efforts to start up a private practice were at first unsuccessful. No one would try a woman doctor, and none of the male doctors would make a referral. After several fruitless months, Lucretia Mott suggested that she give a series of public lectures on physiology and hygiene and offered to preside over them.

Many people were horrified by these lectures, which included a frank discussion of sexual topics, but many came out of curiosity and stayed to learn. Some of her male counterparts began secretly to send their own wives and daughters to her. Gradually she developed a very large practice. The Longshores had moved to Philadelphia, and here Thomas was able to devote himself to writing about reforms, while Hannah earned a generous living for the family, helped to support her younger sister, Jane Viola Myers, through her medical studies, and entertained a stream of visiting reformers.[4]

Mary Frame Myers, Hannah's stepsister, had meanwhile married Owen Thomas and given birth to three children. In 1849 the family was living in Fort Wayne, Indiana, and here Mary Frame and Owen both decided to study medicine privately with a local physician. But Mary Frame soon realized she needed more formal study. In 1853, having made arrangements for the care of the children in her absence, she enrolled in the Penn Medical University of Pennsylvania where Hannah was a lecturer, but she soon had to leave to care for an ill child. She completed her medical education by attending lectures at Western Reserve College in Cleveland (where Owen graduated in 1854), and again at Penn Medical University, where she obtained a degree in 1856.

The Thomases moved to Richmond, Indiana, where they practiced medicine and together served on the Sanitary Commission during the Civil War. Mary Frame Thomas combined a successful career in medicine with an interest in reform, serving on the Richmond board of public health, and as physician for the Home for Friendless Girls, which she helped to found along with Rhoda Coffin. She also worked tirelessly for temperance, women's rights, and suffrage. For two years she edited the *Lily*, the women's rights paper founded by Amelia Bloomer, and later, the *Mayflower*, an Indiana suffrage journal. Although she joined the Methodist church, she did not sever her ties with Friends. An obituary published at the time of her death in the *Friends Intelligencer* said that "she was found in the forefront of every movement the object of which was to elevate women."[5]

Both Hannah Longshore and Mary Frame Thomas had the support of husbands who shared their views on women's rights. Ann Preston, the first woman to become dean of a medical college, remained single. Thirty-seven when she began her training at the Female Medical College, Ann Preston had been active in the antislavery movement and had written a book of rhymed stories for children before becoming a medical apprentice in 1847. Although she devoted the rest of her life to the Female Medical College, she continued to keep in touch with the abolition movement through her close friendship with Lucretia Mott.

Male medical students and doctors professed horror at the idea of women doctors and did everything possible to cause the new Female Medical College to fail. In 1858 the Philadelphia Medical Society ostracized the Female Medical College, making it impossible for its students to be present at any of the teaching clinics. Ann Preston responded by organizing a board of women managers to found a Woman's Hospital, opened in 1861, where women medical students could obtain bedside instruction. Later she won permission for the students of the Female College to attend the teaching clinics at Blockley, the city hospital, and later still at the University of Pennsylvania. At this time the male medical students demonstrated against the admission of the women, throwing rocks and bottles. Far from restraining the students, the male doctors joined them in drawing up a remonstrance protesting the admission of women to medicine. Ann Preston replied with a strong editorial statement in the newspapers, defending women's right to practice medicine:

When once it is admitted that women have souls, and that they are accountable to God for the uses of the powers which he has given them, then the exercise of their own judgment and conscience in reference to these uses becomes a thing which they cannot, rightfully, yield to any human tribunal.

As responsible beings, who must abide by the consequences of our course for time and eternity, we have decided for ourselves that the study and practice of medicine are proper, womanly, and adapted to our mental, moral, and physical condition. . . . We regard this movement as belonging to the advancing civilization of the age. . . .

Speaking to her students at graduation, she compared the distress of the male doctors to that of a "lordly Turk, smoking on his ottoman," were his women to suddenly decide to walk down the street side by side with him to the mosque. Since prejudice was not "amenable to reason," she suggested that the female doctors give up the effort to argue but quietly continue to demonstrate their ability.[6]

Often in ill health and pain due to rheumatism, Ann Preston drew strength from attending Quaker meeting, keeping a journal, and occasionally writing poetry. She died at the age of fifty-eight, leaving her entire estate to the college she loved.

In addition to Hannah Longshore, Mary Thomas, and Ann Preston, pioneer Quaker women doctors included Sarah Dolley, Clara Marshall, Eliza Mosher, and Anna Broomall. Of the first eleven women to become physicians in the United States, five were Quakers. All encountered prejudice in their long struggle to learn and become established in their profession, and all of them devoted some energies during their later years to advancing educational opportunities for women.

Entering the Sciences

Science was another field to which the Quaker pioneers were attracted. Maria Mitchell, the Nantucket astronomer, believed, as did Dr. Joseph Longshore, that women were particularly fitted to be scientists:

Nature made woman an observer. The schools and schoolbooks have spoiled her. . . . So many of the natural sciences are well fitted for woman's power of minute observation that it seems strange that the

Ann Preston. Permission from the Archives and Special Collections on Women in Medicine, Medical College of Pennsylvania, Philadelphia, PA.

Graceanna Lewis. Permission from the Friends Historical Library, Swarthmore College, Swarthmore, PA.

hammer of the geologist is not seen in her hand nor the tin box of the botanist.[7]

Maria Mitchell herself was an acute observer. Working as a partner to her father in astronomical observations, she saw a new comet on the night of October 1, 1847. For this she was elected the following year to the American Academy of Arts and Sciences, and two years later to the Association for the Advancement of Science, while the king of Denmark awarded her a gold medal. In 1865 Matthew Vassar asked her to come to teach at his new Female College near Poughkeepsie, New York. At first she demurred since she herself had no college education. But Matthew Vassar offered to build her an observatory with a twelve-inch telescope, the largest then in the country, and she finally agreed.

As a teacher, she was unorthodox and inspiring, urging her students to question everything and accept no rote learning. Many of her students themselves became pioneer women scientists. Increasingly interested in the education of women, she founded the Association for the Advancement of Women and served twice as its president, chairing its science committee until her death. In 1869 she was elected to the American Philosophical Society, the first woman so honored.

Maria Mitchell never married and lived with her father until his death. In later years, her devoted students formed a warm support community. Plagued by religious doubts, she resigned from the Society of Friends at one point but continued to dress and speak as a Quaker.

Joining Maria Mitchell's Science Committee of the Association for the Advancement of Women in 1876 was Graceanna Lewis, a Quaker from Kimberton, Pennsylvania, and a noted naturalist. Graceanna Lewis had studied at the Kimberton boarding school under Abby Kimber, a botanist and one of the antislavery women who went to London in 1840. After attending Kimberton, Graceanna Lewis taught at her uncle's school at York for two years then, when it folded, spent another year teaching school in Phoenixville before returning to live on her mother's farm. The Lewises were ardent abolitionists, and one of Graceanna's duties was seeing after the needs of the fugitive slaves who stopped at the farm. As a result of this activity, Graceanna Lewis wrote an antislavery tract. At the same time, she began to write down her observations of nature as she watched the life of the birds, animals, and plants around her farm home.

During this period of her life Graceanna Lewis formed a close friendship with Mary Townsend, a gifted young woman who wrote a book called *Life in the Insect World*. Mary's brother, John Townsend, was a naturalist who worked with ornithologist Thomas Nuttall on the identification of birds and mammals. Mary Townsend died in 1849, and Graceanna determined to write a companion book as a sort of memorial to her lost friend.

Following her mother's death in 1862, Graceanna Lewis moved to Philadelphia to study at the Academy of Natural Sciences. As a result of this period of work, she published the first section of a proposed book, *Natural History of Birds*. This and a series of articles and pamphlets on aspects of botany and zoology won her the reputation of being the country's foremost woman naturalist, and she was elected to the Academy. She now felt ready for college teaching, but there were few positions yet available to women, and despite the backing of Maria Mitchell she was turned down by Vassar. Instead, she had to content herself with teaching at the high school level, first at a Friends school in Philadelphia, and then in the Foster School in Clinton Springs, New York.

Protected by her Quaker background from Victorian assumptions about women's delicacy, Graceanna Lewis was shocked by the young ladies at Foster and their squeamish response to her efforts to teach human reproduction as a natural part of life. "I am very tired of *young* ladyism. I want *women* with the souls and destinies of *women*,"[8] she wrote. She continued to lecture on nature in the surrounding areas, including Rochester. Hearing her speak, Dr. Sarah Dolley, the pioneer Quaker doctor, decided to organize a Rochester Society of Natural Sciences. Graceanna Lewis herself was elected an honorary member of the Rochester Academy of Science. She later became a member of the American Philosophical Society also. She returned to Kimberton and lived to a vigorous ninety years of age, still enjoying the birds and flowers of her beloved Chester County. She remained a Quaker and often said that she loved nature because it better helped her to comprehend the Creator.

Entrepreneurs, Writers, Artists

Many Quaker women were successful shopkeepers, and several were outstanding entrepreneurs. As a twenty-nine-year-old widow with six children, Rebecca Pennock Lukens of Chester County, Pennsylvania, inherited a steel mill in 1825 and made it into a famous company manufacturing boiler plates for locomotives and steam ships. Lydia Estes Pinkham, a Friend from Lynn, Massachusetts, developed her homemade natural remedies for female disorders into a nationwide business that grossed $300,000 a year by 1883, an enormous sum for that time.[9]

Since the time of Margaret Fell in the 1600s, Quaker women had been making a reputation for themselves as writers. An examination of a catalog of seventeenth-century published books reveals Quaker women authors out of all proportion to their numbers. This tradition continued in the nineteenth century. In 1821 Deborah Norris Logan wrote a biography of her deceased husband, *Memoir of Dr. George Logan of Stenton*, which is regarded today as a literary achievement as well as a historical source. Since Dr. Logan was active in early American politics and entertained such men as Washington, Jefferson, and others, Deborah Logan's informal glimpses of these leaders have proved invaluable to historians.

Sometime earlier, Deborah Logan had found in the attic at Stenton some tattered and worm-eaten papers that proved to be the correspondence between William Penn and James Logan, his agent in America and the grandfather of her husband. Realizing that these were valuable papers, she copied them carefully and turned them over to the American Philosophical Society. Eventually they were published and earned her the title of one of the first American women historians.

After she completed the monumental task of copying the Penn-Logan correspondence, Deborah Logan began to keep a daily diary—frank, witty, and observant—which gives an intimate glimpse of the life of a wealthy Quaker matron of her time. Like other members of the Quaker establishment, she became Orthodox at the time of the separation and had little use for the antislavery agitation of "fanatics" such as Lucretia Mott and the Grimké sisters. She said little about the role of women and perhaps disapproved of the women's rights activities. Nevertheless, she was very proud of her mother's ability

Hannah Whitall Smith.
Permission from the Quaker
Collection, Haverford College,
Haverford, PA. Photo by Ted
Hetzel.

to manage the family estate after her father died, and was herself a prudent manager of Stenton and a model of a self-respecting Quaker woman.[10]

Many nineteenth-century Quaker women combined writing
with an interest in the reform movements. Phebe A. Hanaford,
a Nantucket Quaker turned Universalist minister, wrote *Lucretia
the Quakeress* as an antislavery brief, and *Women of the Century*
in keeping with her ardent efforts for woman's efforts and for
suffrage.

The most successful Quaker woman author in the nineteenth
century was Hannah Whitall Smith, a descendant of Ann
Cooper Whitall of Revolutionary days. Hannah's father, John
Mickle Whitall, a former sea captain, had developed a glass
manufacturing business in which he prospered, and Hannah
and her two sisters and one brother had a happy childhood
and attended Quaker schools. At nineteen she married Robert
Pearsall Smith, and the couple had two children in the next
three years, much to Hannah's displeasure. Although she later
glorified motherhood, Hannah was restless at first and realized
that she wished she had more education. Robert agreed and

arranged for her to be tutored in history and philosophy with the possibility of enrolling at Haverford College. The death of their first child in 1857, however, ended this project and sent both the Smiths into a religious quest. Finding Quakerism too confining, they began to worship with the Plymouth Brethren and later the Methodists. Later still they were both caught up in the Holiness Movement sweeping the country in the post–Civil War days.

By this time the Smiths had five children: Frank, born in 1854, Mary in 1864, Logan in 1865, Alys in 1867, and Ray in 1868. Frank was Hannah's favorite, but in 1872 he fell ill with typhoid and died within a week. Both parents were shaken by this loss. Hannah attempted to turn her grief to good purpose by writing a memoir of Frank, *The Record of a Happy Life*. Robert at the same time had a nervous breakdown from which he did not quite recover, although he became very active in the Higher Life movement, a wave of religious enthusiasm sweeping England. The couple traveled abroad, participating in revivalistic holiness conferences, and they were for a while a huge success. But Robert became overly affectionate to his young women converts, and scandal rose to such proportions that he had to leave the country.

Hannah had meanwhile poured the enthusiasm of the revival period into a new book, *The Christian's Secret of a Happy Life*, which became immensely popular and ultimately sold over two million copies. Hannah's career as a religious writer was now cut out for her. In the next three decades she wrote over a dozen books as well as booklets and tracts.

An ardent supporter of women's rights, Hannah Whitall Smith frequently wrote about the motherliness of God, saying that she had learned to understand God from her own experience as a mother. She supported the suffrage movement and the WCTU. Her younger sister, Mary Whitall Thomas, was also a feminist and supported her daughter M. Carey Thomas in demanding a college education and then the right to study abroad. Hannah naturally rejoiced in this pioneering niece and was delighted when she became the president of Bryn Mawr College.

In 1888 the Smiths settled in England to be near their married daughter, Mary Costelloe, and her two little girls, Ray and Karin. When Mary ran away to the continent with Bernard Berenson, Hannah took care of the granddaughters. Meanwhile Alys married the young Bertram Russell (later to be divorced), and Logan became a famous essayist. Advocacy of women's rights continued to run strong in this remarkable family, with both of Mary's daughters returning to study at Bryn Mawr and Ray touring for suffrage with Anna Howard Shaw. By this time the family had become part of an intellectual circle in England. Ray ultimately married Oliver Strachey, brother of Lytton Strachey, famous English biographer, and Karin married Adrian Stephens, Virginia Woolf's brother.

One of the most charming of all the Whitall women was Helen Thomas Flexner, younger sister to M. Carey Thomas. Her delightful book *A Quaker Childhood* describes the Thomas family in Baltimore, and her pride in her mother's role as Quaker minister, clerk of the Women's Yearly Meeting, and friend in court for women prisoners. She also told the story of a campaign waged by M. Carey and her mother to persuade James Thomas to allow Carey to go to college. Despite the long tradition of women's equality in the Baltimore Yearly Meeting, Dr. Thomas was not convinced that women needed a college education, or that he could afford such a luxury. Together, Mary Thomas and M. Carey persuaded him to change his mind.[11]

Art was a field from which Quakers had barred themselves for many generations because of their seventeenth-century distaste for uses of art in religious observance. When they reapproached it in the nineteenth century, it was through the medium of natural studies and illustrations. Anna Botsford Comstock wrote and illustrated a whole series of books on entomology and nature study at the turn of the twentieth century. Mary Anne Hallock Foote attended Pratt Institute and wrote and illustrated stories of the American western frontier, while

Alice Barber Stephens, a graduate of the Philadelphia School of Design, became a successful book and magazine illustrator. Gertrude Stanton Kasebier, of Iowa Quaker background, studied at Pratt Institute after she had married and raised three children, and she became the first woman photographer to develop an international reputation. Her photographs of American Indians at the turn of the century are in the Anthropology Archives of the Smithsonian Institution.

Of course, many women besides Quakers entered the professions during the nineteenth century. But in several fields such as medicine, Quakers were among the first, and they gave to the work, as they had given to the reform movements, a certain Quaker flavor. According to estimates made on the basis of *Notable American Women, 1607–1950, A Biographical Dictionary,* thirteen percent of the women doctors, ten percent of the college administrators, sixteen percent of the entrepreneurs, and twenty-two percent of the naturalists were Quakers.[12] Yet even in their heyday, Friends were never more than two percent of the general population, and as the years passed the figure dropped steadily.

What constituted the Quaker flavor? Our sample is relatively small, making conclusions difficult. Quaker women were more apt to be in stable marriages than their non-Quaker counterparts. Often husband and wife served as a team in a profession or a reform activity. They also shared responsibility for educating their children. Quaker women, in keeping with the long tradition of traveling ministers, were free to speak in public and to travel in the service of their concerns. Often a woman's husband would accompany her on her trips. Since education was important to the whole Society of Friends, it was very important to these Quaker pioneers. They were somewhat slower to earn college degrees than their counterparts, because of early Quaker prejudice against higher education, but they overcame this and began to forge ahead in graduate and professional training in the middle and end of the nineteenth century. The first woman to earn a doctoral degree in this country was a

Quaker woman, Helen Magill White, a Swarthmore graduate, who received the degree in 1877.

Because of the long history of Quaker concern for the rights of women, however imperfectly realized, the Quaker women who entered the professions in the nineteenth century had more spiritual and family support than did those of other denominations. Consequently, they set a pattern of wholeness for the women of their age. They were able to manage a home, children, and a career nearly one hundred years before this became a widespread possibility. On the other hand, they accepted those of their number who did not marry, believing such women led full and balanced lives also. And no matter how busy they were, the liberating sense of being led by the Spirit freed their lives from frenzy. Other women commented on their serenity and calm, and some drew from it the courage to try new roles.

11. Meetings and Ministry: The Nineteenth Century

All through the nineteenth century, while some Quaker women were venturing into the reform movements and the professions, large numbers continued to be active as traveling ministers. Some, such as Elizabeth Comstock and Lucretia Mott, combined a traveling ministry with pioneering in reforms, while others, in the spirit of quietism, devoted themselves primarily to religious renewal within their own branch of the Society. Still others traveled to visit the Indians or heads of state abroad. As an evangelical influence gained strength, Quaker men and women began to travel to foreign lands to establish missions or to strengthen small Christian groups. Some idea of the numbers of Quaker women in the ministry is revealed by the fact that forty-eight percent of the women who made names for themselves in American history in the ministry were of Quaker background.[1]

Just as their predecessors had done in the seventeenth and eighteenth centuries, many nineteenth-century Quaker women resisted the call to travel in the ministry. Rachel Hicks of Long Island, a Hicksite, refused the call to the ministry for more than twenty years. Rebecca Dewees of Ohio, a Conservative, suffered for eighteen years after refusing to speak in meeting a second time. Hannah Field, a New York Friend who traveled in England, went through a long trying time in which she "reasoned against the requirements of Truth again and again, and was often involved in a state of great conflict and distress." It was the encouragement she received from other ministers that finally persuaded her to "give up" and appear in the ministry.[2]

The concept of holy obedience, of making oneself into a channel of the Holy Spirit, was always strong in Quaker women's journals. The birth of quietism in the eighteenth century simply reinforced this view. Quaker women in the nineteenth century often wrote of being asked to speak in meeting words that they did not understand, or to take actions that had no apparent meaning, only to learn later what the Lord had in mind. Thus Priscilla Hunt (later Cadwallader) of Indiana felt impelled to say one day in meeting, " 'I am sixty years old today, and I will go to Quaker meeting.' These words were spoken this morning by one who I believe is now present." She then described in detail all the arguments that the person had erected in his or her mind against the Christian religion; proceeded to demolish them, said that the person was now disarmed, and sat down. After meeting a sixty-year-old man approached her and told her she had spoken the words in his mind, as though she could read right into his head.[3]

Ann Branson, a Conservative minister, had many similar experiences. She was sometimes commanded to visit families who were entire strangers to her or to speak to travelers on the road. Once she felt it necessary to preach to the inhabitants of Barnesville, Ohio, from the main street. She tried to disobey but found she was unable to go on without fulfilling the task. During the Civil War, she felt she could experience the sufferings of the people at the front. Visiting one meeting during this time, she stayed week after week, not knowing why this was required of her, until she was given a message to deliver in meeting against paying a bounty tax to induce volunteers into the army. After meeting, a man told her that he felt sure her message had been for him alone. Still bound to this same meeting, she felt, a few days later, that a young woman Friend had something on her mind to deliver, and that it was her duty to help by speaking a few words about the scattering of the seed. The young woman spoke, and again, Ann felt her leading was completely confirmed.[4]

Sometimes the women ministers felt compelled to preach to those who could not understand their language. Mary Swett, the older woman who had accompanied Charity Cook to Germany in 1798, felt that she must return ten years later to visit a group of French villagers who had independently developed a form of worship very similar to Friends. At age seventy-two, despite her lack of French, she set forth and made a successful visit.

Eliza Kirkbride Gurney, the American third wife of Joseph John Gurney, traveled with him in the ministry on the continent of Europe. Together they visited royalty, including the king and queen of France. Eliza had been told that it would be impossible to introduce any serious subjects in the interview, but when they met with the royal family, she recognized with a sinking heart the feeling that she would be called upon to speak about religious matters. She was obedient to the impulse, and the royal family was receptive. Eliza thought she saw tears in the queen's eyes. On another occasion, in Germany, she was frightened by a sense that she must preach, since the translator spoke no English. However, preach she did, Joseph translating from English to French, and the translator from French to German. She also felt compelled to speak in Geneva, despite the strong prejudice against women's ministry. She found both their prohibition and the curiosity of the people toward a woman preacher annoying, and she was "placed in the most painful and apparently indissoluble bonds." But an opportunity arrived to speak to a mixed gathering who had come to the hotel to hear Joseph describe his recent travels. Several days afterwards, at a farewell breakfast for all the pastors of Geneva, Eliza felt she must speak. "It was no small trial to me to be faithful on this occasion, especially as the two ministers who were said to be so entirely opposed to women's ministry were sitting near me; but instead of being offended by what I said, they were as cordial as possible afterwards."[5]

The belief in implicit obedience to divine leading caused Quaker women to be, at times, very blunt. Ann Branson frequently felt called upon to chastise Friends for their misdoings. She visited one family and talked to the father about the "want of true love, Christian patience, and forbearance apparent in the heads of that family." She preached at Philadelphia Yearly Meeting against Gurneyism, which she called a "specious snare to lay waste Quakerism," and she was asked not to speak again.[6]

A strong sense of leading was essential to give Quaker women the courage to travel, for roads in the nineteenth century were still hazardous and lodging uncertain. In Philadelphia, a party of three Quaker women and one man were crossing the Delaware on February 14, 1820. Though the ice appeared solid, the man asked the women if any had uneasy feelings. Apparently none did, for the little party started across, only to have the ice give way under the horses' hooves about halfway to the shore. The man and one woman who was sitting in front leaped to safety, but the carriage went down with the other two.[7]

James Walton, accompanying Priscilla Cadwallader and her companion Rachel Johnson on a trip through New York State and Canada, wrote admiringly of the women's composure:

I may say that these women exceed anything I have any knowledge of; they rode over bridges and causeways, where there were holes so large that if the horses had made a mis-step they would have gone in up to their bodies, and consequently thrown their riders. Here they rode with as much composure as though they were sitting in a house.[8]

Of thirty women ministers who either traveled overseas or were well known in this country during the nineteenth century, twenty-six were married, and of these, all but one had children. While some of these women waited until all their children were fully grown to begin their ministry, others felt called to leave while their children were still young. Sarah Foulke Farquhar Emlen left five children between the ages of one and a half and nine when she went on a five-month trip in 1825. Although she had a housekeeper, it is clear that James Emlen was her chief support at home. She was again pregnant in the fall of 1828 when James was traveling in the ministry in Ohio, and she confessed that "it would be closely trying to me to do without thee when that times comes," the following March.[9]

Sybil Jones, a gifted evangelical minister from South China, Maine, was only thirty-two and the mother of two very small children when, in 1840, she felt she had to make her first trip in the ministry, traveling in Nova Scotia and New Brunswick. Her companion on this as well as her other journeys was her husband, Eli. She wrote in her journal, "We leave our dear children in the best place we could find. . . . Above all, we have felt a humble trust that He who never slumbers will keep them."[10]

The Joneses traveled in the ministry in the United States in 1845, and in 1851, Sybil laid before her monthly and then her yearly meeting "a concern to travel to Great Britain, Ireland, parts of the continent of Europe, Sierra Leone, Liberia, and some islands on the west coast of Africa and in the West Indies." The faithful Eli was once more appointed as his wife's traveling companion. Their extensive itinerary meant that they expected to be away from home for as long as three years.

No one could be found to take care of the children—who now numbered five—for this extended period, so the Joneses determined to break up the family. The youngest girl, Susan Tabor, was left with her paternal grandparents, while the baby, Eli Grellet, was deposited at the nearby home of a friend. The next two children, Sybil Narcissa and Richard Mott, were left at the Friends Boarding School at Providence, while James Parnel, the oldest, now sixteen, went to Haverford College.

After spending eight weeks in Africa visiting mission stations, the Joneses returned to the United States before sailing to Great Britain. After a short reunion with their family, however, they set off again. This time they took the two younger boys, Eli and Richard, to stay with Eliza Gurney in West Hill, Burlington, New Jersey.

The children were not overjoyed at these partings, and the little ones begged their mother not to go. Sybil described the scene in a few lines in her journal. "What tongue can tell my soul's anguish as the tears flowed fast from each child's almost bursting heart? Had it not been for the gentle accents of a Saviour's love, 'it is I, be not afraid; leave thy children with me,' I could not have left them."[11]

It was perhaps more typical for husband and wife to alternate being away from home, as did Rachel and Philip Price of Pennsylvania, the parents of ten children. In the early days of their marriage Philip sometimes traveled to accompany other traveling Quaker ministers, such as Charity Cook and her companion. Later, however, Rachel made extensive trips, leaving Philip home with the family. Like other Quaker husbands in his position, he encouraged his wife not to worry about the family but to continue in her labors:

Although thy company thee knows would be very desirable at home, I hope thou wilt be favoured to be easy about us until thy mind is at full liberty to return with peace. I have been so far much preserved in the patience, beyond what I expected, and I hope I shall be favoured to so continue until the right time for thee to return. . . .

Having set thy hand to the work it will not do to look back, otherwise thou wilt lose the reward which I believe those are favoured to experience who are faithfully given up to it in true sincerity of heart.[12]

Religious Revival

When Sarah Foulke Farquhar came from Ohio to teach at Westtown School as a young widow, she went through a period of depression and religious struggle, which ended with a conversion experience, as we have seen. After weeks of refusing to obey the divine commandment, she finally uttered a short prayer in meeting. This brought her into a state of bliss. In words reminiscent of the first generation of Friends, she wrote

Eli and Sybil Jones. From the private collection of Mary Hoxie
Jones. Photo by Ted Hetzel.

in her journal that night, "My peace flows like a river—O what
a favour, how can I say enough in praise of the Lord."[13]

Many of the nineteenth-century Quaker women journalists,
however, seemed to lack the sense of joy that pervaded the
seventeenth century. Several of the journals are lugubrious.
Sarah Cresson of Haddonfield write frequently that she felt
"poor and stripped," and she was apparently subject to bouts
of depression. Sarah Hunt of West Grove was often troubled
with gloomy thoughts.

To escape the growing quietness and somberness of Quakerism, some turned to other denominations experiencing revival. Laura Haviland, the Michigan abolitionist, found the
Society of Friends too cold and formal when she was growing
up in New York State, and she began to attend Methodist
prayer meetings, despite the opposition of her parents, who

called it "mere religious excitement." She described a conversion experience on the way home from her grandfather's house in words very reminiscent of those of Elizabeth Webb, when she became a Quaker one hundred and fifty years earlier:

I stood a monument of amazing mercy, praising God with every breath, all nature praising instead of mourning as it did a few moments before. O how changed the scene! The birds now sent forth their notes of praise! The leaves of the forest clapped their hands for joy, and the branches waved with praise! Every head of wheat was now bowed in sweet submission.[14]

Although she continued to attend the revival meetings, she did not leave the Society of Friends until 1844, when she and her husband and parents all withdrew over the antislavery issue. She remained a Methodist until 1872 when she felt able to rejoin Friends because of their newly found missionary zeal.

Another Friend turned Methodist who later rejoined the Society was Amanda Way, active in temperance and suffrage. In 1871 she was licensed as a local preacher by the Methodist Episcopal church. But when that group withdrew their support for women preachers in 1880, she returned to the transformed Society of Friends.

Active in the revival movement that changed the face of the Society of Friends was Esther Frame. Of Quaker background on her mother's side, but raised a Methodist, Esther Frame decided to join the Society of Friends when she felt a strong urge to preach. Her husband, Nathan, was opposed: "I could think of no greater calamity that could befall us than for her to become a preacher and in her youth and beauty and womanliness stand before the multitude to be gazed at and criticized as a woman preacher, and be compelled, from the very nature of her calling, to mingle, as a minister, with all kinds of people and classes of society."[15]

Reluctantly, he agreed to her joining the Society of Friends, thinking that she would have less opportunity to preach among the quiet Quakers. They applied for membership to the local

monthly meeting in Salem, Iowa. When the clearness committee of the meeting called on her to examine her readiness for
membership, one of the elders said with typical quietist blunt-
ness, "Esther Frame, it has been given to me to tell thee that
thee does not know the first principles of the Christian religion." Hurt, Esther Frame asked the woman what she meant.
"I have no explanation to make; it was given me to say to thee
that thee does not know the first principles of the Christian
religion," the elder replied.[16]

Despite this rebuff, the Frames finally succeeded in joining
meeting. Moving to Richmond, Indiana, they began to preach
among Friends. Since they were not recorded ministers they
could not appoint meetings, and sometimes their reception was
frosty. However, they began to hold special tract reading meetings for young people, and the meetings soon became popular.
By the summer of 1869, the Frames had a large following and
were able to organize revival meetings in the Fifth Street Meetinghouse, complete with the use of the mourning bench, altar
calls, songs, and outbursts of ecstatic emotion.

From this date on, Esther Frame was in the forefront of a
revival that swept Gurneyite Quakerism in all parts of the country except the Philadelphia Yearly Meeting area. The Frames
traveled to New York and to New England, as well as through
the southern states, preaching to interdenominational audiences. In many communities, Esther was the first woman
preacher the inhabitants had ever heard. Sometimes they were
reluctant to let her speak, but this attitude was soon overcome
by the power of her oratory. One Tennessee minister said that
while he might not favor all women speaking, he had learned
from Esther Frame that God could call a woman to the pulpit.[17]

After ten years of the combined efforts of evangelicals, male
and female, Nathan Frame commented on the results: "There
have been marvelous changes in Friends' Meetings since we
first became members among them. Singing, vocal prayer, testimony, exhortation, reading the Scriptures, preaching, revival,
protracted meetings, the custom of inviting persons to rise in

the public congregations or come to a certain place for prayer have now become very common."[18]

Naturally, not all Friends were pleased with these changes. At one revival meeting in Iowa, an elderly woman Friend climbed on a bench and spoke in meeting for the first and only time in her life: "The Society of Friends is dead. This has killed it."[19]

The most impressive woman evangelical preacher of the era, according to her contemporaries, was Mary Moon Meredith, of North Carolina and later Iowa. Well educated and a gifted speaker, Mary spoke in many interdenominational meetings in communities where a woman had never been known to preach before. Speaking in Reidsville, North Carolina, in 1880, she encountered a storm of opposition to women preaching, and she responded with a strong argument that might have been drawn from Margaret Fell or Lucretia Mott:

There is one thing sure: either God makes a mistake, or Paul makes a mistake, or the people who put Paul in such an awkward position make one. As for me, I shall not place the mistake on God, neither upon that great champion of the cross, the Apostle Paul. . . . People talk about this new departure! Why it is as old as the Church.[20]

Foreign Missions

The revivals accelerated a trend that was already under way within Quakerism: the establishment of foreign missions. Friends had been missionaries in their first burst of zeal in the seventeenth century, when Mary Fisher went to see the sultan. But under quietism the impulse had died. Daniel Wheeler, an English Friend, had traveled to Russia in 1817 at the request of the czar to help drain the swamps around St. Petersburg, but this was an isolated case. The trip made by Sybil and Eli Jones to Liberia in 1851 perhaps marked the beginning of a new era. While the male missionaries of other denominations often took their wives, Quaker women served as equal partners, and sometimes as the most important member of the team. Later, Quaker women pioneered as single women in the mission field.

Following the Joneses, the next Quaker couple to serve as missionaries were Hannah and Joel Bean of West Branch, Iowa. Hannah had grown up in Philadelphia and attended Westtown before teaching at Friends Select School. In 1859 she married Joel Bean and moved to Iowa, where she served as clerk of the women's monthly meeting. In 1861, under a sense of concern, the couple set out to visit the Sandwich Islands (Hawaii) taking their baby daughter with them. Her clothes were packed in a small tin trunk that would serve as a bathtub, or, in the event of her not surviving the trip, a coffin. But survive she did. And Hannah, who had been warned that her health was not good enough to make the trip, bloomed in Hawaii. They visited the mission stations, took charge of a mission school for several months so that the teachers in charge might have a rest, toured the island, and made lifelong friends. They left after nine months but returned twice to visit. This couple also visited Great Britain, taught at the Friends Boarding School in Providence, Rhode Island, and, moving to California in later life, helped to strengthen Quakerism in San Jose.[21]

In 1867 Sarah and Louis Street of Richmond, Indiana, were appointed to join British Friends on an educational mission in Madagascar. They remained ten years, learned the language, and helped to translate the Bible and to publish a local newspaper. Somewhat outspoken about the local government, Louis was asked to leave in 1877, but Sarah stayed on an extra year.

After the Civil War, in which she lost a beloved son, Sybil Jones began to feel an urgent call to visit the Holy Land. In April of 1867 she set forth, accompanied by Eli. The two visited Friends in England, Scotland, and southern France before proceeding to Syria. They spent several months holding meetings and visiting schools throughout Palestine, but they were forced to return to England because of Sybil's delicate health. On a second trip in 1869, they visited the village of Ramallah near Jerusalem. There was already a boys' school in Ramallah but nothing for girls. A young Palestinian woman approached Sybil and asked if she might be helped to start a girls school. The Joneses decided to back this enterprise with some funds that the English Friends had entrusted to them. This was the beginning of the Friends school in Ramallah, still functioning today. A few weeks later, visiting Beirut, the Joneses met a young man, Theophilus Waldmeier, who was teaching in the British Syrian schools. He was so impressed by the Joneses that he enquired about Quakerism, and he eventually joined the Society of Friends. Some years later he opened a Friends school in Brummana, Lebanon.[22]

Throughout the United States, churchwomen of many denominations were becoming active in supporting foreign missions, and Quaker women also joined the movement. In 1881 Eliza Armstrong Cox, a Friend from southern Indiana, visited a Women's Foreign Mission Society of the Methodist Episcopal church and left determined to organize something of the sort for her own group. "A great vista opened to me," she said later. She wrote to a friend and former teacher, Jemima A. Taylor of Mooresville, Indiana, telling of her great idea, and she was astonished to learn that Jemima had also proposed such a group to her monthly meeting and that a first meeting had been held at the home of Rebecca J. Macy. At the next gathering of Western Yearly Meeting the two met informally under a tree with a small group of interested women. Immediately the Women's Missionary Society of Western Yearly Meeting was born, with Eliza Cox as president.

Word of the new organization spread, and women in other Yearly Meetings began to develop foreign missionary societies. Despite the isolation and reservations about evangelicalism in Philadelphia Yearly Meeting, a group began to meet informally and to support a mission in Japan. Sarah Nicholson of Whitall descent took the lead. Iowa women supported mission work in Jamaica. Women in New England, Ohio, North Carolina, Kansas, and New York all joined in. By 1885 the group began to publish a journal, *Friends Missionary Advocate*, and in 1890 they gathered all the groups from all the yearly meetings to establish the Women's Foreign Missionary Union of Friends in America, later to become the United Society of Friends Women.[23]

Spurred on by this organization, a number of Quaker women volunteered for missionary duty. Esther Butler, an Ohio Quaker, went to China in 1892 and remained until her death in 1921, surviving many antiforeign uprisings, including the Boxer Rebellion. One of her many projects was the building of the Peace Hospital in Luho. She was joined in 1892 by Dr. Lucy Gaynor, a medical missionary from Chicago. Esther Baird, a graduate nurse, and Delia Fistler went to Bundelkhand, India, in 1892, and there developed a mission where they provided medical assistance and infant feeding during a famine. Delia Fistler returned home in 1914 because of ill health, but Esther Baird stayed until 1938. Anna Hunnicutt went to Alaska in 1895 to work first in southeastern Alaska and later with the Eskimos of Kotzbue Sound, where she helped to establish a hospital and a school.

As interest in missions increased, the need for some sort of training for evangelical outreach became clear. At the same time, the transformation of many Quaker meetings to Friends churches was creating a demand for trained pastors with some knowledge of the Quaker background. Both these needs were met in 1892 when Walter and Emma Brown Malone, a Quaker couple from Cleveland, Ohio, opened the Friends Bible Institute and Training School, later renamed Malone College, for Bible study and the training of ministers and missionaries.

Emma Malone had grown up in a Canadian Quaker family and was accustomed to women playing an equal role with men. She was a recorded minister, and she and Walter shared the pastoral responsibilities of the First Friends Church in Cleveland, as well as the founding and administration of the school. Emma taught Bible at the new school and was a beloved member of the school community. Her influence helped to keep the concept of the equality of women strong in the evangelical wing of the Society.[24]

Equality in the Business Meeting

While Quaker women were making advances in reforms, professions, and the ministry, their business meetings were still technically separate and unequal within the Society of Friends. Between the sessions of yearly meeting, a body once called Meeting for Sufferings, and later, Representative Meeting, made decisions for the group. Men, not women, formed this meeting. Under the old rules of discipline, the men's meeting was still able to overturn the decisions made by women.

The fact that this situation was inconsistent with the reputation of Friends for equality did not escape the notice of Quaker women. Lucretia Mott started agitating for a change in discipline in 1836. The radical Hicksite groups that split off from the main yearly meetings in the 1840s all put men and women on an equal basis. Elizabeth Comstock wrote her British sister that the women must be on an equal footing with the men since "we profess to be the only pure democracy in the world, men and women being one—on an absolute equality in the Lord Jesus."[25]

In 1877 two yearly meetings changed their discipline to place women in equal numbers on Representative Meeting and to give them full equality in matters of discipline. They were the Philadelphia Hicksite Yearly Meeting, where Lucretia Mott and her colleagues had struggled for forty years for the change, and the Ohio Yearly Meeting at Mt. Pleasant, stirred to action by the evangelical revival. Thereafter, twelve additional meetings made the change by the end of the century. London Yearly Meeting, so long a cause of concern to American Friends, changed its discipline in 1896. Only the Conservative Yearly Meetings resisted, Ohio Conservative being the last to change in 1928.

Men's Yearly Meeting at Race Street, Philadelphia, 1924, shortly before the merger of the men's and women's meeting. Hannah Clothier Hull is bringing a message from the women's yearly meeting. Permission from the Friends Historical Library, Swarthmore College, Swarthmore, PA. Photo by Ted Hetzel.

During the initial period of change, a general conference of all Orthodox-Gurneyite yearly meetings was held at Richmond, Indiana, in 1887. The purpose was to discuss a number of common concerns. The result was the establishment in 1902 of a Five Years Meeting among most of the yearly meetings. One of the questions under discussion at this first meeting was that of Friends having their own foreign mission board. Since the women under the leadership of Eliza Cox Armstrong were developing their own missionary societies in each yearly meeting and nationally, the conference needed to clarify the relationship between the new group and the women's group. Some drew an analogy with the Methodists. At this, Mary Whitall Thomas, clerk of the Maryland Women's Yearly Meeting and a member of the Baltimore delegation, delivered an impassioned speech:

I would be very sorry to see the women of the Society of Friends take the position of those in the Methodist church as auxiliary to any board of men. The women in the Society of Friends hold a different position from that held by them in any other church. Our place is side by side with our brethren. If the women have their local societies which have been very successful, and the Yearly Meeting societies, still it seems to me we should have a general society composed of men and women. Nothing else will agree with the constitution of our church, or will agree with *my* constitution at all. . . . It is time that the men in the Society of Friends should remember the place of the women in it, and they will hear this question brought up again and again and again. The women in the Society of Friends have a position that is not allowed them by their brethren nor given them by man. It is given them by the Head of the church, the Lord Christ Jesus. This society is the only society that professes that woman should have this place, and it is organized on that basis, and we are not going to let you forget it, and it will come up continually, and I do say that the men of the Society of Friends need to be reminded of it. . . . Now brethren and sisters, you say we are not to bring this question of the sexes up: but whom will you have in the constitution of your committees? You say, "the right person." The right person in the judgment of men is generally a man; and you know that there are women just as capable of taking those positions as men. I say that every committee in the Society of Friends should be composed as the committee [delegation] of Baltimore Yearly Meeting of four men and four women. . . . Now this is a serious matter, and I want to urge the women of the Society of Friends to keep this continually in view and to keep the place that God has given you—or take the place—for perhaps we have not yet fully taken it as we ought.[26]

Once their equal status was established, many of the women's yearly meetings began to press for the next logical step: merging the men's and women's meetings. The majority decided to hold joint sessions within ten years. Some of the women's yearly meetings, however, continued to have separate sessions for two or three decades. In the Philadelphia Hicksite Yearly Meeting, men's and women's meetings did not actually give up separate sessions until 1924, while the Orthodox meeting met together from 1923 on but appointed a women's clerk until 1930. The Conservative yearly meetings were also late in joining: North Carolina in 1928, Canada in 1944, and Ohio in 1950.

Some people thought they detected a decided decline in the activity of women in the Society of Friends after the men's and women's meetings merged. Writing in the *American Friend* in 1912, Mary Grove Chawner of Ada, South Dakota, noted with alarm that in the various delegations to the next Five Years Meeting there were only a minority of women represented. In one delegation there were eight male ministers and one woman. Were women in fact taking a lesser share in the business of the society?

Not so many years ago, women were forced to take part in business through the separate women's meeting, though their part may sometimes have been perfunctory. The change to joint meetings was certainly not designed to lessen the activity of women in business, but rather stimulate both men and women by obviating delay and by fusing their interest in common discussion. Much has been gained, no doubt, in the joint meeting; but has all been gained that should be gained and has, perhaps, something been lost?[27]

In Philadelphia, where the women's yearly meetings continued into the 1920s, the Hicksite Meeting was clerked in its final years by a remarkable woman, Jane Rushmore. Jane had been hired in 1911 to staff the Central Bureau of the yearly meeting, which oversaw the work on such issues as peace, temperance, women's suffrage, and the campaign against lynching in the South. In 1918 Jane Rushmore became the recording clerk of the women's yearly meeting, and in 1922, the clerk. When the men's and women's meetings finally joined in 1924, she was chosen to preside over the joint sessions. From this vantage point she compared the two meetings:

In general the Women's meeting had unity without uniformity. It was more progressive than the men's and under much better control. The philanthropic reports found the women's meeting more receptive and new ideas were more likely to be approved.[28]

Elsewhere, the newly united yearly meetings experimented with selecting women as clerks and found they were efficient and popular.[29] As the Society of Friends continued its westward expansion, and new yearly meetings were established, business meetings were conducted with men and women meeting together.

Quaker feminists today tend to look back to the era of the separate women's business meeting with nostalgia. But the minutes of women's meetings give the impression that many of them were shallow and formal affairs, reflecting the fact that they were drained of power and function. Not until the women had struggled for and achieved equal status did their meetings begin to develop strength and creativity. That long struggle itself was a sort of adolescence for Quaker women as a body, preparing them for further leadership within and outside of the Society of Friends.

12. The Quaker Influence in the Final Struggle for Suffrage

All through the years of reform and into the Progressive Era of the early twentieth century, Susan B. Anthony worked tirelessly for suffrage. After 1878 she campaigned everywhere for the federal suffrage amendment that bore her name, while continuing to work for suffrage on a state-by-state basis against discouraging odds. There were seventeen state referenda between 1870 and 1910, of which only two, Colorado in 1893 and Idaho in 1896, were successful. The admission of two more western states, Wyoming and Utah, created the only additional gains to the suffrage column.

Still attuned to the early activists for abolition and women's rights, and to the values that women such as Lucretia Mott had introduced into the struggle for women's rights, Susan B. Anthony continued to try to involve as many different women as possible in the suffrage campaign. She was always interested in enlisting working women and union women, and she still saw the cause of the blacks and of white women closely allied. Whenever she traveled in the South, she spoke in black schools and churches, and she welcomed black women to the suffrage conventions.

Like Lucretia Mott also, she believed that the suffrage platform should be wide enough to encompass many different points of view. Her old friend and colleague Elizabeth Cady Stanton turned her chief attention to proving that organized religion had been the chief impediment to woman's progress and published her *Woman's Bible*, reinterpreting the so-called "anti-woman" texts. In response, the National American Woman Suffrage Association (NAWSA), formed in 1890 by a merger of the two earlier groups, decided in 1896 to disavow any connection with Stanton's controversial work. Susan B. Anthony had taken no part in the development of the *Woman's Bible*, although as a Hicksite Friend she had learned to read Scriptures, she said as "historical, made up of traditions, but not as plenary inspiration." Nevertheless, she considered the repudiation of Stanton's bible a dangerous step:

> The one distinct feature of our association has been the right of individual opinion for every member. . . . I shall be pained beyond expression if the delegates here are so narrow and illiberal as to adopt this resolution. If we do not inspire in women a broad and catholic spirit, they will fail, when enfranchised, to constitute that powerful better government which we have always claimed for them. . . . I pray you vote for religious liberty without censorship or inquisition.[1]

Different winds were now blowing in the suffrage movement, however, and the new young leadership, wealthy and conservative, were determined to permit no issue other than suffrage to be discussed. The resolution against the *Woman's Bible* carried, with some of Susan's beloved coworkers voting for it.

After this defeat, Susan evidently concluded that one could not introduce extraneous issues into NAWSA. At the 1899 convention, held in Michigan, a black member suggested that NAWSA go on record demanding of the railroads that black women no longer be barred from Pullman cars and forced to ride in the dirty smokers. The southern delegates objected to this proposal as introducing the element of race into the suffrage cause. After a heated debate in which Alice Stone Blackwell supported the black woman, Susan B. Anthony said that she was committed as ever to the rights of blacks, but that

> we women are a helpless disfranchised class. Our hands are tied. While we are in this condition, it is not for us to go passing resolutions against railroad corporations or anybody else.[2]

These uncharacteristic words evidently swayed the convention, and it voted against the resolution. This was the beginning of a period during which NAWSA increasingly accommodated itself to the demands of the southern suffragists. Some of these favored arguing for women's suffrage as a means of enforcing white supremacy, and many feared that mixing suffrage with the question of race would result in the failure of suffrage in their home states. The most radical southern suffragists opposed a federal amendment and felt that a state-by-state enfranchisement of white women could be made without giving the vote to black women and thus disturbing the various subterfuges under which most of the southern states had taken the vote away from black men.

More in keeping with Susan B. Anthony's Quaker ideals was the formation of an international suffrage alliance. On a trip to England in 1883 she had met some British suffragists, and on the eve of sailing home she had agreed with them that such an organization must be formed, much as Lucretia Mott and Elizabeth Cady Stanton had agreed on a women's rights convention on the eve of sailing home in 1840. Susan's dream came to fruition in 1888 when the International Council of Women met in the opera house at Washington, D.C., with a large portrait of Lucretia Mott hanging over the podium, and formed itself into a permanent body.

Thereafter Susan gave the world organization increasing attention. She traveled to London in 1899 to represent the United States delegation and to Berlin in 1904. Here with the help of Carrie Chapman Catt, a coworker recruited in 1890, she formed the International Woman's Suffrage Alliance and was elected its honorary president. The German newspapers referred to her as "Miss Anthony of the World," and she told Anna Howard Shaw that she regarded the meetings as the high point of her career.

Following the meetings in Berlin, Susan traveled in Switzerland and then crossed to England. In Manchester she met with some British suffragists and was interviewed for the local papers by Christabel Pankhurst, daughter of Emmeline, the leader of the radical suffragettes. Years later Emmeline Pankhurst wrote of the event:

The visit was one of the contributory causes that led to the founding of our militant suffrage organization, the Women's Social and Political Union. . . . After her [Susan's] departure Christabel spoke often of her and always with sorrow and indignation that such a splendid worker for humanity was destined to die without seeing the hopes of her life-time realized. "It is unendurable," declared my daughter, "to think of another generation of women wasting their lives begging for the vote. We must not lose any more time. We must act."[3]

Susan B. Anthony was eighty-four at the time of this visit. She came home exhausted but rallied sufficiently to attend a national convention in Portland in 1905, and in Baltimore in 1906. Here she spoke of the long galaxy of great women she had known—Lucretia Mott, the Grimké sisters, Elizabeth Cady Stanton, Lucy Stone—and herself as a link in a continuous chain. She was ill throughout the Baltimore meetings, but she forced herself to go on to Washington for a celebration of her eighty-sixth birthday. When a message of congratulations from President Theodore Roosevelt was read, she exclaimed, "When will men do something besides extend congratulations? I would rather have President Roosevelt say one word to Congress in favor of amending the Constitution to give women the vote than to praise me endlessly." At the end she rose again to thank the audience, to speak again of all the women who had gone before her, and to end with the note, "With such women consecrating their lives—failure is impossible."[4] She died a month later at her sister's home in Rochester, still a member in good standing of the Society of Friends.

New Leadership

At the time of Susan B. Anthony's death, many Quaker women held leadership roles in the suffrage movement.

National Woman's Party Members campaigning before the White House. Permission from the Amelia Fry Collection.

M. Carey Thomas joined the National College Equal Suffrage League in 1906, becoming its president in 1908. In this capacity she traveled widely and played a role in the NAWSA. Florence Kelley was elected a vice-president of NAWSA in 1905 and continued to 1910, traveling to attend conventions and to help with referenda campaigns. When she was elected, she said she was born to the work, since her great-aunt, Sarah Pugh, had accompanied Lucretia Mott to the London convention of 1840, and her father, William P. Kelley, a defender of women's rights, had spoken at the early suffrage conventions. When Florence Kelley resigned in 1910, Jane Addams took her place, serving as a vice-president from 1911 to 1914.

Rachel Foster Avery, corresponding secretary of the National Association from 1880, and of the joint NAWSA from 1890 to 1903, had worked with Susan B. Anthony in the development of the International Woman Suffrage Alliance and served from 1904 to 1909 as its secretary. She was also first vice-president of NAWSA from 1907 to 1910, when both she and Florence Kelley resigned in protest over what they regarded as ineffectual leadership on the part of Anna Howard Shaw. Having moved to Philadelphia, Rachel Avery became president of the Pennsylvania Woman Suffrage Association for several years, taking the place of another Friend, Lucretia Longshore Blankenburg, daughter of Dr. Hannah Longshore, who had risked brickbats to hang out her shingle.

When Lucretia Blankenburg resigned the post to Rachel Avery, she devoted herself to helping in a municipal reform movement in Philadelphia that elected her husband, Rudolph Blankenburg, mayor. The two worked so closely together during his term of office that Lucretia Blankenburg was sometimes called "comayor." She also worked in the women's club movement to persuade the General Federation of Women's Clubs to endorse suffrage in 1914.

In New York, Marian Wright Chapman was president of the New York State Society of Woman Suffrage, as well as of the Friends Equal Rights Association. This group had been organized in 1900 to represent the seven Hicksite Yearly Meetings of Philadelphia, Baltimore, New York, Ohio, Indiana, Illinois, and Genesee. Delegates from it attended the National NAWSA meetings and provided liaison with Quaker work for suffrage on the local and state levels. In 1916, when the question of the relationship between the suffrage movement and the war effort was being debated at the National Convention, the Friends were able to present their pacifist views.[5]

The involvement of the Hicksite Friends in the suffrage struggle was so intense that in 1914 the Hicksite Philadelphia Yearly Meeting passed a resolution endorsing the woman suffrage campaign. It was said to be the only religious body to have done so.

In view of the fact that the Society of Friends, by reason of its inheritance and present organization, gives evidence of the advantage which results to the home, to the meeting, and the community, through a full recognition of the dignity of woman and her right to

Alice Paul campaigning in Washington, D.C., after November 1918. Permission from the Amelia Fry Collection.

complete development, the Philadelphia Yearly Meeting of the Religious Society of Friends records its endorsement of equal suffrage as a principle of justice to woman and an opportunity for more effective service. The Yearly Meeting recommends that monthly meetings be watchful for opportunities to influence equal suffrage legislation and encourage their members to give active interest in the accomplishment of this reform.[6]

Alice Paul

After a period of bickering over leadership, the suffrage movement began to move forward again with victories in the states of Washington in 1910 and California in 1911. Harriet Stanton Blatch, the daughter of Elizabeth Cady Stanton, having served an apprenticeship with the Pankhurst organization in England, returned to the United States and organized a Women's Political Union in the state of New York, which galvanized both working women and upper-class women into a rejuvenated campaign. Carrie Chapman Catt reluctantly agreed to return from international suffrage work to the leadership of the NAWSA.

Now that women had the vote in six states, it was time, many of them felt, to resurrect the Susan B. Anthony amendment. The state-by-state route was taking too long, and the active opposition of the antisuffragists, aided by the liquor interests, was making each state battle both grueling and costly. Interest in the federal amendment had been reawakened in 1912, when Theodore Roosevelt had run on the Progressive ticket with woman suffrage a plank in his platform. Some women saw that it was time to use the voting power they had gained so far to press for the amendment.

Despite the efforts of Susan B. Anthony, the suffrage amendment had not been debated on the floor of the Senate since 1887, and never in the House. It had not received a favorable committee report since 1893, and none at all since 1896. A portion of the southern wing of the suffrage movement was opposed to the amendment and threatened to leave NAWSA if it were pushed. Chances of reversing the tide against the amendment appeared slim.

Then, in 1911, a new leader emerged. Her name was Alice Paul, and she was a Hicksite Friend from Moorestown, New Jersey, a graduate of a Friends school and of Swarthmore College. After leaving Swarthmore she had spent a year in New York studying at the New York School of Philanthropy and working in the Henry Street Settlement House. Next she earned a master's degree at the University of Pennsylvania in economics and sociology. Winning a fellowship to Woodbrooke, a Quaker study center near Birmingham, England, she traveled to Europe, spent a summer in Germany, took courses at the University of Birmingham and later at London School of Economics, worked with Quakers in the settlement movement, and studied the working conditions of women.[7]

At Birmingham, she first heard Christabel Pankhurst speak, and the boos that drowned out Pankhurst aroused Paul's anger. Later, in London, she marched in a suffrage procession, listened to Emmeline Pethick-Lawrence, and "was thrilled beyond words." That night she mailed in her twenty-five-cent membership to the Women's Social and Political Union. She worked for suffrage in a minor capacity for some months until she was asked to participate in a militant deputation to the House of Commons to confront the prime minister. Participating might lead to a jail sentence, and Alice Paul wondered how news of such militancy would be received in conservative Moorestown. Should she change her name? She walked around the block several times, thinking, before she mailed a letter accepting the assignment.[8]

As she had suspected, the action led to an arrest. Alice Paul then entered a period of militant action in which she was arrested and imprisoned several times, initiated several hunger strikes, joined the suffragists in such actions as throwing bricks at the windows of public buildings, and once threw a force-feeding tube through a balcony window at the lord mayor of London during a ceremonial banquet. Such actions made the papers in the United States as well as Great Britain, and when she returned to Moorestown in January of 1910, she was prepared for a cold reception.

In fact, many Friends in Moorestown said they could not understand Alice Paul. Others were at first curious. In February, after her return, the young Friends Association held a meeting in Moorestown at which Alice Paul spoke on the "Militant Suffrage Movement in England." She deplored press coverage of the violence, which she explained was generally mounted by the government against the women, and she defended the use of militant actions as necessary. As a reporter paraphrased her speech:

Window smashing is an old historic recognized means in Great Britain of logic. The women used this method on a smaller scale than men have used it. They break but one or two at a time, and those in public buildings which they have helped pay for. It is an encouraging sign that the women of Great Britain have rebelled—it shows that their soul and spirit is alive. In a London prison this quotation is carved on the prison walls: "resistance to tyranny is obedience to God," and this is the spirit that upholds the women of England.

The audience of five hundred gave her rapt attention, according to the reporter, and burst into sympathetic applause. During the question period "several gentlemen" asked her about the Christian nature of window smashing. She replied that "she attached no particular sanctity to a twenty-five-cent window-pane and that she herself had broken forty-eight."[9]

This defense of violence against property did not sit well with the Moorestown community, Quaker and non-Quaker alike, and Alice met hostility just at a time when she needed support. She herself felt critical of the sleepy Society of Friends, particularly in Moorestown, having met much more dynamic social reformers in England. In a speech at Haverford Summer School, she lamented that the Society was failing to respond to the social problems of the day and was losing touch completely with the working class. She called for the development of an American Woodbrooke to "give us the necessary inspiration and vision" for a new dedication to service.[10] Only a few years later a group of young Friends with similar convictions founded Pendle Hill as the American Woodbrooke, and the American Friends Service Committee as an instrument for social change. But for Alice Paul, the changes came too late.

The speech at Haverford was one of her last talks to a Quaker audience. Feeling both critical and criticized, she began to move away from the Society of Friends, although she retained her membership, and her strong sense of self-identity as a Friend all of her life. She took her place in a tradition of Quaker women who were so far ahead of their time that they lost patience with the Society, and yet had a major influence on later generations of Quaker women.

After she returned from England, Alice Paul enrolled in a doctoral program at the University of Pennsylvania, writing her thesis on laws governing women's rights in Pennsylvania. In the summer of 1911, Alice Paul offered to assist the Pennsylvania Suffrage Association in launching a series of open air meetings, a new technique to hold suffrage gatherings not in parlors but on street corners. Alice Paul was joined by a friend from the suffrage campaign in England, Lucy Burns of Brooklyn. The two had shared jail sentences and had a common desire to awaken the American movement to more forceful methods. In Philadelphia they began their efforts by hiring a one-horse cart and a sandwich stand, transformed to a placard, and setting up an impromptu meeting at the corner of Front and Dauphin. Since they had no license for holding this meeting, they were prepared to offer resistance if the police interfered. Nothing of the sort happened, however, and similar meetings were held throughout the summer, drawing larger and larger audiences. On September 30, a crowd of over two thousand gathered in Independence Square to hear eighteen speakers talk about the suffrage campaign.[11]

In the fall Alice Paul had to return to her studies, but in the summer of 1912, when NAWSA held its annual convention in Philadelphia, she and Lucy Burns talked to Jane Addams about offering their services to head the almost moribund congressional committee. Jane Addams agreed and took the suggestion to the national board.

Alice Paul and Lucy Burns were appointed to the committee, along with Crystal Eastman, and later Mary Beard and Dora Lewis. Alice Paul moved to Washington in December of 1912, found a room in a house next door to the Quaker meeting, and rented a little office. From this tiny headquarters she organized a huge procession of women to march through the streets of Washington on March 3, one day before President Wilson's inauguration. Beautifully staged, the parade had an unexpected result. Although a permit had been granted, the police failed to provide adequate coverage, and the women were attacked by a rowdy, antisuffragist mob. The result was near bedlam. Arriving in Washington for his inauguration, President Wilson noticed that the streets were empty. "Where are all the people?" he asked. "Over on the Avenue," he was told, "watching the suffrage parade."[12]

The parade brought an investigation, resulting in the dismissal of the district's chief of police. It also resulted in a great deal of publicity, which Alice Paul used to build a groundswell of interest in the federal amendment. In April she and Lucy organized the Congressional Union, still technically a branch of NAWSA, to work exclusively on the amendment, and in November began issuing a publication, *The Suffragist*. Meanwhile they circulated petitions all over the country calling for the federal amendment, and they organized an automobile cavalcade to bring them to Washington on July 31.

It was inevitable that some of the more conservative members of NAWSA, and the southern group opposed to the federal amendment, objected to Alice Paul's tactics. Efforts were made to bring the Congressional Union under control. In February 1914, Alice Paul was asked to resign from the Congressional Committee. She refused, and the Congressional Union became independent, pursuing its own tactics. In 1914 the suffrage amendment came before the Senate for the first time in twenty-seven years, and before the House for the first time in history.

In Great Britain, Alice Paul had learned from the Pankhursts the idea of holding the political party in power responsible for action or inaction on suffrage. In the United States, with a Democratic president and a Democratic majority in the Congress, she conceived the strategy of asking those women who had the vote in the western states to vote against their local Democratic candidates for Congress, whether or not the person under question had supported suffrage. This technique was hotly argued at the time among suffrage strategists, and it is still debated today among suffrage historians. Election results were mixed, since many women voters did not support the Alice Paul strategy or voted for candidates for other reasons. Nevertheless, the issue of suffrage came up at the next Democratic National Convention for the first time in history. More important, the women involved felt that they had stopped pleading for the vote and had begun to use what power they could muster to achieve their objective.

In 1916 the Congressional Union decided to form the National Woman's Party (NWP), and again to send women west to work in the political campaigns. They also appeared at both the Republican and Democratic national conventions, and they won from the Republican candidate, Charles Evans Hughes, his personal support of suffrage. At the Democratic convention, some one hundred women attempted to stand in silent demonstration, protesting President Wilson's continuing failure to speak for suffrage. They were instead mobbed, and once more women stole the headlines away from the president.

By this time, NAWSA had also decided to campaign for the federal amendment. Nevertheless, it was Alice Paul and her NWP which kept the pressure on the president. This was especially true as the United States prepared to enter World War I and was swept with a patriotic hysteria. Leadership in NAWSA thought they should offer their cooperation to government in the event of war, in return for a tacit understanding that the federal amendment would be passed at the end of the war.[13] Their action duplicated that of Elizabeth Cady Stanton during the Civil War. Alice Paul and her colleagues, however, saw the war as a further opportunity to call for suffrage. "Democracy should begin at home," their banners proclaimed.

In January of 1917, the Paul group began to post silent pickets in front of the White House, carrying signs asking, "Mr. President, What Will You Do for Woman Suffrage? How Long Must Women Wait for Liberty?" After the nation entered the war, their signs became more pointed. One called the president "Kaiser Wilson." Hostile crowds began to collect, and the nervous police decided that picketing the White House was no longer allowed. When the women persisted, 114 were arrested and 66 sentenced to serve terms in the infamous Occoquan workhouse in Virginia or the slightly less obnoxious District of

Columbia jail. While they were incarcerated, other women from all over the country came immediately to take their places. In prison, the leaders demanded to be treated as political prisoners and refused to eat. When they were force-fed, they managed to spread the news. "Miss Paul and Rose Winslow are being forcibly fed—inhuman and abominable," Dora Lewis, a proper Philadelphia matron, wrote to her family.[14] As the ringleader, Alice Paul was moved to the federal psychiatric hospital and examined by a psychiatrist. His report was that she was sane but had a will of iron. "She would die for her cause but she would never give up."[15]

Many of the women in prison were from wealthy and prominent families, and the resulting public protest was soon felt in the White House. President Wilson sought to defuse the situation by pardoning all the women, but they defeated this strategy by refusing to accept the pardon. By November the administration had no alternative but to unconditionally release all the prisoners. One week later the House set a date, January 10, to vote on the amendment.

Nevertheless, the NWP would not rest until Wilson himself used his influence to cause Congress to vote in favor of the amendment. The women kept up their demonstrations, including burning the president in effigy and burning his words publicly, and they were arrested time after time until the passage of the amendment was at last assured.

The NWP at its largest never included more than 50,000 persons, at most two percent of the membership of NAWSA. Whether credit for the final passage of the nineteenth amendment can be claimed for this group, rather than for the efforts of countless women everywhere, remains a matter for debate. It is clear from the record that the tactics of the Woman's Party goaded Wilson to action, despite his explicit disclaimers. But the more important point is that Alice Paul must be credited for bringing the techniques of nonviolence, peaceful protest, and the acceptance of prison terms and suffering, to play on the issue of women's rights for the first time since experiments with nonresistance in the days of Lucretia Mott, and to an extent never attempted before.

A number of Quaker women joined Alice Paul in the Woman's Party. Florence Kelley worked with Mary Beard to produce a research paper entitled *Why Women Demand a Federal Suffrage Amendment: Difficulties in Amending State Constitutions; A Study of Constitutions in Nonsuffrage States*, published in 1916 by the Congressional Union. Amelia Himes Walker, another Woman's Party member, was a Swarthmore classmate of Alice Paul's, and one of the picketers who went to jail. Another Quaker member was Martha Moore, also a Swarthmore graduate, who was active in the woman's suffrage committee of the yearly meeting. Florence Sanville, a Pennsylvanian who crusaded for protection for working women and children, marched with the Paul group but escaped imprisonment. M. Carey Thomas joined the NWP in 1920.

Introducing ERA

No sooner was the federal amendment safely ratified, than Alice Paul turned to the next step, the introduction of an Equal Rights Amendment. Her exhaustive studies of laws discriminating against women had convinced her that only such an amendment could make equality real. Beginning in 1920, she worked tirelessly to build a coalition of women to work with the Woman's Party on the ERA.

Now, however, many of her former colleagues opposed her actions. The demand for protective legislation for working women was central in the lives of such women as Florence Kelley, Jane Addams, and Florence Sanville. Indeed, Alice Paul herself had backed such legislation until it began to be clear that a federal equal rights amendment would eliminate such positive, as well as negative discrimination. For several years Alice Paul tried to hold a coalition together, suggesting that a "construing" clause might be added to the amendment to ex-

Alice Paul on August 26, 1920, at National Woman's Party
headquarters, celebrating the passage of the nineteenth amendment.
Permission from the Amelia Fry Collection.

empt women's industrial protections. But the lawyers for Florence Kelley's Consumer League were dubious, and in the end
that group formally announced their opposition to the ERA and
published a pamphlet attacking it. The National Women's
Trade Union League, the WCTU, and the League of Women
Voters (the successor to NAWSA) followed suit, as well as many
other women's organizations. Of the prominent Quaker women who had supported Alice Paul, only M. Carey Thomas
announced that she believed that in the long run women would
benefit from equal treatment under the law.

Embattled and isolated, Alice Paul decided to take time out
from the NWP while she attended law school. Meanwhile, a
team of women lawyers wrote equal rights laws for the various
states, correcting discrimination and calling for statewide equal
rights amendments. These were then introduced to state leg-

islatures by local NWP chapters, and in some cases they were passed. However, antifeminist legislatures and courts often rescinded the changes. Having earned three law degrees in short order, Alice Paul returned to the Woman's Party more convinced than ever that a federal amendment was necessary. Let industrial protections be extended to men, rather than written exclusively for women, she urged.

With her usual flair for pageantry, in July of 1923 she arranged a reenactment of the Seneca Falls Convention held seventy-five years earlier, and there she announced her new amendment, which she named the Lucretia Mott Amendment. In the fall it was introduced into Congress. From 1923 to 1972, when the Equal Rights Amendment finally passed Congress and went to the states for ratification, she and her colleagues lobbied for it at every session of Congress.

For many years, NWP was small and probably involved few Quakers. Most active women Friends were involved in one of the peace organizations that had developed in the wake of World War I, including the American Friends Service Committee. Others gave their time to the League of Women Voters on both the local and national level. Anna Lord Strauss, great-granddaughter of Lucretia Mott, served for six years as president of the New York City branch of the League, before becoming national president in 1944. Others put their major efforts into improving race relations, working with the NAACP or the Urban League or the Community Relations Division of the AFSC. Rachel Davis Dubois, a Quaker woman from New Jersey, was for many years widely known in this field.

Alice Paul knew many of these women, but her singleminded pursuit of equal rights did not permit her to give time to either peace efforts or work for racial equality. If challenged on such questions, she would answer that both peace and racial justice would be secured when women had equal access to power, and that these other goals should not be allowed to interfere in any way with the great work at hand.[16]

Mildred Scott Olmstead, a Friend and a former executive secretary of the Women's International League for Peace and Freedom, worked in a Washington office next to that of Alice Paul. She remembers Alice's singlemindedness. "She used to ask us to join her and we would say, 'First, let's see that no young men are drafted before we expose young women to the draft.' But today, of course, WILPF supports the ERA, although we still put our major emphasis on peace. Alice was a woman many decades ahead of her time, and to be such a woman is not easy."[17]

Although some Quaker women have chosen to work on a single issue, most have agreed with Abby Kelley Foster, who said that "all human rights are bound up in one great bundle," and it is impossible to make choices. Theologically, the Quaker concept of turning oneself into a direct channel for the Holy Spirit makes the human choice of a single objective contradictory.

But one of the glories as well as the difficulties of the Society of Friends has been its great variety. As one recent Quaker leader has said, "It is never either/or. It is always both/and."[18] Alice Paul may not have been a typical Quaker woman, nor worked faithfully at Quaker religious practice, but she always considered herself a Friend. Interviewed at the age of ninety-one, she spoke of her Quaker heritage:

Women are still voiceless. We have to wait until complete equality becomes a reality. I grew up in a Quaker family and the Quakers believe in the equality of the sexes. It is hard to grow up in such a family and never hear about anything else. When you put your hand to the plow, you can't put it down until you reach the end of the row.[19]

13. Building a Peace Movement

One beautiful August morning in 1914, Jane Addams was looking out over the waters of Frenchman's Bay from the cottage at Bar Harbor, Maine, where she spent part of each summer with her friend Mary Smith. Among the usual sailing yachts and lobster boats, she saw to her astonishment a large ocean liner. It was the *Kronprinzcessin Cecilie*, a German ship carrying a cargo of bullion. War had been declared two days earlier, and the captain of the ship, fearing capture, had turned back. Jane wrote later of her reactions:

The huge boat in her incongruous setting was the first fantastic impression of that strange summer when we were so incredibly required to adjust our minds to a changed world. . . . It is impossible now to reproduce that basic sense of desolation, of suicide, of anachronism, which that first news of the war brought to thousands of men and women who had come to consider war as a throwback in the scientific sense.[1]

Since the Civil War, the United States had been involved in no major conflicts. Peace-minded Americans had opposed the Spanish-American War and the annexation of the Philippines, and they increasingly believed that all international conflicts would be arbitrated at the World Court established at the Hague in 1899. With the optimism of the Progressive Era, they believed that humankind would now press on with more important business: perfecting democracy and achieving economic justice.

During the fifty years between wars, peace societies had grown. The venerable American Peace Society continued to work for international arbitration and to arrange peace conferences. The more radical Universal Peace Union espoused such related causes as the end of the death penalty, prohibiting military training in the schools, and justice for native Americans. It also espoused the annual celebration of Mother's Day as a time for women to pledge themselves to peace, an idea originally launched by Julia Ward Howe but carried on primarily by Quaker women. Following the Civil War, Lucretia Mott had decided to put most of her energies into the Universal Peace Union and its affiliate, the Pennsylvania Peace Society, of which she became president. "Even the woman question, as far as voting goes, does not take hold of my every feeling as does war," she wrote a friend.[2]

Another Quaker woman leader in the peace movement was Hannah Bailey of Maine. In 1887 she became the head of the Department of Peace and Arbitration of the WCTU and later of the same department for the World WCTU. From her home in Maine she published two monthly periodicals, *Pacific Banner* for adults and the *Acorn* for children, pressing for arbitration and the end of prizefighting and lynching as well as capital punishment. She urged mothers to avoid giving their children martial toys and opposed military drill in the schools and conscription. Many Quaker women used her materials to introduce the subject of peace in clubs and literary societies in their local communities.

Birth of WILPF and AFSC

For women like Hannah Bailey as well as Jane Addams, the beginning of World War I came as a distinct shock, an interruption to more important business. Some of the women in the leadership of the suffrage movement went on with their campaigns as though nothing had happened, but for others it was time to take more drastic action for peace. Spurred on by Rosika Schwimmer of Hungary, secretary for the International Suffrage Alliance, and Emmeline Pethick-Lawrence, a leader of the suffragettes of England, Jane Addams and Carrie Chapman

Jane Addams. Permission from
the Swarthmore College Peace
Collection, Swarthmore, PA.

Emily Greene Balch. Permission
from the Swarthmore College
Peace Collection, Swarthmore, PA.

U.S. delegation to the International Congress of Women, the
Hague, 1915. Permission from the Swarthmore College Peace
Collection, Swarthmore, PA.

Catt, then president of the International Suffrage Alliance, called a convention of three thousand women to meet in Washington in January of 1915 to consider what might be done to press for peace negotiations. The group constituted itself as the Women's Peace Party, with Jane Addams as chair, and it issued an eleven-point program, including a call for continuous mediation.

In April delegates from the Women's Peace Party along with women from other organizations set sail for the Netherlands on board the Dutch ship *Noordam* to attend an International Congress of Women held in the Hague. Among the Quaker-related women on board were Jane Addams, who had accepted the position of chair of the congress; Grace Abbott; Lucy Biddle Lewis, a delegate of the Philadelphia Yearly Meeting (Hicksite); and Emily Greene Balch, a professor of economics at Wellesley College, a frequent attender of Quaker meetings.

War hysteria was beginning to affect the United States, and the mission was denounced as "silly and base" by former president Theodore Roosevelt and others. Jane Addams replied through the papers that the women did not believe that they could settle the war but that they thought it was of value to state a new point of view. "We do think it is fitting that women should meet and take counsel to see what may be done."[3]

The British government objected to the congress, prevented a delegation of 180 British women from attending, and held the *Noordam* off Dover for some days. France and Russia did not send delegates. There were, however, fifteen hundred women present representing twelve countries: Austria, Belgium, Canada, Denmark, Germany, Great Britain (a few women had managed to travel before the congress was banned), Hungary, Italy, the Netherlands, Norway, Sweden, and the United States. Despite the high tensions of the times, the group was able to meet peacefully and to agree on a platform that has been called a forerunner of Wilson's Fourteen Points and of some of the principles of the League of Nations. One of the planks was of course equal political rights for women. Another was continuous mediation. Looking ahead, even beyond the current war crisis, the women named themselves the International Committee for Permanent Peace.

In order to pursue mediation after the congress, the delegates were divided into two groups, one to call on the heads of state of the belligerent nations, and one to visit the comparable offices in the neutral nations. It seemed a bold venture. "Never since Mary Fisher, the Quakeress, set out on her mission to preach Christianity to the Grand Turk was such an adventure undertaken by women," one commentator said.[4]

Surprisingly, they were received by twenty-one ministers, the presidents of two republics, a king, and the pope in Rome. Everyone was cordial and seemed to think that the opinion of a large body of women was worth considering. Perhaps in the gloom of the hour these officials were refreshed by the mere presentation of new ideas. The most encouraging example of this reaction was that of the prime minister of Austria. Jane Addams, in reporting the interview, remembered him as formidable, and his silence, after he had heard their mission, was ominous.

I said to him, "It perhaps seems to you very foolish that women should go about in this way, but after all, the world itself is so strange in this war situation that our mission may be no more strange nor foolish than the rest."

He banged his fist on the table. "Foolish?" he said. "Not at all. These are the first sensible words that have been uttered in this room in ten months. . . . That door opens from time to time, and people come in to say, 'Mr. Minister, we must have more ammunition, we must have more money or we cannot go on with this war.' At last the door opens and two people walk in and say, 'Mr. Minister, why not substitute negotiations for fighting? They are the sensible ones.' "[5]

Back in the United States, Jane Addams and Emily Balch spent the summer trying to persuade President Wilson to call a conference of mediation. He agreed with their objectives but said he had his own plan. Instead, the women succeeded in enlisting the support of Henry Ford, who insisted that he was going to help them conduct a conference of neutrals to be held in Stockholm, Sweden. Ford then chartered a Peace Ship and set sail for Europe with the slogan "Get the boys out of the trenches by Christmas," thereby bringing on his head, and that of some of the women who undertook the trip, ridicule and sarcasm from the press. Jane Addams had intended to sail, despite deep misgivings about Ford's real intentions, but she came down with pneumonia. Emily Greene Balch went in her place to the Stockholm Conference.

The Women's Peace Party continued to work for mediation until the United States entered the war in April of 1917. By then there were other important issues to deal with at home: the protection of civil liberties of pacifists and provision for the conscientious objectors who were forced to choose between the army and prison. One week after the declaration of war by the United States, a member of the Women's Peace Party, Frances Witherspoon, established a Bureau of Legal Advice for Conscientious Objectors in New York, forerunner of both the American Civil Liberties Union and the Central Committee for Conscientious Objectors. Later Frances Witherspoon worked with several other women to establish the War Resisters League. The Fellowship of Reconciliation had been organized in November of 1915, with Jane Addams as one of its founding members, and it, too, worked for civil liberties. Quaker women served on the boards and committees of these various groups.

In the war hysteria, nevertheless, Jane Addams was expelled from the Daughters of American Revolution, and Emily Greene Balch, who had supported some of the more radical peace groups oriented toward socialism, was not reappointed to her teaching post at Wellesley. It was a painful blow to a fifty-two-year-old woman who loved teaching. In dealing with the resulting stress, she turned more and more to the spiritual refreshment offered by the Society of Friends, joining the group in 1921.

In May of 1919, the International Committee for Permanent Peace met in Zurich, Switzerland, after a four-year lapse and renamed itself the Women's International League for Peace and Freedom. Among Quaker women present were Florence Kelley, Lucy Biddle Lewis, and Emily Greene Balch. The women criticized the Versailles Treaty, called for the lifting of the Allied blockade, and for international relief in countries facing starvation. On the last day, they elected Jane Addams as international president and Emily Greene Balch as secretary-treasurer.

For the next three years, from headquarters in Geneva, Emily Balch lobbied in the League of Nations for an enlarged League membership and a more democratic structure, as well as for women's rights, while establishing guidelines for WILPF. Thereafter she served the new organization in a variety of capacities, succeeding Jane Addams as president of the American section in 1931 and as honorary international president in 1937.

Jane Addams herself saw the League as the crowning achievement of her career. She asked that on her tombstone be engraved the legend, "Jane Addams of Hull-House and the Women's International League for Peace and Freedom." Although she continued to be active in many causes until her death in 1935, she never gave up the post as international president of WILPF, chairing every international conference. In 1931 she was awarded the Nobel Peace Prize, sharing it with Nicholas Murray Butler of Columbia. Her $16,000 was immediately given to WILPF. Fifteen years later, Emily Greene Balch received the prize for herself and for WILPF. The following year it was awarded to the American Friends Service Committee and the Friends Service Council of London.

The American Friends Service Committee was born on April 30, 1917, just twenty-two days after the United States entered the war. Developed to provide "a service of love in wartime" for conscientious objectors and others, the committee was made up of representatives of the three major Quaker groups—Orthodox, Hicksite, and Five Years Meeting. Three women, Anna G. Walton, Arabella Carter, and Lucy Biddle Lewis, were among the founders. A fourth, Rebecca Carter (later Rebecca Carter Nicholson), soon became the first paid staff member.[6]

Begun just when the Orthodox Philadelphia Yearly Meeting had at last established equality for women, AFSC was the first major philanthropic effort in which Quaker men and women worked together on equal terms. The reforms of the eighteenth century, in which Quaker men began to make good deeds rather than political power their basic form of self-expression, were now bearing their full fruit. The organization at first reflected the working methods of Philadelphia businessmen. The chair of the board was always a man, and the executive secretary also, except for a few months in 1927, when Anna Griscom Elkinton served as acting secretary. Nevertheless, in the field, where actual relief work was carried on, it was often women who took the lead and became AFSC's heroes. This in turn helped move the organization forward toward true equality.

In the spring of 1917, the AFSC set to work immediately on its twin mission: arranging for conscientious objectors—primarily Quaker, but also Mennonite and Brethren—to be furloughed to its care, and developing units to be sent overseas to do relief work in France and later elsewhere in Europe. Although women were not subject to the draft, young Quaker women were also eager to serve and were sent to relief projects overseas.

In June of 1917, six women went to Russia to work in areas surrounding Buzuluk, a wheat depot on the Samara-Tashkent railroad. Here war refugees had crowded in from the front, straining the supplies of food and water already reduced by drought and famine. English Quakers were already at work in this area, providing medical services, and the six American women helped in the clinics and established workrooms where one member of each refugee family could gain employment: weaving, spinning, sewing, or embroidering. They also set up schools for refugee children.

After the Russian Revolution in 1918, part of this mission group went on to Siberia, while two members made their way to Moscow and there fed hungry children for a short time. In 1920 two of the AFSC women, Anna Haines and Nancy Babb, returned to Samara to do what they could about severe famine conditions. They reported that "the fields were as black as though a fire had swept them," and as they approached the local orphanage, they could hear the cries of the children two blocks away. The only help they could offer was to sort the dead from the dying. Over ninety percent of the children under three died that year. Eating became an ordeal as starving children looked in through the windows with hungry eyes. Yet the workers had to eat in order to help unload and distribute the grain that came in far too small and too few shipments to their area. Several staff members came down with typhus. Nevertheless, they stayed on until 1923 when conditions were somewhat improved. For all these women, the months on the steppes were to be remembered as a high point of their lives.[7]

In the spring of 1919, three American women entered Germany to investigate the conditions of children under the Allied blockade. They were Jane Addams and Alice Hamilton, both of whom had done service with the AFSC unit in France, and Carolena Wood, a young Friend from New York, a part of the group interested in transforming the Society and ridding it of the cleavages of earlier years. The three had $30,000 and twenty-five tons of new clothing to distribute, but more important, they had a mission to fulfill. On the basis of their reports, AFSC would decide how much to be involved in German relief. Jane Addams and Alice Hamilton wrote a careful report, but Carolena Wood's letters were galvanizing:

The first week or ten days I was in Germany was given to visiting hospitals, orphan asylums, day nurseries, and clinics for children to gather an impression of the physical suffering which is here by seeing some of the little wasted bodies due to the ravages of tuberculosis and rickets, and which must result in death, invalidism, or a lot of dwarfs.

All is directly due to under-nourishment. When I saw the destruction left in the battle-fields of France I wished that all the world might go there to see what war is, but this is no less a battle-field with its deep, awful lesson.[8]

Following these reports, AFSC decided to do what it could to feed the hungry in Germany. The original idea was to undertake a small-scale demonstration project, but Herbert Hoover, then director of the American Relief Administration, and a Quaker, asked instead if the Friends would be willing to distribute food to children throughout Germany. It was impossible to say no. A group of workers skilled in either medicine, social work, or administration was recruited and sent to begin to establish feeding stations. Five of the original eighteen workers were Quaker women. As staff and resources grew, the project was expanded until AFSC was maintaining 2,271 kitchens, supplying 8,364 feeding stations, and feeding a million children. Many of the men and women who participated in this project felt they were realizing the William James quest for a moral alternative to war, fighting disease, suspicion, and hunger. Many went on to devote their lives to this sort of work.

Unlike the traveling ministers who were their spiritual forebears, the Quakers who served in the AFSC projects did not proselytize. They believed that their projects and their lives should speak for them. In addition, from the first they had welcomed men and women of different faiths who shared their interest in finding an alternative to war. Respect for these differences inhibited a missionary approach. Nevertheless, in Germany and France, as well as other European countries, war-weary men and women were encouraged by the silent help of the Friends and began to inquire about the spiritual roots of Quakerism. From this inquiry grew small but dynamic groups of Quaker meetings on the continent.[9] For the more evangelical Friends, however, the refusal of AFSC workers to perform the more traditional missionary role was disappointing and grew in time to become a source of friction.

AFSC project in Russia. Anna Louise Strong sits at table in center.
Permission from the AFSC Archives.

Peacemaking Between Wars

Between WILPF and the AFSC, the opportunities for Quaker
women to work for peace after World War I were many and
varied. WILPF quickly developed a nationwide organization
with state and local chapters concentrating on educating themselves and the public about alternatives to war and causes and
cures to international tensions. One method was to bring so-
called enemies into American communities, letting people see
for themselves that the Germans and the Bolsheviks were, after
all, human. Large numbers of Quaker women served on WILPF
committees throughout the country, and a few were always in
top leadership positions, paid or unpaid.

In addition to the annual congresses, WILPF women were
involved in special peacekeeping missions abroad. In 1925
some Haitian women who were members asked the executive

committee to look into conditions on their island, occupied by the U.S. Marines since 1915. Emily Greene Balch gathered a group of six persons, four women and two men, who spent three weeks on the island, surveying political, economic, social, and financial conditions. They worked as closely as they could with the Haitian people rather than the occupation forces. The result of the trip, published in book form as *Occupied Haiti*, had an enormous impact, and it was thought to be a factor leading to U.S. withdrawal four years later.

The AFSC also absorbed the energies of many Quaker women. From the first, local Quaker meetings worked to raise money and to gather clothing and bedding for the overseas projects. Older women who could not be active knitted layettes and made blankets for shipment abroad. In addition, it became traditional for younger Quaker women to offer a year or two of service. After the worst of the postwar emergency was over in Europe, AFSC opened service opportunities in settlement houses, southern schools for blacks, and Indian reservations throughout the United States. The organization also began, in 1927, to send young men and women across the country each summer in peace caravans, to bring messages of international reconciliation to the small towns of the United States. During the Depression, AFSC undertook a major project of childfeeding in the Appalachian coalfields, suggested originally by Grace Abbott, and here the first workcamps were initiated, in which young men and women spent their summer in unpaid volunteer labor to aid underprivileged communities.[10]

Like WILPF, AFSC was interested in probing opportunities for reconciliation. In 1927 a mission was sent to Nicaragua to see what might be done to make peace in the wake of the intervention of the United States Marines, and to see General Augusto Sandino, who alone had not capitulated after the American intervention. Carolena Wood (one of the first three Americans to enter Germany) was part of this mission, wearing, according to a friend, her old corduroy knickers for the trip. Her goal was to look into conditions of women, not only in Nicaragua but in the other Central American countries the group visited. The four persuaded General Sandino's father to go with them into the interior to make contact with the Sandino forces, but they were discouraged by the American chargé d'affaires. Nevertheless, they made plans to proceed with the trip and would have done so, if a new U.S. Marine offensive had not made the trip impossible. From Managua they cabled President Coolidge to protest the campaign against Sandino, then came home to speak to the American people about the danger of further meddling in Central American affairs.[11]

Many women found the activities of WILPF and the AFSC complementary and were able to serve both organizations. Hannah Clothier Hull, a suffragist and a Friend, worked on the committee guiding the AFSC childfeeding program in Germany and Austria, and she served as vice-chair of the AFSC board, as well as a member of the peace section, while filling the post of national chair of WILPF for many years.

Entering the Nuclear Arm

Throughout the 1920s, Friends persisted in an attitude of hope. Surely, with all this effort and goodwill, the world would learn its lesson and never again be involved in the barbarism of war. By the early 1930s, however, the peace was again threatened by the rise of fascism. The AFSC sent workers to feed children on both sides of the Spanish Civil War and began a long effort to help the Jews and other victims of persecution escape from Nazi Germany. The WILPF worked for universal disarmament, the Kellogg-Brian Pact, and a negotiated peace in Spain. At home all pacifists threw themselves into a unified effort to persuade Americans never again to enter a world war. The success of Gandhian methods of nonviolence in working toward independence for India helped to convince many Quakers that pacifism need not mean surrender to evil, but that the positive forces of truth and love could be used to oppose violence. This was the same message as the nonresisters of the

Lady Borton on Pulau Bidong in 1980. Photo by Peter Fleischl. Permission from the AFSC Archives.

nineteenth century had articulated, but few Friends had understood. In the spirit of nonviolence, AFSC sent a mission to the Gestapo to speak against persecution of the Jews, the only Protestant church group to so act.

During World War II, which broke like a storm upon all the hopes for peace, Quaker women devoted themselves to such enterprises as maintaining hostels for refugees from Germany, protesting the relocation of Japanese-Americans from the West Coast, and finding new homes and schools for both groups. Many also served, along with their husbands or brothers, in the Civilian Public Service camps established for conscientious objectors, in mental hospitals, forestry camps, or medical experiment stations. Some trained at Haverford College for postwar reconstruction.

In the postwar years, these women and many other Quaker workers returned to Europe and Japan to try to undo some of the damage of war. In addition to relief, AFSC promoted off-the-record conferences for diplomats and other leaders, as well as student exchanges, in an effort to provide reconciliation and probe the causes of war. At the headquarters of the United

Nations, both WILPF and AFSC worked for a less vindictive peace than that of Versailles and a reasonable hope for international accord.

The news of the first explosion of the atomic bombs on Nagasaki and Hiroshima in 1945 brought dismay to American pacifists, as indeed to many men and women of goodwill. As part of its postwar work, AFSC sent Esther Rhoads, a Philadelphia Quaker and a longtime teacher at the Friends School in Tokyo, to Japan to take part in the work of Licensed Agencies for Relief in Asia (LARA). She wrote that almost everyone who called at the Friends Center had lost some member of the family, but that somehow these people had the "gift of forgiveness. If they blame anything for the tragedies through which they have passed, it is *war* and not Americans." The emperor of Japan had requested that an American woman tutor his son, and in the fall of 1946 Elizabeth Gray Vining, an author and a Quaker, arrived in Tokyo to take up this duty. Her letters back to AFSC were poignant:

At meeting for worship one Sunday, I could see through the window women washing sweet potatoes and laying them out to dry in the sun on the concrete steps that are all that is left of the Friends Meetinghouse. Sweet potatoes keep better that way—and sweet potatoes were just about all they had to eat. . . . The devastation from the incendiary bombs covers acres and miles. People have cleaned up the debris very well, and have planted little vegetable patches among the piles of stone and the remains of stone foundations and the rusted piles of twisted iron and tin. Little shacks built out of wood, if people are lucky, or of old iron and tin, are going up everywhere, there will be no way to keep them warm this winter, for fuel is scarce and there is no charcoal ration.[12]

The emergence of atomic weapons added urgency to the peace movement. The AFSC developed regional offices throughout the country to support local peace work. The WILPF recruited a new generation of pacifist women. Among them was Kay Camp, a graduate of Swarthmore and a Friend, who joined in the 1950s and later became national chair. In 1957 a new organization, SANE, a National Committee for a Sane Nuclear Policy, was developed, with leadership from both AFSC and WILPF. One of its most dynamic board members has been Mildred Scott Olmstead, for many years previously the executive secretary of WILPF. In 1961 a group of housewives organized a nationwide strike calling for the government "to end the arms race, not the human race." Women Strike for Peace, thus born, has worked closely with WILPF and has included many Quaker women.

As the devastating decade of the 1960s crept forward and the United States became more deeply enmeshed in the war in Vietnam, the United States peace movement became increasingly focused on that conflict. In 1966 the AFSC established a rehabilitation center for civilian victims in Quang Ngai, an area held by the South Vietnamese forces, while sending medical aid to victims in North Vietnam and areas held by the National Liberation Front. In 1968 AFSC made the first of a series of visits to Hanoi to deliver medical supplies and discuss possible peace terms. Within the United States, WILPF protested the Vietnam war with petitions, marches, lobbying, and civil disobedience, its members blocking trucks laden with napalm bound for Vietnam. In 1971 a WILPF delegation, including Kay Camp, went to both Saigon and Hanoi to discuss the possibility of peace.

A group of Quakers eager to use nonviolent methods in direct action against the war formed A Quaker Action Group. One of AQAG's civil disobedience projects was sailing the yacht *Phoenix* loaded with relief supplies for both North and South Vietnam into Haiphong harbor. Aboard was a Wisconsin Quaker woman, Elizabeth Boardman.[13] Increasingly, individual Quakers also felt led to commit civil disobedience and accept the resulting jail sentences as a personal statement of protest. Elizabeth Gray Vining was one of many Quaker women to take this action.

In 1969 a young Quaker woman, Lady Borton, whose father had worked in Germany with AFSC after World War I, went to Quang Ngai to serve in the Quaker rehabilitation center. While there, she took pictures and wrote stories of the Vietnamese people she came to know, hoping to transfer her feeling for them to the American public back home. Returning to the United States in 1971, she continued to be haunted by the faces of the victims of the war. In 1980 she decided to return for a six-month tour of duty with AFSC on the island of Pulau Bidong, then crowded with boat people who had for one reason or another left the Republic of Vietnam. Here, in the incredible crowding and tensions of the refugees, she kept a journal in which she was able to reflect about both experiences. The result was a book published in 1984, *Sensing the Enemy*.[14]

Many commercial vessels came to Bidong with a load of refugees plucked from the sea. One day such a boat hailed the island when Lady Borton was standing on the jetty.

"You must be a Quaker," the captain told her when they were within hearing.

"Why do you think that?" Lady asked.

"Because you are a woman, and you are here."[15]

With the winding down of the Vietnam war, the large-scale antiwar movement, which was also a student protest movement, began to dissolve, but the solid core of peace movements remained strong. The 1970s and 1980s have witnessed significant new developments. One has been the proliferation of departments of peace studies and peace research on college campuses at both the undergraduate and graduate levels. Led by Elise Boulding, a Quaker sociologist who served for years as international president of WILPF, a Consortium on Peace Research and Development was founded at the University of Colorado in Boulder in May of 1970. Another project led by Elise Boulding has been the creation of a U.S. Peace Academy to study strategies for peace. This academy was established by Congress in 1984 but has not been adequately funded at this writing.

A second development during this period has been the increased interest in refusing to pay taxes for war. Quakers have always been opposed to war taxes, but most have paid them obediently when taxes supported both war and civilian purposes. Elizabeth Redford, a Quaker woman, was rebuked in 1695 by the Men's London Yearly Meeting for suggesting otherwise.[16] For many years, a few individual Friends have been troubled enough about supporting war with their dollars to be tax refusers. Marion Bromley, an Ohio Quaker woman, was one of the founders of a group called Peacemakers, which began in 1948 to refuse to pay taxes for war. In the past decade, Quakers of all persuasions have become more interested in protesting the payment of war taxes and have pressed for a separate and alternative peace tax fund into which conscientious objectors could pay that portion of their income tax that currently supports war, just as young men who are conscientious objectors are able to render alternative service to the military. Evangelical as well as pastoral and silent meeting Friends have joined in an enterprise called New Call to Peacemaking, which embraces Mennonites and Brethren churches, and which is searching for a common approach to the problem of peace churches paying for war.

The development of a feminist movement in the 1960s has affected the peace movement also, with the emergence of specifically feminist peace organizations and actions, all embracing Quaker women. Several international feminist conferences on nonviolence have been held, attended by women of many nations interested in exploring the connections between feminist and nonviolent theory. In 1980 a group of feminist women encircled the Pentagon with the help of scarves and were arrested for refusing to move. This was the first of several such demonstrations of a group calling itself *Women's Pentagon Action*, dedicated to feminist methods of protesting militarism.

The encampment of women in England at the U.S. Air Force Base at Greenham Common, protesting the deployment of cruise missiles in Great Britain and in Europe, has been supported by many pacifist feminists, and it has inspired several similar actions in the United States. One was the summer 1983 encampment of women near the Seneca army base in upper New York State. The WILPF and the Nationwide Women's Program of AFSC were among the sponsors of this encampment, and a number of Quaker women took part in the gathering and in committing civil disobedience by climbing the fence on the border of the army base. The local community, heavily dependent on the base for employment, was not happy with the encampment, and there were provocative stories in the papers and several unpleasant confrontations.

In July 1983, just when these developments were coming to a head, Lucretia Mott was inducted into the Women's Hall of Fame in the village of Seneca Falls, New York. Present for the ceremonies were some women from the encampment. Dressed for the occasion, they were not identified immediately as campers and were amused to hear people comment that they liked the objectives of the campers, but not their methods. As one of the entertainers at the ceremony pointed out, that same remark had been made at the same place, one hundred and thirty-five years earlier.

14. Quaker Women Today

Today there are 115,000 Quakers in the United States and approximately 200,000 in the world, a tiny proportion of the general population. Many Americans think that Quakers were a part of the history of this country and are now more or less an extinct species. "Are you really a Quaker?" one newspaperman asked a contemporary Quaker woman. "Can I take your picture?"

The movement of women into higher education and into the professions, which Quaker women led in the nineteenth century, has long since become commonplace for middle-class American women; and the causes for which Quakers fought— the end of slavery, woman's rights to her own earnings, suffrage, temperance—have an old-fashioned ring. In effect, Quaker women have become obscured by their own success. Other women from other religious persuasions have caught up and forged ahead of them. When the first three volumes of *Notable American Women: 1607–1950, A Biographical Dictionary* was published in 1971, it was noted that 6.3 percent of the women covered were Quaker, whereas Quakers at their most numerous had never been more than 2 percent of the population. A fourth volume of the dictionary, published in 1980, which covers the lives of women who had made their mark after 1920, shows no such preponderance of Quakers.

Quaker women approve of these statistics, since most of them have never been interested in high achievement for its own sake. (Neither have Quaker men, as sociologist Digby Baltzell points out.)[1] The religious values that led these women to pioneer in many areas stemmed from a personal sense of responsibility having little to do with the usual measures of worldly success. If today their leadings take them in obscure

directions, they are content to follow, confident that what matters still is being faithful to the Light. A Quaker woman from
Georgia puts it well:

I strongly identify with the position of [Quaker women] breaking new
ground and then moving aside to allow others to take over and follow
through. I believe women these days, especially Quaker women, are
following the leadings and doing many courageous things. . . . Many
[Quaker] women are serving in ways that are not directly related to
women's issues but have provided examples of productive, functional
creative women to the mainstream of society. This is a very important
evolution from the point of view of the early women's movement. . . .
As the feminine is incorporated, a more balanced culture may emerge.[2]

The current women's movement, emerging in the 1960s,
caught Quaker women largely by surprise. Preoccupied by
their opposition to the war in Vietnam and their participation
in the civil rights movement, they felt detached from the new
burst of feminist energy that seemed focused on a personal
experience of sexism. Having grown up in homes with a strong
tradition of parents who shared responsibility, and having had
without question equal opportunities for education and career
choices, many Quaker women felt that they had been spared
any personal experience with patriarchy. If they could sym-
pathize with women's struggles for equality, it was at a remove
from their own lives. The question of the role of women had
been settled within the Society of Friends long ago, they felt,
and the new movement was irrelevant to their personal experience. Interviewed in 1975 in regard to her views on wom-
en's liberation, a seventy-year-old Quaker woman in New
England, twice widowed, active in Quaker organizations on the
national level, said that she had never felt "unliberated."

There has been a Quaker tradition of equality, and I've never felt the
need to push for jobs or anything. I've never felt unliberated. It is not
that I don't believe in it, but I've never had occasion to feel unliberated. Neither of my two husbands liked separating men's and wom-
en's activities, so maybe that's another reason I haven't felt the need
to join.[3]

This woman was interviewed as part of a survey of nineteen active Quaker women in a local Massachusetts monthly meeting. Of these women, only two defined themselves as feminists, although the interviewer felt that they were all living as feminists and serving as role models to other women in the meeting and the community.[4]

A second survey, including women who were active in the AFSC and the YWCA in the years 1945 to 1960, has been completed and is currently being evaluated. Most of the AFSC women were Quakers. The preliminary impression of the researcher was that these women also did not regard themselves as feminists but had committed their lives to social causes. "All were independent, believed they had a right to define their own lives independently of husband and family, and had no second thoughts about the choice they had made."[5]

Indeed, Quaker women born in the 1920s and 1930s built on the experience of their foremothers. Quaker husbands and sons in the twentieth century have generally been willing to share household tasks, and Quaker women have managed to combine family duties with full-time careers, either as paid professionals or full-time volunteers to peace or social change organizations, in a style that many younger women of today might envy. Few aspired to be superwomen; rather they simplified their lives by dressing casually, eschewing expensive entertaining, and involving the whole family in household chores, just as Lucretia Mott did 150 years ago.

For all the advantages that this head start in liberation undoubtedly gave Quaker women, they, along with Quaker men, have suffered from blind spots. The Society of Friends does not exist in a vacuum. Its own testimony for equality has always been shaped and tempered by the attitudes of the larger society. It has been inevitable that unconscious forms of sexism have crept into Quakerism itself.

Younger Quaker women, meeting the new feminism on college campuses or in activist groups, have been challenging Quaker meetings and Quaker organizations to examine themselves for hidden forms of patriarchy. If it is true that men and women are really equal, then why are more men in administrative positions while more women are secretaries, they ask. Or why are women asked to serve the covered dish suppers and run the First Day schools, while men predominate on the financial and property committees? And why is the language used in meeting for worship patriarchal?

Quaker men as well as Quaker women share a commitment to the concept of equality. But Quaker men, enjoying at least some of the conventional masculine privileges, are less apt to see inequality unless it is brought forcefully to their attention. When questions of sexism were first raised, many Quaker men, and not a few women also, reacted with the fear that the new feminism was both too separatist and too strident to have much relevance for the Society of Friends. Despite the many years of separate women's meetings, Friends have continued to be slow to understand or accept the need for some of the Quaker feminists to meet separately in order to share and to free themselves of the hidden bonds of sexism.

Some of these younger women have come to Quakerism from other backgrounds and have experienced the force of patriarchy in their formative years. Others are not quite so sure that their own Quaker childhood was as free of sexist attitudes as they once believed. Their need to meet and sometimes worship separately has been strong, despite the initial opposition of older Friends, some of whom view the return to separate meetings as a setback in the long struggle toward integration.

Quaker feminists are sensitive to these feelings and have always emphasized that while they need to meet separately, they are not withdrawing from communal worship or communal business meetings. They are rather developing their own strengths in order to participate more fully in the common human enterprise of building community within the Society of Friends.

The question of stridency and of anger has also continued to surround the development of a new feminism within the

Society of Friends. One of the Massachusetts women interviewed in 1975 spoke of these feelings in describing a conference where feminist issues surfaced.

There was so much anger. Not that there shouldn't be anger, but I
thought it was too bad to mix anger with the desire to expand wom-
en's role. There were so many expressions of hostility against men in
general. There was a funny ironic kind of masculinity about the
women. As if at one time they were hating men but emulating them.[6]

The Quaker devotion to nonviolence has sometimes made it
difficult for Quakers to know how to handle anger, and some
of this reaction to feminism is a result of that difficulty. To view
an agent of change as strident is of course to project one's own
fears upon the other; Friends considered Lucretia Mott strident,
and John Woolman, now regarded as nearly a saint, was
thought irritatingly "peculiar." In the past several decades, the
Black Power movement and its corollaries among Indians, La-
tinos, and other people with whom Friends work have helped
to give them a liberal education in the value of anger. Quakers
have also come to acknowledge that their own homes are not
as free of violence as they might wish.[7] Courses in marriage
enrichment, nonviolent parenting, and nonviolence for children have proliferated and have helped Friends to learn more
about their feelings.

Another source of resistance to the new feminism within the
Quaker fold was the perception that it posed a threat to conventional marriage patterns. From the days of Fox and Fell,
marriage has been very important to Friends as a means of
transmitting Quaker values through a family setting, and of
enriching and sustaining the Quaker meeting community.
Many Quaker couples have been partners in reform. While
Friends have also always accepted men and women who chose
to stay single or select a person of the same sex as a life partner,
they have continued to emphasize the extreme care with which
the state of matrimony should be entered. Modern meetings
appoint clearness committees to discuss marriage plans with

young couples, just as in earlier times, and these committees take their job very seriously, ask probing questions, and sometimes delay a marriage if they feel the couple has not thought through potential sources of problems.

In the Philadelphia Yearly Meeting's book of *Faith and Practice*, published in 1972, one of the "Advices" states the ideal of responsibility sharing in modern language:

Friends are reminded that it is the experience and testimony of our Society that there is one teacher, namely Christ, and that in his Spirit there are no distinctions between persons, nor any reason of age, sex, or race that elects some to domination. Live in love and learn from one another. Combativeness in family life, whereby man and wife or parents and children strive to assert a supremacy of will is not compatible with the conviction that there is that of God in everyone.[8]

But while clinging to the ideal of building egalitarian marriages within the larger meeting structure, the more liberal Friends groups have also been ready to deal with new forms of marriage relationships. Meetings have struggled over the question of how to react to the fact that many couples coming to them for marriage preparation have been living together. Generally this widespread practice has been accepted, and Friends have put their emphasis on counseling that such relationships must never be exploitative, nor entered into without a spiritual as well as physical commitment. Pendle Hill, a Quaker study center near Philadelphia, has held lectures and group discussions of new forms of marriage relationships. And a few meetings have helped lesbian or gay couples in their desire to enter into a lifelong commitment with the support of their religious community. This has not been true of the evangelical meetings, which continue to feel that homosexuality is expressly forbidden by Scripture.

Despite some areas of resistance, Friends have come to see the new feminism as a logical extension of their historic testimony, and to make institutional changes. Quaker institutions have made genuine efforts to add women to boards that were previously all-male, to make sure that women are hired and paid on the same scale as men in Quaker schools and service agencies, and to institute affirmative action when needed. Haverford College became coeducational in 1979. A Quaker woman, Asia A. Bennett, became the executive secretary of AFSC; and another, Kara Cole, was appointed to the comparable position for the Friends United Meeting (FUM), a new name for the Five Years Meeting. In 1985 Marty Walton was chosen as general secretary of the Friends General Conference. At the local meeting level, women have been added to financial and property committees, and men take their turn in serving tea.

The hardest change to effect has been language. Friends have resisted such change on the grounds that the word *man* is inclusive; that God the Father also means God the Mother, and that Christ was after all, male. When feminists have persisted in asking for a more inclusive terminology, they have been told that this matter is trivial. It is a strange response for a Society that has been known for its use of plain language—the refusal to use honorifics or to swear oaths—a matter that the justices of Puritan England regarded as offensively trivial.

Here and there, however, changes in language have been made. The AFSC uses nonsexist terminology exclusively. A Quaker songbook has been written with alternative, nonsexist language included for some of the old favorites, thanks largely to the efforts of Elizabeth Watson, a Quaker Bible scholar and strong feminist. As this is being written, a number of yearly meetings are in the process of revising their books of discipline to eliminate sexist language and to include specific statements on discrimination based on sex.

Within the pastoral and evangelical wings of modern Quakerism, there has been a strong surge of interest in the legacy of the traveling women ministers and the feminism inherent in the Quaker message. As the Earlham School of Religion in Richmond, Indiana, many young Quaker women have prepared themselves to become pastors of Friends churches, sometimes sharing the post with their husbands, sometimes alone. Many of these women have studied the history of Quaker women and have sought to reintroduce the concept of Quaker feminism to their congregations. The evangelical women also have developed great interest in Quaker women's history. A group of these women have recently formed a Task Force on Women that is producing a newsletter called *The Priscilla Papers*. Through the newsletter and workshops it continues to expose Friends to the egalitarian heritage of the Society.

Many meetings formed women's support groups in the early 1970s. Some of these have survived and grown strong. Others have died out as the women involved have become busy putting their feminism into action. Many such women are involved today with organizations providing services to abused women, pregnant teenagers, women and girls who have suffered rape, or women needing legal advice. Some have worked with the National Organization for Women (NOW), and some with the new feminist peace movement. The AFSC's Nationwide Women's Program has provided a network to link up working women and minority women, not only in the United States, but in many of the countries to which women's jobs have been exported. In Philadelphia, several Quaker women were involved in the founding of Women's Way, a funding organization for women's service agencies—the first, the largest, and most successful of its kind. Its annual Lucretia Mott banquet honors each year an American woman who has made a significant contribution to the advancement of women.

Quaker women acknowledge, however, that they do not always find it easy to work with feminists of a more secular persuasion. Habits of competition, of striving for power, of distrust and hostility, copied from the commercial world with its dominant masculine values, seem to them to sometimes surface in the new feminist organizations, despite feminist theory to the contrary. The years of withdrawal have taught Quakers a different style of interpersonal relationships. In the "real world," even when that real world is a feminist world, they are sometimes too uncomfortable to try to speak up for their own values of consensus decision making and nonviolence in personal relations.

Their reluctance is lamentable, for some of these Quaker values were inherent in the birth of the women's movement in the nineteenth century and need to be reintroduced by spiritually minded women of whatever persuasion. The Quaker woman who chooses to participate in feminist politics but to keep silent when her own values are violated is not being true to the tradition of the valiant traveling ministers, nor is she offering what is perhaps her unique contribution to the modern movement. For this reason some Quaker women feel that one should not "graduate" from the meeting-based women's group, after all, but use it as a source of strength in pursuing feminist Quaker values in the larger movement.

Quaker women also feel that by spending their energies in non-Quaker community activities, they have failed to educate the whole Society of Friends in the relationship between feminism and the spiritual message of the Society of Friends. Most Quakers continue to see feminism more as an expression of equal rights than as an avenue of growth for both men and women. Yet feminism, properly understood, is a call for authentic spiritual development, based on the authority of one's own experience of the Light. It is a rejection of hierarchy (which has generally meant male authority), and an embracing of community. It is a turning away from divisions of all kinds, and a search for wholeness. It is a dream of a future based on preservation, not exploitation; cooperation, not competition; the weaving of a web of networks, not their destruction by conflict. It is a vision of the divine Spirit that nurtures and supports each individual as a mother might and gives to humans the wonderful gift of personal affirmation and creativity.

Nor has the relevance of feminism to the peace movement, long a central issue in the Society of Friends, been fully understood. Feminists within that movement, both male and female, have pointed out that many of its strategies have mirrored the strategies of war. The Pentagon decides to create a new missile. The peace movement decides to oppose the new missile. The Pentagon looks for the political power to provide more support for weapons. The peace movement mounts a political campaign to defeat the Pentagon's strategies. Feminist pacifists, including many younger Quaker women, have suggested a new strategy, a search for those human issues that unite people in their love of children and of the earth, an organization based on local affinity groups rather than nationwide task forces, and inclusion of many issues, rather than the rigorous narrowing down to one focus. These ideas, and the actions that are planned on the basis of them, are in an initial stage, but to some people they appear to hold promise. In commenting on the women using nonviolence to protest the deployment of U.S. missiles on Greenham Common, one British woman said: "Perhaps it is the long unheard and ignored voices of women that may rescue the world in time from the nuclear madness which is absorbing all thought and action."[9]

The future vision of the feminists is very similar to the future vision of any scholar who has tried to imagine how the world might be organized in a postindustrial, postnuclear time. Dr. Kenneth Boulding, a Friend and noted economist and the husband of Dr. Elise Boulding, wrote a pamphlet some time ago with the provocative title *The Evolutionary Potential of Quakerism*.[10] In it he argued that the time for values of Quakerism to flower fully lay in the future, when humankind would need to understand peace, equality, and community to survive in the postindustrial age. Dr. Elise Boulding, herself a futurist, leads groups in envisioning a future as they would have it, and then working backward to the present to see what strategies are needed to make that future come true. Again, it is the perfectionist values of Quakerism that seem necessary for survival. To live today as though the Kingdom of God, or the Holy Community, had already been established is to begin to build that community within the framework of the old society. This link-

age between Quakerism and feminism in future planning has
not been widely discussed or understood within the Society of
Friends.

Perhaps the Quaker bent toward action rather than theory
accounts for some of this failure to explore the ramifications of
feminist thought in relationship to Quaker belief. But Friends
have long discovered that action itself can be a means of search
and a channel to belief. Following the Vietnam War, many
young men and women, searching for a spiritual basis of their
lives, turned to the Society of Friends, which they knew originally as an antiwar organization. There they entered into a
deeper religious experience. Similarly, some of the young
women committed to the new feminism have discovered the
Quakers as a spiritual home.

Such a woman is Lenny Lianne of Alexandria, Virginia. After
working as a state lobbyist for the National Organization for
Women, Lianne decided to undertake more radical personal
action for the Equal Rights Amendment. She joined a group of
women who, on August 26, 1981, the anniversary of the passage of the Nineteenth Amendment, chained themselves to the
White House fence as a symbol of women's determination to
win ratification. This was the beginning of twenty-one nonviolent actions in support of the amendment. The group committed itself to a code of nonviolence, according to Lianne:

This included not only non-violence to the body, but also to the spirit.
We respected the police as people and not as stereotypically enemy.
I was the police liaison. We also had a consensus form of decision-
making. This was a new process for many of the women used to
majority votes.

After being arrested on Mother's Day, 1982, Lianne attended
a Friends meeting for the first time. She had been on a spiritual
journey throughout the actions. A member of the group, Mary
Ann Beall, who had fasted for ERA in Illinois, had been arrested at the Seneca encampment, and had joined in all the

nonviolent actions, was both a devoted Quaker and a strong feminist. Talking with her, Lianne thought she ought to see if the Religious Society of Friends had the answer for her.

It was home almost immediately. I have since become a member. . . . What led me to become a Friend was the respect for each individual's spiritual values and journey, no hierarchy, and the equality of all members.[11]

How many other women or men may have come to Quakerism for its historic and contemporary support for the equality of all persons is hard to judge. The Quaker stress on individual responsibility and individual faithfulness makes it a demanding religious path. Friends do not expect to become a mass movement in the foreseeable future. But Lianne's story is not unique. She joins a long parade of Quaker women who have acted on the basis of the Light, sure that more light will come. It is a strengthening and liberating belief. From Margaret Fell to Mary Fisher, May Dyer, Elizabeth Haddon, Susanna Morris, Charity Cook, Rebecca Jones, Angelina and Sara Grimké, Sarah Douglass, Abby Kelley Foster, Lucretia Mott, Elizabeth Comstock, Hannah Bean, Rhoda Coffin, Emma Malone, Susan B. Anthony, Ann Branson, Mary Meredith Hobbs, Sybil Jones, Hannah Whitall Smith, Alice Paul, Emily Greene Balch, Kay Camp, Elise Boulding, Kara Cole, and Mary Ann Beall, the parade continues, bringing to each generation the same message, that in Christ there is neither male nor female, and in souls there is no sex.

Quaker women were among those demonstrating for the ERA who chained themselves to the White House fence on August 26, 1981. Mary Ann Beall is on the left, Lenny Lianne on the right. Photo by Celia Barteau. Permission from Mary Ann Beall.

Michelle Avery, AFSC staff member and Quaker woman, at the Seneca, New York, nonviolent action in the summer of 1983. Permission from the AFSC Archives.

Bibliography

Manuscript Sources

Quaker Collection, Haverford College

Allinson, Martha Cooper. Extracts from journal. Allinson Family Papers.

Baltimore Yearly Meeting. Papers. Includes:
    Blackwater Monthly Meeting, Virginia. Minutes.
    Virginia Yearly Meeting. Women's Minutes, 1763–1825.
    Women's Association for Visiting the Penitentiary. Minutes.

Cresson, Sarah. Diary, 1771–1829.

Ellis, Margaret. Diary of Travels in the Ministry, 1739–55.

Fisher, Sarah Logan. Letterbook.

Haverford College. Minutes, Board of Managers, Vol. 1.

Hudson, Elizabeth. "An Abstract of the travels of Elizabeth Hudson," with some other remarks from 22nd of 1st month, 1743.

Jones, Rebecca. Letterbook, will.

Lindsey, Sarah. Notes accompanying her husband on religious visits, 1857–61.

London Yearly Meeting. Morning Meeting of Ministers, 1695; Minutes, 1784. Microfilm.

Maryland Half-Yearly Meeting of Women Friends. Microfilm.

"Ministering Friends of America Who Have Visited Foreign Parts in Truth's Service" [1685–1835].

Moore, Ann. Journal, 1756–78.

Morris, Margaret Hill. Journal, 1751–68.

New England Yearly Meeting. Women's Minutes. Microfilm. Collection includes:
    Dover Quarterly Meeting Women's Minutes. Microfilm.

Philadelphia Yearly Meeting. Women's Minutes, from 1681. Hicksite and Orthodox from 1827.
    Buckingham, Pa., Monthly Meeting. Women's Minutes. Microfilm.
    Chester, Pa., Monthly Meeting. Women's Minutes. Microfilm.
    Radnor Monthly Meeting. Women's Minutes. Microfilm.

Rhode Island Quarterly Meeting. Women's Minutes. Microfilm.

Sandwich Quarterly Meeting. Women's Minutes. Microfilm.

Scattergood, Rachel. Diary, 1840, 1850. Scattergood Family Papers.

Smith, Hannah Logan. Miscellaneous Papers.

Swett, Mary Howell. Diaries, 1797–99.

Whitall, Ann Cooper. Journal (typescript).

Wilbur, Julia. Journal.

Friends Historical Collection, Guilford College

North Carolina Yearly Meeting. Women's Minutes, 1812–63. Microfilm.

Friends Historical Library, Swarthmore

Cook, Margaret. Journal.

Emlen, Sarah Foulke Farquhar. Journal, 1811, 1845.

Goshen Monthly Meeting. Records of Birth and Deaths, William Wade Hinshaw Index.

Mott, Lucretia to Mary P. Allen, 6-5-1877. Mott Manuscript Collection.

Nantucket Monthly Meeting. Women's Minutes. Microfilm.

New York Yearly Meeting. Women's Minutes. Microfilm. Collection includes:

Flushing Yearly, Quarterly, and Monthly Minutes. Microfilm.

Westbury Monthly Meeting. Women's Minutes. Microfilm.

Historical Society of Pennsylvania

Mifflin, Anne Emlen. "Notes on the Bible and Religion," also "Notes on Religion." Pemberton Papers.

Philadelphia Female Anti-Slavery Society. Minutes (In Pennsylvania Abolition Society Papers).

Wistar, Mary Waln. Correspondence.

Westtown Treasure Room

Budd, Rebecca. Journal, 1799–1801.

Wilson, Mercy. Letters, 11-1844, 9-1846.

Unpublished Papers

Brady, Marilyn. " 'The Friendly Band': Quaker Women's Benevolence and the Poor in Late Eighteenth Century Philadelphia." Master's thesis, University of Oklahoma, May 1978.

Emlen, Sarah Foulke Farquhar. Unpublished typescript of her diaries in possession of the Emlen family and lent to the author courtesy of Robert and Cora Emlen.

Fry, Amelia R. "Alice Paul and the South." Paper delivered to the Southern Historical Association, Louisville, Ky., November 12, 1981.

————. "The Divine Discontent: Alice Paul and Militancy in the Suffrage Campaign," a paper delivered to the Fifth Berkshire Conference, Vassar College, June 16–18, 1981. Available through the Schlesinger Library, Radcliffe.

Hamm, Thomas, D. "The Holiness Movement and the Great Revival Among Orthodox Friends." Paper presented at the meeting of the Quaker Historians and Archivists, Moses Brown School, Providence, Rhode Island, 6-16-1984.

Jones, Barbara, "Deborah Logan." Master's thesis, University of Delaware, 1964.

Lynn, Susan. "Women, Reform, and Political Consciousness: The Young Women's Christian Association and the American Friends Service Committee, 1945–1960." Ph.D. diss., Stanford University, 1986.

Paul, Alice, and Amelia R. Fry. "Conversations with Alice Paul: Woman Suffrage and the Equal Rights Amendment." Transcript of a tape-recorded interview conducted by Amelia R. Fry. Berkeley, Calif.: Regional Oral History Office of the Bancroft Library, 1976.

Smedley, Katherine. "Martha Schofield."

Spann, Anna Louise. "The Ministry of Women in the Society of Friends." Ph.D. diss., University of Iowa, 1945.

Stoneburner, Carol, Charlotte Simkin Lewis, and Ruth Fulp "A Comparison of 85 Quaker Women and a Sample Group of Non-Quaker Women as Described in the *Dictionary of Notable American Women.*" Study prepared for symposium on "American Quaker Women as Shapers of Human Space," Guilford College, Greensboro, N.C., March 16, 17, 18, 1979.

Taber, William, Jr. "The History of Ohio Yearly Meeting, Conservative, from its Beginnings until 1947." Master's thesis, Earlham School of Religion, 1965.

Ullman, Claire Frances. "The Quaker Spirit and the Ethic of Feminism: The Influence of Quaker Religious Beliefs on the American Woman's Rights Movement, 1848–1860." Senior paper, Harvard, 1984.

Walker, Elizabeth. "Feminism and Contemporary Quaker Women." Senior paper, Hampshire College, 1975.

Wellman, Judy. "The Mystery of the Seneca Falls Women's Rights Convention: Who Came and Why?" Manuscript of a pamphlet to be published by the New York State Historical Commission.

Published Sources

Meeting Minutes, 1870–1930

Affiliation noted with Friends General Conference (Hicksite), FGC; Friends United Meeting (Orthodox), FUM; Conservative Friends Alliance, Conservative; and Evangelical Friends Alliance, EFA or Independent.

Baltimore Yearly Meeting, FGC; Baltimore Yearly Meeting, FUM; California Yearly Meeting, FUM; Canada Yearly Meeting, Conservative; Canada Yearly Meeting, FUM; Central Yearly Meeting, Independent; Epistle to Women Friends in Philadelphia, 1842; Genesee Yearly Meeting, FGC; Illinois Yearly Meeting, FGC; Indiana Yearly Meeting, FGC; Indiana Yearly Meeting, FUM; Iowa Yearly Meeting, Conservative; Kansas Yearly Meeting, EFA; Lake Erie Yearly Meeting, Independent; Missouri Valley Yearly Meeting, Independent; Nebraska Yearly Meeting, FUM; New England Yearly Meeting, Conservative; New York Yearly Meeting, FGC; New York Yearly Meeting, FUM; North Carolina Yearly Meeting, Conservative; North Carolina Yearly Meeting, FUM; Ohio Yearly Meeting, Conservative; Ohio Yearly Meeting, FGC; Ohio Yearly Meeting, EFA; Oregon Yearly Meeting, EFA; Philadelphia Yearly Meeting, FGC; Philadelphia Yearly Meeting, Orthodox; Western Yearly Meeting, Conservative; Western Yearly Meeting, FUM; Wilmington Yearly Meeting, FUM. Also printed Minutes, London Yearly Meeting of Women Friends, 1886–1907.

Quaker Records: Books of Discipline

Baltimore Yearly Meeting, 1982.
Iowa Yearly Meeting, 1932.
New York Yearly Meeting (Hicksite), 1830.
Philadelphia Yearly Meeting, 1972.

Quaker Records: Miscellaneous

London Yearly Meeting During 250 Years. London: Religious Society of Friends, 1919.

Proceedings of the Friends Conference in Richmond, Indiana, 1887. Stenographic Report, Richmond, 1887.

Testimonies to Deceased Ministers. Philadelphia: Philadelphia Yearly Meeting, 1787.

Biographies and Journals of Quaker Women

JANE ADDAMS

Addams, Jane. *The Second Twenty Years at Hull House*. New York: Macmillan, 1930.

Addams, Jane, Emily Greene Balch, and Alice Hamilton. *Women at the Hague*. New York: Macmillan, 1915.

Tims, Margaret. *Jane Addams of Hull House, 1860–1935, A Centenary Study*. New York: Macmillan, 1961.

SUSAN B. ANTHONY

Anthony, Katherine. *Susan B. Anthony: Her Personal History and Her Era*. New York: Doubleday, 1954.

DuBois, Ellen Carol, ed. *Elizabeth Cady Stanton, Susan B. Anthony: Correspondence, Writings, Speeches*. New York: Schocken Books, 1981.

EMILY GREENE BALCH

Randall, Mercedes M. *Improper Bostonian: Emily Greene Balch*. New York: Twayne Publishers, 1964.

JANE BILES

"Jane Biles." In *Quaker Biographical Sketches*, ed. Willard Heiss. Indianapolis: Willard Heiss, 1972.

ELIZABETH BOARDMAN

Boardman, Elizabeth. *The Phoenix Trip: Notes on a Quaker Mission to Haiphong*. Celo, N.C.: Celo Press, 1985.

LADY BORTON

Borton, Lady. *Sensing the Enemy: An American Woman Among the Boat People of Vietnam*. New York: Dial Press, 1984.

ANN BRANSON

Branson, Ann. *Journal of Ann Branson*. Philadelphia: W. H. Pile's Sons, 1892.

PATIENCE BRAYTON

A Short Account of the Life and Religious Labours of Patience Brayton. New York: I. Collins, 1837.

PRISCILLA CADWALLADER

Cadwallader, Priscilla. *Memoir of Priscilla Cadwallader*. Philadelphia: T. Elwood Zell, 1862.

ELIZABETH BUFFUM CHACE

Chace, Elizabeth Buffum. *Anti-Slavery Reminiscences*. Boston: Fremont and Sons, 1891.

Wyman, Elizabeth Chace. *Elizabeth Buffum Chace and Her Environment*. 2 Vols. Boston: W. B. Clarke, 1914.

LEA GORDON CHANCE

Chance, Lea Gordon. *Repentant Rebel*. New York: Vantage Press, 1969.

ELIZABETH MARGARET CHANDLER

Jones, Mary Patrick. "Elizabeth Margaret Chandler—Poet, Essayist, Abolitionist." Ph.D. diss., University of Toledo, 1981. Microfilm.

RHODA COFFIN

Johnson, Mary Coffin. *Rhoda M. Coffin: Her Reminiscences, Addresses, Papers, and Ancestry*. New York: Grafton Press, 1910.

ELIZABETH COLLINS

Collins, Elizabeth. *Memoir of Elizabeth Collins*. Philadelphia: Friends Bookstore, 1873.

ELIZABETH COMSTOCK

Hare, C. *Life and Letters of Elizabeth Comstock*. London: Headley Brothers, 1895.

CHARITY COOK

Newlin, Algie. *Charity Cook, A Liberated Woman*. Richmond, Ind.: Friends United Press, 1981.

PRUDENCE CRANDALL

Fuller, Edmund. *Prudence Crandall: An Incident of Racism in Nineteenth-Century Connecticut*. Middletown, Conn.: Wesleyan University Press, 1971.

ANNA DICKINSON

Giraud, Chester. *Embattled Maiden: The Life of Anna Dickinson*. New York: Putnam, 1951.

ANN DILWORTH

"Ann Dilworth." In *Quaker Biographical Sketches*, ed. Willard Heiss. Indianapolis: Willard Heiss, 1972.

ELIZABETH DRINKER

Biddle, Henry Drinker, ed. *Extracts From the Journal of Elizabeth Drinker, from 1757 to 1807*. Philadelphia: J. B. Lippincott, 1889.

MARGARET FELL

Ross, Isabel. *Margaret Fell: Mother of Quakerism*. London: Longman's, 1949.

HELEN FLEXNER

Flexner, Helen. *A Quaker Childhood*. New Haven, Conn.: Yale University Press, 1940.

MARY HALLOCK FOOTE

Paul, Rodman W., ed. *A Victorian Gentlewoman in the Far West: Reminiscences of Mary Hallock Foote*. San Marino, Calif.: Huntington Library, 1971.

ABBY KELLEY FOSTER

Bacon, Margaret Hope. *I Speak for My Slave Sister: The Life of Abby Kelley Foster*. New York: Thomas Y. Crowell, 1975.

ESTHER FRAME

Reminiscences of Nathan T. Frame and Esther G. Frame. Cleveland Ohio: Britton Printing Company, 1907.

ABBY HOPPER GIBBONS

Emerson, Sarah Hopper. *Life of Abby Hopper Gibbons*. 2 Vols. New York: G. P. Putnam, 1897.

ANGELINA AND SARAH GRIMKÉ

Lerner, Gerda. *The Grimké Sisters from South Carolina: Pioneers for Women's Rights and Abolition*. New York: Schocken Books, 1971.

ELIZA GURNEY

Mott, Richard F. *Memoir and Correspondence of Eliza P. Gurney*. Philadelphia: J. B. Lippincott, 1884.

CORNELIA HANCOCK

Cornelia Hancock. *Record of Wrightsville: An Experiment in the Care of Property*. Philadelphia, 1889.

Jacquette, Henrietta, ed. *South After Gettysburg: The Story of a Civil War Nurse*. New York: Thomas Y. Crowell, 1937.

LAURA S. HAVILAND

Haviland, Laura S. *A Woman's Life-Work; including thirty years' service on the underground railroad and in the war* . . . Cincinnati: Walden & Stowe, 1881.

RACHEL HICKS

Hicks, Rachel. *Memoir of Rachel Hicks*. New York: G. P. Putnam, 1880.

ELIZABETH HOOTEN

Manners, Emily. *Elizabeth Hooton: First Quaker Woman Preacher, 1600–1672*. London: Headley Brothers, 1914.

JANE HOSKENS

"Life of Jane Hoskens." In *Friends Library*, 1:463. Philadelphia, 1837.

EMILY HOWLAND

Breault, Judith C. *The World of Emily Howland: Odyssey of a Humanitarian*. Millbrae, Calif.: Les Femmes, 1976.

SARAH HUNT
Hunt, Sarah. *Journal of Life and Religious Labors of Sarah Hunt.* Philadelphia: Friends Book Association, 1892.

HELEN HUNT JACKSON
Odell, Ruth. *Helen Hunt Jackson.* New York: Appleton Century, 1939.

REBECCA JONES
Allinson, William J. *Memorial of Rebecca Jones.* Philadelphia: H. Longstreth, 1849.

SYBIL JONES
Jones, Rufus M. *Eli and Sybil Jones: Their Life and Work.* Philadelphia: Henry T. Coates, 1889.

FLORENCE KELLEY
Goldmark, Josephine. *Impatient Crusader: Florence Kelley's Life Story.* Urbana, Ill.: University of Illinois Press, 1953.

GRACEANNA LEWIS
Warner, Deborah Jean. *Graceanna Lewis, Scientist and Humanitarian.* Washington, D.C.: National Museum of History and Technology, 1979.

REBECCA LUKENS
Wolcott, Robert W. *A Woman in Steel—Rebecca Lukens.* Princeton, N.J.: Princeton University Press, 1940.

EMMA MALONE
Osborne, Bryon L. *The Malone Story.* Canton, Oh.: Malone College, 1970.

MARIA MITCHELL
Wright, Helen. *Sweeper in the Sky: The Story of Maria Mitchell.* New York: Macmillan, 1949.

MARGARET MORRIS
Jackson, John W. *Margaret Morris: Her Journal with Biographical Sketch and Notes.* Philadelphia: George MacManus, 1949.

LUCRETIA MOTT
Bacon, Margaret Hope. *Valiant Friend: The Life of Lucretia Mott.* New York: Walker, 1980.

Greene, Dana. *Lucretia Mott: Her Complete Speeches and Sermons.* Lewiston, N.Y.: Edwin Mellen Press, 1980.

ALICE PAUL
Irwin, Inez Hayes. *The Story of Alice Paul and the National Woman's Party.* Fairfax, Va.: Denlinger's Publishers, 1977.

HANNAH PENN
Drinker, Sophia H. *Hannah Penn and the Proprietorship of Pennsylvania.* Philadelphia: Society of Colonial Dames, 1958.

CATHERINE PHILLIPS

Phillips, Catherine. *Memoirs of the Life of Catherine Phillips.* London: J. Phillips and Son, 1797.

LYDIA PINKHAM

Stage, Sarah. *Female Complaints: Lydia Pinkham and the Business of Women's Medicine.* New York: W. W. Norton, 1979.

RACHEL PRICE

Price, Philip. *Memoir of Philip and Rachel Price.* Philadelphia: Phillip E. Price, 1852.

JANE RUSHMORE

Johnson, Emily Cooper. *Under Quaker Appointment: The Life of Jane Rushmore.* Philadelphia: University of Pennsylvania Press, 1953.

FLORENCE SANVILLE

Sanville, Florence. *The Opening Door.* Philadelphia: Franklin Publishing Company, 1967.

HANNAH WHITALL SMITH

Smith, Hannah Whitall. *The Open Secret.* Chicago: Revell, 1885.

Strachey, Barbara. *Remarkable Relations: The Story of the Pearsall Smith Women.* New York: Universe Books, 1982.

Strachey, Ray, ed. *Religious Fanaticism: Extracts from the Papers of Hannah Whitall Smith.* London: Faber & Gwyer, 1976.

M. CAREY THOMAS

Dobkin, Marjorie Housepan. *The Making of a Feminist: Early Journals and Letters.* Kent, Oh.: Kent State University Press, 1969.

ANN WARDER

Cadbury, Sarah, ed. "Extracts from the Diary of Ann Warder." *Pennsylvania Magazine of History and Biography* 17 (January 1894): 444–61; 18 (April 1894): 51–63.

ELIZABETH WEBB

"A Letter from Elizabeth Webb to Anthony William Boehm." In *Friends Library,* ed. William Evans and Thomas Evans, 13:163. Philadelphia: Joseph Rakestraw, 1837.

Women's History

Alsop, Gulielma Fell. *The History of the Woman's Medical College.* Philadelphia: J. B. Lippincott, 1950.

Altschuler, Glenn C., and Jan M. Saltzgaber. *Revivalism, Social Conscience, and Community in the Burned-Over District: The Trial of Rhoda Bement.* Ithaca, N.Y.: Cornell University Press, 1983.

Bacon, Margaret Hope. *As the Way Opens: The Story of Quaker Women in America*. Richmond, Ind.: Friends United Press, 1980.

———. "A Widening Path: Women in the Philadelphia Yearly Meeting Move Toward Equality, 1681–1929." In *Friends in the Delaware Valley*, ed. John M. Moore. Philadelphia: Friends Historical Association, 1981.

Banks, Olive. *Faces of Feminism: A Study of Feminism as a Social Movement*. Oxford: Martin Robertson, 1981.

Berg, Barbara. *The Remembered Gate: Origins of American Feminism*. New York: Oxford University Press, 1978.

Berkin, Carol Ruth, and Mary Beth Norton. *Women of America: A History*. Boston: Houghton Mifflin, 1979.

Brailsford, Mabel. *Quaker Women*. London: Duckworth, 1915.

Cadbury, Henry J. "George Fox and Women's Liberation." *Friends Quarterly* 18 (Autumn 1974): 370–76.

Calvo, Janis. "Quaker Women Ministers in Nineteenth-Century America." *Quaker History* 63 (1974): 75–93.

Chambers-Schiller, Lee Virginia. *Liberty, A Better Husband: Single Women in America*. New Haven, Conn.: Yale University Press, 1984.

Clarke, A. Chambers. *Seedbed of Reform: American Social Service and Political Action, 1918–1933*. Minneapolis: University of Minnesota Press, 1963.

Dunn, Mary Maples. "Saints and Sisters." In *Women in American Religion*. ed. Janet Wilson James. Philadelphia: University of Pennsylvania Press, 1980.

———. "Women of Light." In Berkin and Norton, *Women of America: A History*.

Epstein, Dena. "Lucy McKim Garrison: American Musician." *Bulletin of the New York Public Library* 67 (October 1963): 529–46.

Evans, Elizabeth. *Weathering the Storm*. New York: Scribners, 1975.

Flexner, Eleanor. *Century of Struggle: The Woman's Rights Movement in the United States*. Cambridge, Mass.: Belknap Press, 1959.

Freedman, Estelle B. *Their Sisters' Keepers: Women's Prison Reform in America, 1830–1910*. Ann Arbor: University of Michigan Press, 1981.

Fry, Amelia. "Alice Paul and the Divine Discontent." In *Women in New Jersey History*. ed. Mary R. Murrin. Trenton, N.J.: New Jersey Historical Commission, 1985.

Gadt, Jeannette Carter. "Women and Protestant Culture: The Quaker Dissent from Puritanism." Ph.D. diss., University of California at Los Angeles, 1974. Microfilm.

Hadley, Freda, and Naomi Pyle. *U. S. F. W.—Growth Unlimited: The Story of the United Society of Friends Women, 1890–1960.* Richmond, Ind.: United Society of Friends Women, 1960.

Hanaford, Phebe A. *Daughters of America, or The Women of the Century.* Augusta, Maine: True and Company, 1883.

Hardesty, Nancy. *Women Called to Witness: Evangelical Feminism in the Nineteenth Century.* Nashville, Tenn.: Abingdon Press, 1984.

Harris, Dorothy. "Baltimore to Waynesville in 1805; Extracts from the Memoirs of Rebecca Wright Hill." *Bulletin of the Friends Historical Association* 40 (Spring 1951): 24–33.

Hersh, Blanche Glassman. *The Slavery of Sex: Feminist-Abolitionists in America.* Urbana, Ill.: University of Illinois Press, 1978.

Hewitt, Nancy A. *Women's Activism and Social Change, Rochester, New York, 1822–1872.* Ithaca, N.Y.: Cornell University Press, 1984.

Holmes, Kenneth L., ed. *Covered Wagon Women.* Glendale, Calif.: Arthur H. Clark, 1983.

Howard, Elizabeth Fox. *Women in the Church and in Life.* Malten, England: E. E. Taylor. 1911.

Irwin, Inez Hayes. *The Story of Alice Paul and the National Woman's Party.* Fairfax, Va.: Delinger's Publishers, 1977.

Irwin, Joyce. *Womanhood in Radical Protestantism, 1525–1676.* New York: Edwin Mellen Press, 1979.

James, Janet Wilson, ed. *Women in American Religion.* Philadelphia: University of Pennsylvania Press, 1980.

Katzenstein, Caroline. *Lifting the Curtain: The State and National Woman Suffrage Campaigns As I Saw Them.* Philadelphia: Dorrance, 1955.

Kerber, Linda. *Women of the Republic: Intellect and Ideology in Revolutionary America.* Chapel Hill, N.C.: University of North Carolina Press, 1980.

King, Ursula. *Voices of Protest; Voices of Promise: Exploring Spirituality in a New Age.* London: Hibbert Trust, 1984.

Kraditor, Aileen. *Ideas of the Woman Suffrage Movement, 1890–1920.* New York: Columbia University Press, 1965.

———. *Means and Ends in American Abolitionism.* New York: Vintage Press, 1967.

Lakey, George. "Technique and Ethos in Nonviolent Action: The Woman Suffrage Case." *Sociological Inquiry* 38 (Winter 1968): 37–42.

Leach, Robert. *Women Ministers: A Quaker Contribution.* Wallingford, Pa.: Pendle Hill, 1979.

Mack, Phyllis. "Women As Prophets During the English Civil War." *Feminist Studies* 8 (Spring 1982): 19–45.

McLaughlin, Eleanor, and Rosemary Ruether. *Women of Spirit: Female Leadership in Jewish and Christian Traditions.* New York: Simon & Schuster, 1979.

Melder, Keith E. *Beginnings of Sisterhood: The American Woman's Rights Movement, 1800–1850.* New York: Schocken Books, 1977.

Mott, Lucretia. *Discourse on Women.* Philadelphia: Merrihew & Thompson, 1849.

Norton, Mary Beth, and Carol Berkin. *Women of America, A History.* Boston: Houghton Mifflin, 1979.

Noun, Louise R. *Strong-Minded Women: The Emergence of the Woman Suffrage Movement in Iowa.* Ames, Iowa: Iowa State University Press, 1969.

O'Neill, William. *Everyone Was Brave: The Rise and Fall of Feminism in America.* Chicago: Quadrangle Books, 1969.

Ruether, Rosemary Radford, and Rosemary Keller. *Women and Religion in America.* Vol. 1, *The Nineteenth Century: A Documentary History.* San Francisco: Harper & Row, 1981.

Scott, Ann. *Making the Invisible Woman Visible.* Urbana, Ill.: University of Illinois Press, 1984.

Smith, Hulda. *Reason's Disciples.* Urbana, Ill.: University of Illinois Press, 1982.

Smith-Rosenberg, Carroll. *Disorderly Conduct: Vision of Gender in Victorian America.* New York: Alfred A. Knopf, 1985.

Stanton, Elizabeth, Susan B. Anthony, and Matilda Joslyn Gage. *History of Woman Suffrage.* New York: Fowler, 1881.

Woody, Thomas. *A History of Women's Education in the United States.* New York and Lancaster, Pa.: Science Press, 1929.

Quaker History

Baltzell, E. Digby. *Puritan Boston and Quaker Philadelphia.* New York: Free Press, 1979.

Barbour, Hugh. *The Quakers in Puritan England.* New Haven, Conn.: Yale University Press, 1964.

Barclay, Robert. *An Apology for the True Christian Divinity, As the Same is Held Forth and Preached by the People, called Quakers.* Manchester, England, 1869.

Beamish, Lucia Katherine. *Quaker Ministry, 1691–1834.* Oxford, England, circa 1967.

Benjamin, Philip. *The Philadelphia Quakers in the Industrial Age, 1865–1920.* Philadelphia: Temple University Press, 1976.

Besse, Joseph. *An Abstract of the Sufferings of the People Called Quakers.* London: J. Soule, 1733.

Boulding, Kenneth. *The Evolutionary Potential of Quakerism.* Wallingford, Pa.: Pendle Hill, 1964.

Bradley, A. Day. "Progressive Friends in Michigan and New York." *Quaker History* 52 (1963): 95–103.

Braithwaite, William. *Second Period of Quakerism.* New York: Macmillan, 1919.

Brinton, Howard. *Quaker Education in Theory and Practice.* Wallingford, Pa.: Pendle Hill Pamphlets, No. 9, 1940.

Bronner, Edwin R. "An Early Example of Political Action by Women." *Bulletin of the Friends Historical Association* 43 (1954): 29–32.

Brookes, George S. *Friend Anthony Benezet.* Philadelphia: University of Pennsylvania Press, 1937.

Cadbury, Henry J. *Friendly Heritage: Letters from the Quaker Past.* Norwalk, Conn.: Silvermine Publishers, 1972.

Cox, John, Jr. *Quakerism in the City of New York, 1657–1930.* New York, 1930.

DiStefano, Judy Mann. "A Concept of the Family in Colonial America: The Pembertons of Philadelphia." Ph.D. diss., Ohio State University, 1970. Microfilm.

Duane, William, ed. *Extracts from the Diary of Christopher Marshall.* Albany, N.Y.: J. Munsell, 1877.

Dymond, Jonathon. *Essays on the Principles of Morality.* New York: Harper & Brothers, 1834.

Elliott, Errol T. *Quakers on the American Frontier.* Richmond, Ind.: Friends United Press, 1969.

Fox, George, *Works.* Philadelphia: Marcus Gould; New York: Isaac Hopper, 1831.

Frost, J. William. *The Quaker Family in Colonial America.* New York: St. Martins Press, 1973.

Grubb, Isabel. *Quakers in Ireland, 1654–1900.* London: Swarthmore, 1927.

Gummere, Amelia Mott. *The Quaker, A Study in Costume.* Philadelphia: Ferris & Leach, 1901.

Gurney, Joseph John. *Observations on the Distinguishing Views and Practices of Friends.* London: J. and A. Arch, 1834.

Harrison, Eliza Cope, ed. *Philadelphia Merchant: The Diary of Thomas Pym Cope, 1800–1851.* South Bend, Ind.: Gateway Editions, 1980.

Hill, Christopher. *The World Turned Upside Down.* New York: Viking, 1972.

Hill, Richard. *Letters of Doctor Richard Hill and his Children.* Philadelphia. John J. Smith, 1854.

The History of Pennsylvania Hall which was Burned by a Mob on the 17th of May. Philadelphia: Merrihew and Gunn, 1838.

Hole, Helen. *All Things Civil and Useful.* Richmond, Ind.: Friends United Press, 1980.

———. *Westtown Through the Years.* Westtown, Pa.: Western Alumni Association, 1942.

Jones, Mary Hoxie. *Swords into Plowshares.* New York: Macmillan, 1937.

Jones, Rufus M. *A Service of Love in Wartime.* New York: Macmillan, 1920.

Kennedy, Thomas C. "Southland College: The Society of Friends and Black Education in Arkansas." *Arkansas Historical Quarterly* 42 (Summer 1983): 207–13.

Klain, Zora. *Educational Activities of New England Quakers.* Philadelphia: Westbrook Publishers, 1928.

———. *Quaker Contributions to Education in North Carolina.* Philadelphia: Westbrook Publishers, 1925.

Levick, James. "Emigration of Early Welsh Quakers to Pennsylvania." *Pennsylvania Magazine of History and Biography* 17 (1893): 404.

Lloyd, Arnold. *Quaker Social History, 1669–1738.* London: Longmans, Green & Co., 1950.

McDaniel, Ethel Hittle. *The Contribution of the Society of Friends to Education in Indiana.* Indianapolis: Indiana Historical Society, 1939.

Marietta, Jack D. *The Reformation of American Quakerism, 1748–1783.* Philadelphia: University of Pennsylvania Press, 1984.

Moulton, Philip, ed. *Journal and Major Essays of John Woolman.* New York: Oxford University Press, 1971.

Myers, Albert. *Hannah Logan's Courtship.* Philadelphia: Ferris & Leach, 1904.

Nickalls, John L., ed. *Journal of George Fox.* London: Religious Society of Friends, 1975.

Norton, John. *The Heart of New England Rent.* London: J. H. for J. Allen, 1660.

Nuremberger, Ruth. *The Free Produce Movement.* Durham, N.C.: Durham University, 1942.

Nuttall, Geoffrey F. *The Holy Spirit in Puritan Faith and Experience.* Oxford: B. Blackwell, 1946.

Osborne, Bryan L. *The Malone Story: The Dream of Two Quaker Young People.* Canton, Ohio: Malone College, 1970.

Penn, William. *Just Measures*. London: Thomas Northcott, 1692.

Pickett, Clarence E. *For More Than Bread*. Boston: Little, Brown and Company, 1953.

Sharpless, Isaac. *The Story of a Small College*. Philadelphia: John C. Winston, 1918.

Swift, David E. *Joseph John Gurney, Banker, Reformer and Quaker*. Middletown, Conn.: Wesleyan University Press, 1962.

Taber, William, Jr. *Be Gentle, Be Plain: The History of Olney*. Celo, N.C.: Celo Press, 1976.

Taylor, Ernest. *The Valiant Sixty*. London: Bannisdale Press, 1951.

Teeters, Negley K. *They Were in Prison: A History of the Pennsylvania Prison Society, 1787–1937*. Philadelphia: John C. Winston, 1937.

Thomas, Allen C. "Congregational or Progressive Friends: A Forgotten Episode in Quaker History." *Bulletin of Friends Historical Association* 10 (1920): 21–32.

Thomas, K. V. "Women and the Civil War Sects." *Past and Present* 13 (1958), pp. 42–62.

Thornburg, Opal. *Earlham: The Story of the College, 1847–1947*. Richmond, Ind.: Earlham College Press, 1963.

Thorne, Dorothy Gilbert. *Guilford, A Quaker College*. Greensboro, N.C.: Guilford College, 1937.

Wahl, Albert. "Progressive Friends of Longwood." *Bulletin of Friends Historical Association* 19 (1953): 11–33.

Walzer, Michael. *The Revolution of the Saints*. Cambridge: Harvard University Press, 1965.

Weeks, Stephen. *Southern Quakers and Slavery: A Study in Institutional History*. Baltimore: Johns Hopkins Press, 1896.

Wells, Robert. *A Demographic Analysis of Some Middle Colonies' Quaker Families in the 18th Century*. Ph.D. diss., Princeton, 1969. Microfilm.

———. "Quaker Marriage Patterns in a Colonial Perspective." *William and Mary Quarterly* 29 (1972): 415–41.

Willauer, G. F., Jr. "First Publishers of Truth in New England, a Composite List, 1656–1775." *Quaker History* 65 (Spring 1976): 35–44.

Woody, Thomas. *Early Quaker Education in Pennsylvania*. New York: Arno Press, 1969.

———. *Quaker Education in the State of New Jersey*. Philadelphia: University of Pennsylvania Press, 1923.

Worrall, Arthur J. *Quakers in the Colonial Northeast*. Hanover, N.H.: University Press of New England, 1980.

Wright, Louis. *Middle-Class Culture in Elizabethan England*. Chapel Hill, N.C.: University of North Carolina Press, 1935.

Zuckerman, Michael, ed. *Friends and Neighbors: Group Life in America's First Plural Society*. Philadelphia: Temple University Press, 1982.

Notes

Introduction

1. Estelle B. Freedman, *Their Sisters' Keepers: Women's Prison Reform in America, 1830–1910* (Ann Arbor, Mich.: University of Michigan Press, 1981), p. 24; Mary M. Dunn, "Women of Light," in *Women of America*, ed. Carol Berkin and Mary Norton (Boston: Houghton Mifflin, 1979), p. 132. See also Blanche G. Hersh, *The Slavery of Sex: Feminist-Abolitionists of America* (Urbana, Ill.: University of Illinois Press, 1978), for the role of Quakers in the development of the women's rights movement.
2. William Penn, a seventeenth-century British Quaker who founded the colony of Pennsylvania, wrote in *Fruits of Solitude* (London: Northcott, 1693), "Sexes made no Difference; since in Souls there is none: and they are the Subjects of Friendship" (p. 33).
3. Grace Malley to author, 8-22-1984.

Chapter 1

1. William Gouge, *Of Domesticall Duties* (London, 1622), quoted in Jeannette Carter Gadt, "Women and Protestant Culture" (Ph.D. diss., University of California, 1974), p. 32.
2. Geoffrey F. Nuttall, *The Holy Spirit in Puritan Faith and Experience* (Oxford: B. Blackwell, 1946), p. 87.
3. William Penn, preface to the original edition, *The Journal of George Fox*, ed. John L. Nickalls (London: London Yearly Meeting, 1975), p. xxxix.
4. Nickalls, *Journal of George Fox*, p. 673.
5. Ibid., p. 11.
6. Ibid., p. 24.
7. George Fox, "An Encouragement to All Faithful Women's Meetings" (letter 320), in *The Works of George Fox* (Philadelphia: Marcus Gould; New York: Isaac Hopper, 1831), 8:92–97.
8. Penn, preface to Fox's journal, p. xliv.
9. Isabel Ross, *Margaret Fell, Mother of Quakerism* (London: Longman's, 1949), p. 11.
10. Ibid., p. 200.
11. Fox's journal, p. 557.
12. Joseph Besse, *An Abstract of the Sufferings of the People Called Quakers* (London: J. Soule, 1733), vol. 1, sec. 5, p. 136.
13. Phyllis Mack, "Women as Prophets During the English Civil War," *Feminist Studies* 8 (Spring 1982): 19–45.
14. Fox, letter 313, in *Works*, p. 76. For a better version, see Fox's letter of 1-30-1675, in *Kendal Early Records Book*, p. 59, as quoted in William C. Braithwaite's *Second Period of Quakerism* (New York and London: Macmillan, 1919), p. 274.

15. Fox, letter 320, *Works*, p. 93.
16. Ibid., p. 115.

Chapter 2

1. Percentage of women in New England churches from Gerald F. Moran, " 'Sisters' in Christ," in *Women in American Religion*, ed. Janet Wilson James (Philadelphia: University of Pennsylvania Press, 1980), p. 48.
2. Charles F. Adams, ed., *Antinomianism in the Colony of Massachusetts Bay, 1636–38* (Boston: Prince Society, 1894), p. 329, quoted in Gadt, "Women and Protestant Culture," p. 77.
3. Emily Manners, ed., *Elizabeth Hooten: First Quaker Woman Preacher* (London: Headley Brothers, 1914), p. 32.
4. Gadt, "Women and Protestant Culture," p. 147. For a full exposition on this subject, see chap. 3, "Attitudes Toward Women in the New World: The Opposites of Quaker and Puritan."
5. Linda Ford, "William Penn's Views on Women: Subjects of Friendship," *Quaker History* 72 (Fall 1983): 94; also A. Ruth Fry, *Quaker Ways* (London: Cassell and Company, 1933), p. 69.
6. G. J. Willaurer, Jr., "First Publishers of Truth in New England: A Composite List, 1656–1775, *Quaker History* 65 (Spring 1976): 39–44.
7. Quoted in Mabel Brailsford, *Quaker Women* (London: Duckworth, 1915), p. 147.
8. *Memoirs of the Life of Catherine Phillips* (London: J. Phillips & Son, 1797), pp. 109–10.
9. "Life of Jane Hoskens," in *Friends' Library* (Philadelphia: Rakestraw, 1837), 1:463.
10. "A Letter from Elizabeth Webb to Anthony William Boehm," in *Friends' Library* (1849), 13:163.
11. Goshen Monthly Meeting records note the birth of Peter, son of Margaret and Nathan on 1-26-1753, "at the dwelling of Robert Pilus in the County of Gloucester near the city of Bristol in Great Britain as certified by Sarah Cunningham and six other women." Abstracts of Goshen Monthly Meeting Records, William Wade Hinshaw Index, Friends Historical Library (hereafter FHL), Swarthmore College. A passage in the journal of Margaret Ellis, Margaret Lewis's traveling companion, notes: "On the 20th (of 11 month) we came to Bristol and lodged at our Friend Richard Champions and stayed there about four months." Journal of Margaret Ellis, Quaker Collection, Haverford College Library (hereafter QC), p. 32.
12. Algie I. Newlin, *Charity Cook: A Liberated Woman* (Richmond, Ind.: Friends United Press, 1981), p. 47.
13. "The Life of Patience Brayton," in *Friends' Library* (1845), 10: p. 441–80.
14. "Ann Dilworth," *Quaker Biographical Sketches*, ed. Willard Heiss (Indianapolis, 1972), p. 45.
15. Diaries of Mary Howell Swett, 1797–99, entry for 10-13-1798, QC.
16. An Abstract of the Travels, with Some Other Remarks of Elizabeth Hudson, from 22nd of 1st mo. 1743, entry ca. 1746, QC.
17. "Memorial of Jane Biles," *Quaker Biographical Sketches*, p. 53.

18. Elizabeth Hudson, ca. 1747.
19. Minutes, London Yearly Meeting, 1784, microfilm, QC.
20. Israel Pemberton to "Esteemed Friend," Pemberton Papers, Historical Society of Pennsylvania (hereafter HSP), vol. 11, pp. 25–26.

Chapter 3

1. Minutes, Radnor Monthly Meeting for Women, microfilm, QC.
2. Minutes, Blackwater Monthly Meeting, Baltimore Yearly Meeting Papers, QC; Algie Newlin, *Charity Cook*, p. 26.
3. Radnor Minutes, QC.
4. Minutes, Rhode Island Quarterly Meeting of Women Friends, 4-17-1775, East Greenwich, Rhode Island, microfilm, QC.
5. Minutes, Maryland Half-Yearly Meeting of Women Friends, 6-1678, microfilm, QC.
6. Minutes, Flushing Yearly, Quarterly, and Monthly Meetings of Women Friends, 1729–52, microfilm, FHL.
7. William Penn, *Just Measures* (London: Northcott, 1692), p. 8.
8. Edwin R. Bronner, "An Early Example of Political Action by Women," *Quaker History* 43 (Spring 1954): 29–32.
9. Minutes, Philadelphia Yearly Meeting of Women Friends, 1766, QC.
10. Ibid., 1803.

Chapter 4

1. John Bevan, "John Bevan's Narrative," in James Levick, "Emigration of the Early Welsh Quakers to Pennsylvania," *Pennsylvania Magazine of History and Biography* 17 (1893): 404.
2. Philip Moulton, ed., *Journal and Major Essays of John Woolman* (Oxford: Oxford University Press, 1971), p. 25.
3. Albert Myers, ed., *Hannah Logan's Courtship* (Philadelphia: Ferris & Leach, 1904), p. 161; Richard Hill, *Letters of Doctor Richard Hill and His Children* (Philadelphia: John J. Smith, 1854), p. 156.
4. Robert Wells, "Quaker Marriage Patterns in a Colonial Perspective," *William and Mary Quarterly* 29 (1972): 415–42.
5. Ibid.
6. Mary Pemberton to James Pemberton, December 12, 1748, Pemberton Papers, HSP, 6:178.
7. John W. Jackson, ed., *Margaret Morris: Her Journal, with Biographical Sketch and Notes* (Philadelphia: George MacManus, 1949), p. 31.
8. Elizabeth Collins, *Memoirs* (Philadelphia: Friends Bookstore, 1873), p. 39.
9. Extracts from the Journal of Martha Cooper Allinson, Allinson Papers, QC.
10. Wells, "Quaker Marriage Patterns," p. 426; Philip S. Benjamin, *The Philadelphia Quakers in the Industrial Age, 1865–1920* (Philadelphia: Temple University Press, 1976), p. 159.
11. J. William Frost, *The Quaker Family in Colonial America* (New York: St. Martin's Press, 1973), pp. 98–99.

12. Myers, *Hannah Logan's Courtship*, p. 8.
13. Elizabeth Hudson, ca. 1744.
14. Elizabeth Estaugh, "Testimony to the Memory of Her Beloved Husband, John Estaugh, Deceased," in *Testimonies to Deceased Ministers, Philadelphia Yearly Meeting* (1787), p. 119.
15. Sophia H. Drinker, *Hannah Penn and the Proprietorship of Pennsylvania* (Philadelphia: Society of Colonial Dames, 1958).
16. Journal of Ann Cooper Whitall, 1760–62, QC.
17. William Duane, ed., *Extracts from the Diary of Christopher Marshall* (Albany, 1877), pp. 157–58.

Chapter 5

1. Sarah Cadbury, ed., "Extracts from the Diary of Ann Warder," *Pennsylvania Magazine of History and Biography* 18 (April 1894): 51.
2. Letterbook of Sarah Logan Fisher, QC.
3. Anne Emlen Mifflin, "Notes on Religion," Historical Society of Pennsylvania.
4. Henry Drinker Biddle, ed., *Extracts from the Journal of Elizabeth Drinker* (Philadelphia, 1889), pp. 93–100.
5. Ibid., p. 409.
6. Whitall journal, QC.
7. Minutes, Blackwater Monthly Meeting, 5-17-1793, QC.
8. Marilyn Dell Brady "The Friendly Band: Quaker Women's Benevolence and the Poor in Late Eighteenth Century Philadelphia" (Master's thesis, University of Oklahoma, 1978).
9. John Cox, *Quakerism in the City of New York* (New York, 1930), pp. 176–77.
10. For an interesting discussion of the significance of the Quaker move into philanthropy see Mary Maples Dunn, "Women of Light," in *Women of America,* ed. Carol Ruth Berkin and Mary Beth Norton (Boston: Houghton Mifflin, 1979), pp. 131–33.
11. Helen C. Hole, *Westtown Through the Years* (Westtown, Pa., 1932), p. 161.
12. Margaret Bacon, *Valiant Friend: The Life of Lucretia Mott* (New York: Walker, 1980), p. 26.
13. Jonathon Dymond, *Essays on the Principles of Morality* (New York: Collins & Brother, c. 1825), pp. 251–52.
14. William J. Allinson, comp., *Memorial of Rebecca Jones* (Philadelphia: H. Longstreth, 1849), pp. 231–32.
15. Ibid., p. 296.

Chapter 6

1. Dorothy Harris, ed., "Baltimore to Waynesville in 1805: Extracts from the Memoirs of Rebecca Wright Hill," *Quaker History* 40 (Spring 1951): 24–33.
2. Journal of Sarah Foulke Farquhar Emlen. Typescript in the possession of the Emlen family.

3. "Letters from a Quaker Woman," in *Covered Wagon Women*, ed. Kenneth L. Homes (Glendale, Calif.: Arthur H. Clark Co., 1983).
4. Ethel Hittle McDaniel, *The Contribution of the Society of Friends to Education in Indiana* (Indianapolis: Indiana Historical Society, 1939), p. 20.
5. Howard Brinton, *Quaker Education in Theory and Practice* (Wallingford, Pa.: Pendle Hill, 1967), pp. 31–40.
6. McDaniel, *Contribution of the Society of Friends*, p. 38.
7. Margaret Hope Bacon, "A Widening Path: Women in Philadelphia Yearly Meeting Move Toward Equality, 1681–1929," in *Friends in the Delaware Valley*, ed. John M. Moore (Philadelphia: Friends Historical Association, 1981), p. 185.
8. Lucretia Mott to Mary P. Allen, 6-5-1877, FHL, Swarthmore.
9. Joseph John Gurney, *Observations on the Distinguishing Views and Practices of Friends*, rev. ed. (London: J. and A. Arch, 1834), pp. 277–78.
10. David Swift, *Joseph John Gurney, Banker, Reformer, and Quaker* (Middletown, Conn.: Wesleyan University Press, 1962), pp. 209–10.
11. Isaac Sharpless, *The Story of A Small College* (Philadelphia: John C. Winston, 1918), pp. 38–39; minutes of the Board of Managers of Haverford College, vol. 1, QC.
12. Minutes, Board of Managers, Haverford College, 5-30-1870, QC.
13. Dorothy Gilbert Thorne, *Guilford, A Quaker College* (Greensboro, N.C.: Guilford College, 1937).
14. Opal Thornburg, *Earlham, the Story of the College, 1847–1947* (Richmond, Ind.: Earlham College Press, 1947).

Chapter 7

1. Ruth Nuermberger, *The Free Produce Movement* (Durham, N.C.: Durham University Press, 1942), p. 6.
2. Mary Patrick Jones, *Elizabeth Margaret Chandler—Poet, Essayist, Abolitionist* (Ph.d. thesis, University of Toledo, 1981), p. 2.
3. Bacon, *Valiant Friend*, p. 38.
4. Keith E. Melder, *Beginnings of Sisterhood: The American Woman's Rights Movement, 1800–1850* (New York: Schocken Books, 1977), pp. 59–60.
5. Ibid., p. 64.
6. Minutes, Philadelphia Female Antislavery Society, HSP.
7. Gerda Lerner, *The Grimké Sisters From South Carolina: Pioneers for Woman's Rights and Abolition* (New York: Schocken Books, 1971), p. 192.
8. Ibid., p. 246.
9. *The History of Pennsylvania Hall Which Was Burned by a Mob on the 17th of May* (Philadelphia: Merrihew and Gunn, 1838).
10. Elisabeth Griffith, *In Her Own Right: The Life of Elizabeth Cady Stanton* (Oxford: Oxford University Press, 1984), p. 38.
11. Glen C. Altschuler and Jan M. Saltzgaber, *Revivalism, Social Conscience, and Community in the Burned-Over District: The Trial of Rhoda Bement* (Ithaca, N.Y.: Cornell University Press, 1983).
12. Aileen S. Kraditor, *Means and Ends in American Abolitionism* (New York: Vintage, 1967), p. 87.

13. Eliza Cope Harrison, ed., *Philadelphia Merchant: The Diary of Thomas Pym Cope, 1800–1851* (South Bend, Ind.: Gateway Editions, 1978), p. 602.
14. Lucretia Mott, *Discourse on Women* (Philadelphia: T. B. Peterson, 1850).
15. Dana Greene, ed., *Lucretia Mott: Her Complete Speeches and Sermons* (New York: Edwin Mellen Press, 1980), p. 218.
16. Susan B. Anthony Papers, Radcliffe College, as quoted in Hersh, *The Slavery of Sex*, p. 146.
17. Elizabeth Cady Stanton, *Eighty Years and More: Reminiscences, 1815–1897* (New York: Schocken Books, 1971), p. 161; Hersh, *Slavery of Sex*, p. 137.

Chapter 8

1. Margaret H. Bacon, *I Speak for My Slave Sister: The Life of Abby Kelley Foster* (New York: Thomas Y. Crowell, 1974), p. 194.
2. Laura Haviland, *A Woman's Life-Work: Labors and Experiences* (Cincinnati: Walden & Stowe, 1881), pp. 245–387.
3. C. Hare, *Life and Letters of Elizabeth L. Comstock* (London: Hedley Brothers, 1895), p. 180.
4. Richard F. Mott, *Memoir and Correspondence of Eliza P. Gurney* (Philadelphia: Lippincott, 1884), p. 322; Henry J. Cadbury, *Friendly Heritage: Letters from the Quaker Past* (Norwalk, Conn.: Silvermine Publishers, 1972), p. 86.
5. Dena J. Epstein, "Lucy McKim Garrison: American Musician," *Bulletin of the New York Public Library* 67 (October 1963): 545.
6. Katharine Smedley, "Martha Schofield," unpublished manuscript.
7. Thomas C. Kennedy, "Southland College: The Society of Friends and Black Education in Arkansas," *Arkansas Historical Quarterly* 42 (Summer 1983): 211.
8. *Extracts of Minutes, Ohio Yearly Meeting (Orthodox)*, (Damascus, Oh., 1874), p. 13.
9. Elizabeth Cady Stanton, Susan B. Anthony, and Matilda Joslyn Gage, *History of Woman Suffrage* (New York: Fowler, 1881), 2:215–16.
10. Bacon, *Abby Kelley Foster*, p. 65.
11. Katharine Anthony, *Susan B. Anthony: Her Personal History and Her Era* (Garden City, New York: Doubleday, 1954), p. 296.
12. Stanton, *Eighty Years and More*, p. 316.
13. *New York Daily Tribune*, November 15, 1876, quoted in Smedley, "Martha Schofield," p. 108.
14. Stanton, Anthony, Gage, *Woman Suffrage*, 3:28–35.
15. Carol Stoneburner, Charlotte Simkin Lewis, and Ruth Fulp, "Comparison of 85 Quaker Women And a Sample Group of 85 Non-Quaker Women as Described in *The Dictionary of Notable American Women*" (Prepared as background material for symposium on "American Quaker Women as Shapers of Human Space," Guilford College, Greensboro, N.C., March 16, 17, and 18, 1979).

Chapter 9

1. Thomas Woody, *The Education of Women in America* (New York and Lancaster, Pa.: Science Press, 1929), 2:368.

2. Roberts Vaux to Mary Waln Wistar, n.d., HSP.
3. Minutes, Women's Association for Visiting the Penitentiary, 1846–58, Baltimore Monthly Meeting, Baltimore Yearly Meeting Papers, QC.
4. Sarah Hopper Emerson, *The Life of Abby Hopper Gibbons* (New York: Putnam, 1896), 2:300.
5. Negley Teeters, *They Were in Prison: A History of the Pennsylvania Prison Society, 1787–1937* (Philadelphia: John Winston, 1937), p. 257.
6. Rhoda Coffin, "Sarah J. Smith—A Modern Friend," *American Friend* 6 (1-11-1900): 31–32.
7. Cornelia Hancock, *Record of Wrightsville: An Experiment in the Care of Property* (1889), FHL.
8. A. Chambers Clarke, *Seedbed of Reform: American Social Service and Social Action, 1918–1933*, (Minneapolis: University of Minnesota Press, 1963), p. 51; Josephine Goldmark, *Impatient Crusader: Florence Kelley's Life Story* (Urbana, Ill.: University of Illinois Press, 1953).

Chapter 10

1. Greene, *Mott* p. 150.
2. *Friends Intelligencer and Journal* 46, no. 6 (1889), pp. 90–91, 141.
3. Gulielma Fell Alsop, *History of the Woman's Medical College* (Philadelphia: Lippincott, 1950), p. 26.
4. *Friends Intelligencer and Journal* 58, no. 43 (1901), p. 686.
5. *Friends Intelligencer and Journal* 46, no. 6 (1889), pp. 90–91, 141.
6. Alsop, *Woman's Medical College*, p. 82.
7. Helen Wright, *Sweeper in the Sky* (New York: Macmillan, 1949), p. 141.
8. Deborah Jean Warner, *Graceanna Lewis, Scientist and Humanitarian* (Washington, D.C.: National Museum of History and Technology, 1979), p. 116.
9. Robert W. Wolcott, *A Woman in Steel: Rebecca Lukens* (Princeton: Princeton University Press, 1940); Sarah Stage, *Female Complaints: Lydia Pinkham and the Business of Women's Medicine* (New York: W. W. Norton, 1979).
10. Barbara Jones, *Deborah Logan* (Master's thesis, University of Delaware, 1964).
11. Helen Flexner, *A Quaker Childhood* (New Haven, Conn.: Yale University Press, 1940).
12. Stoneburner, Lewis, and Fulp, "Quaker Women," p. 3.

Chapter 11

1. Stoneburner, Lewis, and Fulp, "Quaker Women," p. 3.
2. *Piety Promoted* (Philadelphia: Friends Bookstore, 1890), 5:74.
3. *Memoir of Priscilla Cadwallader* (Philadelphia: T. Elwood Zell, 1862), pp. 12–13.
4. *Journal of Ann Branson* (Philadelphia: W. H. Pile's Sons, 1892).
5. Richard Mott, ed., *Memoir and Correspondence of Eliza P. Gurney* (Philadelphia: J. B. Lippincott, 1884), pp. 94, 95, 104, 105.
6. *Ann Branson*, pp. 213, 228, 259.

7. *Memoirs of Elizabeth Collins*, pp. 118–19.
8. *Priscilla Cadwallader*, pp. 34, 38–39.
9. "Journal of Sarah Foulke Farquhar Emlen," 9-8-1828 and 10-15-1828.
10. Rufus Jones, *Eli and Sybil Jones: Their Life and Work* (Philadelphia: Henry T. Coates, 1889), p. 42.
11. Ibid., p. 81.
12. *Memoir of Philip and Rachel Price* (Philadelphia: Phillip E. Price, 1852), p. 39.
13. Emlen Journal, 9-30-1813.
14. Haviland, *Life-Work*, p. 20.
15. *Reminiscences of Nathan T. Frame and Esther G. Frame* (Clevland, Ohio: Britton Printing Company, 1907), p. 34.
16. Ibid., p. 39.
17. Ibid., pp. 418–20.
18. Ibid., p. 426.
19. Darius B. Cook, *Memoirs of the Quaker Divide* (Dexter, Iowa: *Dexter Sentinal*, 1914), pp. 70–71.
20. *Christian Worker* (1-15-1880), p. 34.
21. "Joel and Hannah Elliott Bean," *Quaker Biographies*, 2d. ser., ed. Book Committee, Philadelphia Yearly Meeting (Philadelphia, 1926), pp. 226–42.
22. Jones, *Eli and Sybil Jones*, pp. 193–98.
23. Freda M. Hadley and Naomi D. Pyle, eds., *U. S. F. W.—Growth Unlimited: The Story of the United Society of Friends Women, 1890–1960* (Indianapolis: United Society of Friends Women, 1960).
24. Anna Louise Spann, *The Ministry of Women in the Society of Friends* (Ph.D. thesis, University of Iowa, 1945).
25. Hare, *Elizabeth Comstock*, p. 272.
26. *Proceedings of the Friends Conference in Richmond, Indiana, 1887* (Richmond: Richmond Friends Conference, 1887).
27. *The American Friend* vol. 119 (Ninth Month 1912), p. 610.
28. Emily Cooper Johnson, *Under Quaker Appointment: The Life of Jane P. Rushmore* (Philadelphia: University of Pennsylvania Press, 1953), p. 154.
29. Pioneer women clerks of Hicksite yearly meetings included: Sarah Fox, Ohio, 1901; Elizabeth Koser, Maryland, 1902; Elizabeth Darlington, Indiana, 1917; and Luella Flitcraft, Illinois, 1928. Among the pastoral meetings, Wilmington, Ohio, was the pioneer with a woman clerk, Mary Mills, in 1916. Compiled by author from printed yearly meeting records.

Chapter 12

1. Katherine Anthony, *Susan B. Anthony*, p. 497.
2. Aileen Kraditor, *The Ideas of the Woman Suffrage Movement, 1890–1910* (New York: Columbia University Press, 1965), p. 172.
3. Katherine Anthony, *Susan B. Anthony*, p. 483.
4. Ibid, p. 498.
5. Quaker women in the leadership in this organization included: Anne Webb Janney, Elizabeth Passmore, Mary Bentley Thomas, and Lucy Sutton in Baltimore; Effie L. D. McFee and Francena Maine, New York; Rebecca Webb

Holmes and Ellen Price, Philadelphia; Louisa Janney Zell, Indiana; Henrietta Hadley, Illinois.

6. *Proceedings of the Philadelphia Yearly Meeting* (1914), pp. 66, 100.

7. Amelia R. Fry, "Alice Paul and the Divine Discontent," in *Women in New Jersey History*, ed. Mary R. Murrin (Trenton, N.J.: New Jersey Historical Commission, 1985).

8. Alice Paul, "Conversations with Alice Paul: Woman Suffrage and the Equal Rights Amendment," transcript of a tape-recorded interview conducted by Amelia R. Fry, 1976, Regional Oral History office of the Bancroft Library, University of California, Berkeley.

9. "Woman Suffrage at Moorestown," *Friends Intelligencer and Journal 67*, no. 8 (2-19-1910), pp. 121–22.

10. Alice Paul, "The Church and Social Problems," *Friends Intelligencer and Journal 67*, no. 34 (8-20-1910), pp. 513–15.

11. Caroline Katzenstein, *Lifting the Curtain: The State and National Woman Suffrage Campaigns in Pennsylvania As I Saw Them* (Philadelphia: Dorrance and Company, 1955).

12. Inez Hayes Irwin, *The Story of Alice Paul and the National Woman's Party* (Fairfax, Va.: Delinger's Publishers, 1977), p. 31.

13. Amelia R. Fry, "The Divine Discontent: Alice Paul and Militancy in the Suffrage Campaign," (Paper delivered to the Fifth Berkshire Conference, Vassar College, June 16–18, 1981). Available through the Schlesinger Library, Radcliffe.

14. Louise Lewis Page, "Political Prisoner: The Story of My Grandmother, Dora Lewis," unpublished manuscript.

15. Irwin, *Alice Paul*, p. 294.

16. Amelia R. Fry, "Alice Paul and the South," (Paper presented to the Southern Historical Association, November 12, 1981).

17. Mildred Scott Olmstead, speech delivered on March 4, 1985, at Friends Meeting House, Philadelphia, in celebration of Women's History Week.

18. Margaret Hope Bacon, "Let This Life Speak: The Heritage of Henry J. Cadbury," *Friends Journal 29* (December 15, 1983): 15.

19. *Newsweek*, March 23, 1970, p. 18.

Chapter 13

1. Jane Addams, *The Second Twenty Years at Hull-House* (New York: Macmillan, 1930), pp. 118–19.

2. Lucretia Mott to Richard Webb, 1-22-1872, Boston Public Library.

3. *Chicago Record-Herald*, April 13, 1915, quoted in Mercedes Randall, *Improper Bostonian: Emily Greene Balch* (New York: Twayne Publishers, 1964), p. 144.

4. Ibid., p. 167.

5. Jane Addams, Emily Greene Balch, and Alice Hamilton, *Women at the Hague* (New York: Macmillan, 1915), pp. 96–97.

6. *To See What Love Can Do* (Philadelphia: American Friends Service Committee, 1977).

7. Marvin Weisbord, *Some Form of Peace* (New York: Viking, 1967). Also Rufus M. Jones, *A Service of Love in Wartime* (New York: Macmillan, 1920).

8. Jones, *Service of Love*, p. 258.
9. Mary Hoxie Jones, *Swords into Plowshares* (New York: Macmillan, 1937).
10. *To See What Love Can Do*, pp. 6–7.
11. Report of the Mission to Central America, 1927, AFSC Archives, Philadelphia.
12. Clarence E. Pickett, *For More Than Bread* (Boston: Little, Brown, and Company, 1953), pp. 238–40.
13. Elizabeth Jelinek Boardman, *The Phoenix Trip: Notes on a Quaker Mission to Haiphong* (Celo, N.C.: Celo Press, 1985).
14. Lady Borton, *Sensing the Enemy: An American Woman Among the Boat People of Vietnam* (New York: Dial, 1984).
15. Ibid., pp. 59–60.
16. Minutes, Morning Meeting of Ministers, Friends House Library, London, microfilm, QC. See also Arnold Lloyd, *Quaker Social History, 1669–1738* (London and New York: Longmans, Green and Co., 1950), pp. 92–93.

Chapter 14

1. Digby Baltzell, *Puritan Boston and Quaker Philadelphia* (New York: Free Press, 1979).
2. Judy Lumb, answer to questionnaire on Quaker women and feminism, 6-1984.
3. Elizabeth Walker, "Feminism and Contemporary Quaker Women" (Senior paper, Hampshire College, 1975), p. 75.
4. Ibid.
5. Susan Lynn to author, 5-5-1985.
6. Walker, "Feminism," p. 70.
7. Judy Brutz, "How Precious Is Our Testimony?" *Friends Journal* 30 (Oct. 1, 1984), pp. 8–9, and Demie Kurz, "Violence and Inequality in the Family," *Friends Journal* 30 (Oct. 1, 1984): 10–12.
8. *Faith and Practice* (Philadelphia: Philadelphia Yearly Meeting, 1972), p. 200.
9. Dora Wilson quoted in Ursula King, *Voices of Protest—Voices of Promise: Exploring Spirituality in a New Age* (London: Hibbert Trust, 1984), p. 5.
10. Kenneth Boulding, *The Evolutionary Potential of Quakerism* (Wallingford, Pa.: Pendle Hill, 1964).
11. Lenny Lianne to the author, Autumn 1984.

Index